SUPPORT

FOR PARENTS AND INFANTS

SUPPORT
FOR PARENTS AND INFANTS

A Manual for
Parenting Organizations
and Professionals

edited by C. F. Zachariah Boukydis
Department of Medicine
Harvard Medical School

ROUTLEDGE & KEGAN PAUL
NEW YORK AND LONDON

First published in the USA in 1986 by
Routledge & Kegan Paul Inc.
in association with Methuen Inc.
29 West 35th Street, New York, NY 10001

Published in Great Britain by
Routledge & Kegan Paul Ltd
11 New Fetter Lane, London EC4P 4EE

Set in Linotron Sabon and Helvetica
by Input Typesetting Ltd, London SW19 8DR
and printed in Great Britain
by T J Press (Padstow) Ltd
Padstow, Cornwall

Library of Congress Cataloging in Publication Data

Support for parents and infants.
Includes bibliographies and index.
1. Infants. 2. Parenting—Societies, etc. 3. Self-
help groups. I. Boukydis, C. F. Zachariah.
[DNLM: 1. Parents—psychology. 2. Parent-Child
Relations. 3. Professional-Family Relations. 4. Social
Environment. WS 15.5.F2S959]
HQ744.S86 1986 649'.'1'06   86-618

British Library CIP Data also available
ISBN 0–7102–0038–2

Contents

Contributors

C. F. Zachariah Boukydis, PhD, Research Associate, Department of Medicine, Harvard Medical School and Children's Hospital, Boston, MA.

Linda Gilkerson, PhD, Coordinator of High Risk Intervention Services, Division of Developmental and Behavioral Pediatrics, Evanston Hospital, Evanston, IL.

Page Talbott Gould, PhD, Vice President, Intensive Caring Unlimited, Merion, PA.

Jane Israel Honikman, BA, Director, Santa Barbara Birth Resource Center, Santa Barbara, CA.

Michael Kalinowski, PhD, Associate Professor, Department of Consumer and Family Studies, University of New Hampshire, Durham, NH.

Laurie Lowen, BA, President, Parents of Prematures, Bellevue, WA.

Maureen Lynch, MA, Formerly Executive Director, Parents of Premature and High-Risk Infants International, Inc., New York, NY.

Richard Marshall, MD, Professor, Washington University School of Medicine and Director, Division of Neonatology, St Louis Children's Hospital, St Louis, MO.

Carolyn Mebert, PhD, Assistant Professor, Department of Psychology, University of New Hampshire, Durham, NH.

Mary A. Moran, PhD, Director, Early Childhood Services, Easter Seal Society of New Hampshire and Vermont, Manchester, NH.

Lenette S. Moses, BA, President, Intensive Caring Unlimited, Erdenheim, PA.

Stephanie Porter, RN, Co-Director, NICU Parent Support, Inc., and Board of Directors, Parent Care (PPHRIII), Milton, MA.

Foreword: Importance of parental support from the viewpoint of a clinician

Richard Marshall, MD

The freedom of living in contemporary society provides enriching opportunities for many kinds of fulfillment that were impossible for our ancestors. Education and challenging careers are available, provided we are willing to go to where these openings lead. On occasion we are almost bewildered with choices as space and time seem to shrink and expand around us. Distances diminish with jet planes; and events from all over the world are brought into our homes by television shortly after they occur. Yet despite our mastery of so much, it is felt by many that we have lost some precious qualities of stability as a price for the flexibility we have achieved. Extended family contacts are less frequent with increased mobility, and it is more difficult to maintain long-standing networks of friendships as we move around. If we accept that "people need people," as Barbara Streisand tells us, then we need to find and create substitutes for nurturing relationships that were available in times of lesser mobility. Support groups based upon a shared experience, often focusing upon a crisis in the life cycle such as birth, illness or death, have emerged as substitutes for family and friends.

In my field of work with families, parents of premature or sick newborns have begun to form such support groups centered upon the mutual experience of having had a child in a Neonatal Intensive Care Unit (NICU), (Boukydis, 1982). Participants have described how such groups help them process the bewildering and overwhelming experiences they endure when they become part of the NICU world. Parents describe themselves as caught in a trap. They are undergoing a "grief reaction" characterized by isolation, hopelessness, sadness, loss of control, confusion, grief and anger (Nance, 1982; Harrison, 1983). At the same time, parents recognize that they are expected by the NICU staff to behave in ways that indicate that they are acceptable parents. No matter how responsible the NICU caregivers are to the families' needs, there is inherent tension between the parents and the staff focused upon the control and power that the doctors and nurses exert over their children. Veteran parents who have experienced similar feelings can relate as peers to the families with children in the NICU. A certain kind of concern and mutual support is available only from those peers in whom issues of authority and power are not important considerations.

Professionals can benefit from working with parent support groups or parenting networks in a variety of ways, and I would like to use my own experience as a neonatologist to illustrate these possibilities. Perhaps most importantly, professionals can learn from parent groups what it is that parents need and require when they have children in the NICU. From attending the first two national conferences bringing together parents and professionals concerned with care of families of premature and high-risk infants (Parent Care: Parents of Premature and High Risk Infants International, Inc.) in 1984 and 1985, I have been able to discuss and learn about the parent's perspective away from the everyday pressure and tension of the NICU. Hopefully, I can use this information to be more aware and more responsive to the individual needs of different families. More specifically, I have had an opportunity to learn about the needs of parental grief by meeting with the members of the St Louis AMEND (Aiding Mothers Experiencing Neonatal Death) group. Our neonatal social worker told me that our unit was not sensitive to the needs of grieving families. After curbing my initial anger at the suggestion of my imperfection, it became clear that she was right. And so, for a period of about six months, we invited members of the AMEND group to meet with neonatologists and house staff to tell us what they would like us to do to be helpful. The AMEND members were gracious and forthright. We then began to implement a policy towards neonatal death, described elsewhere (Marshall and Cape, 1982), that has been well received by families. Looking back, it seems obvious to ask consumers how we can better serve their needs, and yet in our professional training we are not taught to use such humility and common sense.

When parent support networks help professionals see parents as colleagues and members of the team, many other beneficial results can follow. Improved communication with families enhances personal satisfaction for the professional. As barriers break down, some of the almost inevitable tension diminishes. If there is more trust and frankness, then the parents are more satisfied. In this day of unbridled litigation, there will be fewer malpractice suits if professionals and families work together. Moreover, parenting networks can provide needed financial and political support for neonatal programs. In our community, the Life Seekers, parents who have had infants with perinatal or neonatal problems, have given significant money to our neonatal unit for equipment. Their help has been indispensable. Other appreciative families have generously donated equipment for neonatal research. In addition, some years ago insurance was available in Missouri that specifically excluded newborn infants. In conjunction with the Life Seekers, we were able to get that law changed so that the exclusion was removed.

It is difficult to establish and maintain parent support groups. There are competing pressures from jobs, families, and other responsibilities. There are financial requirements and delicate relationships with professionals and organizations. But if, as I believe, such groups are an essential resource, then it is imperative that people who have successfully formed and maintained parent groups, as well as scholars who have analyzed such groups, share that experience. That is precisely what Dr Zachariah Boukydis and his colleagues have done. They have given us a detailed picture of what it takes to start and run parenting networks. They deserve our thanks and gratitude since this book will help both professionals and parents work together to improve the care of infants and their families.

References

Boukydis, C. F. Z. (1982). "Support groups for parents with premature infants in NICU's" in R. Marshall, C. Kasman, and L. Cape (eds), *Coping with caring for sick newborns*, Philadelphia: Saunders.
Harrison, H. (1983). *The premature baby book*, New York: St Martin's.
Marshall, R. and Cape, L. (1982). "Coping with neonatal death" in R. Marshall, C. Kasman, and L. Cape (eds), *Coping with caring for sick newborns*, Philadelphia: Saunders.
Nance, S. (1982). *Premature babies: A handbook for parents*, New York: Arbor House.

Introduction

C. F. Zachariah Boukydis

Over the past twenty years, there has been a rapid rise in a-professional, mutual aid or self-help organizations in most industrialized countries. In the United States for instance, directories compiled by the National Self-Help Clearinghouse (Gartner and Reissman, 1979) list thousands of self-help organizations in local communities. The diversity and range of focus of such groups is remarkable. A brief scan of titles of self-help organizations includes names such as Burns Recovered, Concerned Relatives of Nursing Home Patients, Fly Without Fear, Gamblers Anonymous, Mastectomy Recovery Plus, Smokenders, and Womenpause.

Recent directories list dozens of national organizations, and thousands of local organizations, devoted to issues related to children and families. Some deal with general parenting concerns (i.e. Family Resource Coalition) while others take into account the unique concerns of a specific population (i.e. Parents of Premature and High Risk Infants International Inc.). A useful resource guide, titled *Programs to strengthen families* (Family Resource Coalition, 1983), makes the following distinctions in types of organizations for families with young children: prenatal and infant development; child abuse and neglect prevention; early childhood education; parent education and support; home, school, and community linkages; families with special needs; neighborhood-based, mutual help and informal support; and family-oriented day care.

The primary focus of this book will be on developing parenting networks based on a cooperative mutual aid, or peer self-help model. In some situations, this may require a so-called "parent–professional collaboration," but the basic assumption is that no one person or discipline has the total range of skills or experience necessary. Therefore constructive *collaboration* between individuals, whether they be concerned parents or professionals, is required.

Resource material listed in this manual will aid the reader in finding particular organizations which they may wish to contact or use as models for developing a similar parenting network or organization. The structure of this book includes chapters which address *specific issues* involved in developing a parenting organization (Chapter 1: Support for early parenting: Research and theoretical perspectives; Chapter 2: How to start a parents' organization; Chapter 5: Fund raising and networking for parenting organizations; Chapter 6: Advocacy skills for parenting organizations; Chapter 7: Peer counseling training; Chapter 8: Innovative models of parenting networks at the national level; Chapter 9: Tools for planning a parenting network; Chapter 10: Parenting organizations and resources), and chapters which portray issues involved with developing a network in a *particular population* of parents and infants (Chapter 3: Organizing support groups for parents of premature infants; Chapter 4: Support networks for fathering in the postnatal period; Chapter 8: Innovative models of parenting networks at the national level). The emphasis is not on parenting group meetings *per se*, but on a variety of potential networking structures (one-to-one peer counseling, parenting telephone hotlines, parenting information and resource exchanges, advocacy groups, etc.) which have arisen and which have been found to be useful.

Some basic characteristics of self-help networks or organizations in general are that they: (1) stress the benefits of *peer psychological support*; (2) provide *positive models* of members who have coped adequately with their situation; (3) provide different structures to improve *networking* among members in an attempt to reduce social isolation and stress; (4) operate with some form of *cooperative decision making* where the power of decision making lies with members of the group who share the life experience that is the focus of the group; (5) "*fill the gap*" in existing services, complement existing services, or provide coherent alternatives to specialized, competing services; (6) provide "*a-professional models*" which do not reflect the mode of operation inherent in any discipline, yet draw from knowledge and resources related to several disciplines.

While the specific focus of many contemporary self-help organizations may be new, there is nothing unique about people bonding together in small groups to exchange resources, benefit from special talents, and provide protection and emotional confirmation.

In every phase of human history, and in every culture, one can see diverse examples of mutual aid groups. The word therapy, which we now tend to associate with a highly specialized, one-to-one counseling relationship, derived from the Greek root *therapeutae*. In early Christian history, the *therapeutae* were small extended family villages, which were organized to provide material help to the poor and disabled. Therefore, the early understanding of a therapeutic relationship extended to providing a network of life support for those who were isolated or otherwise rejected, from other small groups. The therapeutic relationship involved redressing a balance in the individual's interconnection within a community context.

Vignettes about parental support

An understanding of the particular kind of support that parents can give to each other, may be derived from the following vignettes.

Vignette 1

Recently, a series of discussion groups at the Wilhelmina Gasthuis Hospital, in Amsterdam, led to the formation of a national organization, the "Association of Parents of Incubator Babies." In an article on the formation of the national organization, de Leeuw (in press) said:

> The association, that unites experienced parents of former incubator infants, also aims to help new parents. For this they (experienced parents) are trained by professionals in listening and talking. The contribution of the experience of other parents may be a very important one; a contribution the hospital may never be able to give.

The national organization was developed: to match "veteran" parents with "new." parents in different parts of the country (parent-to-parent match-ups), to develop local parenting groups in different parts of the country where parents choose to meet on a regular basis, to develop useful information on premature/high risk infant development for parents, and to increase community and professional awareness of the concerns of families with premature/high risk babies.

Similar organizations are currently under way in England, Scotland, Ireland, West Germany, Canada, and the United States (to name a few countries where identifiable "national" networking organizations exist). In addition, Parent Care (Parents of Premature and High Risk Infants International), based in the United States, is making efforts to develop communication between *different* national parenting networks and local groups in different countries.

Vignette 2

In a recent study on the behavioral development of premature babies (Boukydis, Lester and Hoffman, 1986), we had a two-pound premie who had to remain in the hospital for eight weeks. This baby was brought to Boston while his parents remained in Gloucester, a coastal fishing town, forty-five miles away. Right after the baby was born, his grandmother called a family counsel in Gloucester. Fifty-four people attended the meeting. They planned a schedule in which someone drove the baby's parents to and from Boston each day, child care was arranged for the other four children, and all meals and housework were covered during the period of the baby's stay in hospital. There was also an emergency back-up person assigned twenty-four hours a day. This was a coherent, functioning family network. It combined the "natural" resources one might expect from an extended family with a conscious decision to meet and schedule people's time, and contributions, to the parents in crisis. The staff on our study were moved to hear how much coordinated effort went into enabling these people to be able to visit their baby in the NICU each day. Our strong feeling extended to other parents in our study who were holding together extreme situations in their life without such viable network support.

An austere contrast to this family was another mother in our study whose second child was a two-and-a-half pound premie. This baby had a relatively easy course during her hospitalization, without serious illness associated with her prematurity, but when she arrived at home she was fussy and impossible to soothe for long periods of time. Her feeding pattern was unpredictable, and she was overall a very tense, hyper-reactive baby. The father was an artist who could not stand the crying and moved out to live in his studio after the first week. This mother was holding on for days, waiting for her own mother to arrive from far away. However, when the grandmother finally came, she stayed only one night, and then left to visit other relatives. It was at this point that the mother couldn't bear the strain and asked us for help in arranging back-up resources to cope with her baby and her difficult situation. This mother had been able to cope with the stress of having a difficult baby and being a single parent as long as she had the expectation that her mother would arrive eventually to help her out. When her mother left so quickly, the woman felt she had exhausted all possible resources, and asked our help to find a visiting nurse and an older parent with experience to get her through this difficult phase.

Vignette 3

Parents with babies in different circumstances claim that there is a unique understanding that only other parents in similar situations can have. A most sad and poignant example of this special understanding was captured in a photograph which appeared on the front page of the *Boston Globe* (February 5, 1983). The photograph showed two fathers and a tiny casket at a memorial service at Children's Hospital, Boston. One father had traveled with his newborn son from South Africa so that his child might have a crucial heart operation for "hypoplastic left ventricle syndrome" at Children's Hospital. While waiting for the operation, the father from South Africa met another father from Putnam Valley, New York, whose infant son was also being prepared for the same operation. The two men became friends while sharing the anxiety, fear and hopes connected with the impending operations. Two days later, the baby from South Africa died following surgery. A quote from the article, which was exemplary of the support the two men gave each other, read: "He and I have latched onto each other" (the father from South Africa said after the memorial service); "We'll be friends for life. There's probably no one else who can understand the experience."

Recent literature on the transition to parenthood in industrialized countries has differed in the depiction of the process. The portrayal runs from the transition as a "normal developmental process" to a potentially "stressful event" which must be negotiated with the utmost care (Rossi, 1968). No doubt there are important mediating influences which affect the lives of individuals as they bear their children. Important themes include a higher rate of geographic, and socioeconomic mobility with attendant separation from extended family, and even from long-term friends. Such mobility increases the possibility of stressful isolation and influences the passing on of child-rearing lore from one generation to the next. The rise of the childbirth education, or prepared childbirth, movement in the late 1960s and early 1970s was an effort to provide new structures of continuity to a growing segment of the population of potential parents who had never witnessed a child being born, and who had little experience of infant care. The prepared childbirth classes that I participated in as a resource person in the mid-1970s often had one postpartum class in which parents could tell others about their experience of having their baby. These postpartum meetings were an exciting gathering of new parents and babies. We quickly saw, however, that these one-time meetings gave rise to a new, unforeseen demand for continuity. Parents moved from telling their birth stories to sharing the joys and stresses of early parenting. There was an implicit demand for more information, resources, and emotional support. Many informal child care exchanges, and ongoing meetings of new parents arose out of these one-time postpartum gatherings. Over the years, childbirth education organizations began to develop postpartum, or early parenting classes. The chapter by Jane Honikman in this volume arises from her experience with developing networks to support early parenting as a follow through to childbirth preparation classes.

Once again, the rapid rise of literature and media resources on parenting is a kind of replacement for the oral transmission of parenting lore and the experiential base for learning parenting in the extended family. The media explosion extends now from books, pamphlets, and manuals, through parenting newsletters and magazines, to instructional videotapes and television series on how to parent. In a recent study we conducted on the development of infants and their families (Boukydis, Lester and Hoffman, 1986), we asked parents to rank relative importance for them of different sources of information about child care. Books were listed as equally important to family and friends as a crucial resource in these lower-middle, and middle-class families. Other information in this study showed the importance of family and friends in mediating the stresses of early parenthood, but this one finding points toward the increasing impact of the media. This influence is not always neutral, or necessarily benign. Quite often parents are left to sort out the "rights" and the "lefts" of parenting philosophy and the conflicting political ideologies implicit in the material (Hardyment, 1983).

Family sociologists have pointed to the decline of the nuclear family as the expected configuration for early parenting (Uzoka, 1979). In economic terms, the nuclear family is no longer the predominant unit of consumer activity and production. Trends indicate that during this decade one out of every two children will live in a family where there is one parent, or where there has been separation and divorce. In two-parent families, women are returning to the work force and parents are seeking day care with infants of increasingly younger ages. The pressure for more than one salary in two-parent families translates into more extreme pressure on women and men to balance the demands of early parenting and productive work. The situation for single parents (Weinraub and Wolf, 1983), and adolescent parents (Crockenberg, 1986) is increasingly complex and stressful.

A major portion of this book will be devoted to building structures to provide psychological support to parents, yet it is expected that other functions of parenting networks will involve advocating for more and better services for new families. The chapter by Mary Moran deals with advocating for families with children who require special services, but many principles she outlines will be useful for anyone advocating broader resources for families.

While the structures portrayed in this book sometimes smack of modern psychological culture (a group for every social ill), it is important to consider that: (1) innovative structures for providing support have arisen, and are tried and tested more frequently in human communities during periods of rapid social transition; and (2) we can look back historically to see how elements of recent structures are reflected in past "social" organizations. Parenting organizations are to this extent social experiments. As such, they may or may not exist at a distance from other cultural, or religious institutions in different communities. People who read this book may gain some momentum and useful ideas for providing more support and resources for parents within an existing defined (political, economic, or religious) community, or to fill a vacuum in a "secular" community context. At a deeper level, these parenting organizations provide a community forum where people are attempting to "rebuild the social infrastructure" (Weiss, 1983). For some this implies an attempt to return to past values concerning family life and raising children, and for others, it has meant identifying what is essential in human living, in the support and growth of parents and children, and learning to provide innovative structures which will function to facilitate this growth, whatever the family configuration.

References

Boukydis, C. F. Z., Lester, B. and Hoffman, J. (1986) "Parenting and social support networks for parents of preterm and full term infants" in C. F. Z. Boukydis (ed.), *Research on support for parents and infants in the postnatal period*. New York: Ablex.

Crockenberg, S. (1986). "Support for adolescent mothers during the postnatal period: Theory and practice" in C. F. Z. Boukydis (ed.), *Research on support for parents and infants in the postnatal period*. New York: Ablex.

Family Resource Coalition (1983). *Programs to strengthen families: A resource guide*. Family Resource Coalition, 230 N. Michigan Ave., Suite 1625, Chicago, IL 60601.

Gartner, A. and Reissman, F. (1979). *Help: A working guide to self-help groups*. New York: New Viewpoints.

Hardyment, C. (1983). *Dream babies: Three centuries of good advice on child care*. New York: Harper & Row.

de Leeuw, R. (in press). "Neonatal intensive care: Impact on families." *Journal of Psychosomatic Obstetrics and Gynaecology*.

Rossi, A. (1968). "Transition to parenthood." *Journal of Marriage and the Family*, 26–39.

Uzoka, A. (1979). "The myth of the nuclear family." *American Psychologist*, 34(1), 1095–106.

Weinraub, M. and Wolf, B. (1983). "Effects of stress and social supports on mother–child interactions in single- and two-parent families." *Child Development*, 54, 1297–311.

Weiss, H. (1983). "Introduction" in *Programs to strengthen families: A resource guide*. Family Resource Coalition, 230 N. Michigan Ave, Suite 1625, Chicago, IL 60601.

PART 1

Overview – The importance of support for parenting

CHAPTER 1

Support for early parenting: Research and theoretical perspectives

C. F. Zachariah Boukydis

Introduction

Current research is attempting to examine the complex balance between emotional support and instrumental, or resource, support for early parenting. In a review of research on social support, Barrera (1981) distinguished three areas of focus: (1) the potential or actual *providers* of support available to a person; (2) a person's internal *appraisal* of the availability and effectiveness of support; and (3) the *activities* involved in the provision of social support. Generally, past research on the effects of social support examined the relationship between numbers of contacts with family and friends and indicators of stress in early parenting. While it was assumed that there would be direct relationships such that, for instance, having a high number of contacts would be associated with lower levels of stress, this was often not the case. Important mediating factors such as: (1) the functional status or ascribed personality of the particular person in relation to the extended family network; (2) the coherence or density of the network; (3) help with household tasks and child care; (4) the presence of ongoing illness and stress; and (5) personal factors (previous experience with infant care, age of parent, presence of significant other, infant characteristics such as easy or difficult temperament), were found to be important in examining the complex role that social support plays in mediating the stresses of early parenting.

Importance of informal networks

I Social support and pregnancy outcome

In research on pregnancy outcome, Nuckolls examined the relationship between social support (or "psychosocial assets"), social stress as measured by a cumulative life change rating scale, and the normal or complicated outcome of pregnancy (Nuckolls, Cassel and Kaplan, 1972). For women who experienced a great deal of life change during pregnancy, having a high number of social support resources was strongly related to favorable pregnancy outcome. Women who had relatively few social support resources had three times as much incidence of pregnancy and birth complications. However, for women who experienced moderate or low amounts of life change during pregnancy, the relationship between social support or psychosocial assets was not predictive of pregnancy outcome. Again, it is important to remember that only in women's lives where there was a great deal of reported life change, was social support predictive of pregnancy outcome.

It was from studies such as this that social support began to be discussed as a complex mediator of social stresses. Norbeck and Tilden (1983) also studied the effects of life stress and social support on pregnancy outcome in 117 women who were healthy obstetric patients at a large, urban medical center. They found that high life stress and low social support (emotional support from family and friends) were strongly related to feelings of stress and emotional disequilibrium around the time of childbirth. High life stress during the previous year was related to the overall number of complications during childbirth. Further, women who had high stress, but who had adequate "resource" support (not necessarily "emotional" support) during pregnancy, had less obstetric complications, while those women with high stress and low resource support had many more obstetric complications when their babies were born.

II Social support and infant temperamental characteristics

Crockenberg (1981) studied the influence of social support, infant irritability and maternal responsiveness on the development of infant–mother attachment at one year of age. The sample included working-, and middle-class families. Infant irritability was assessed during the newborn period using the Brazelton Neonatal Assessment Scale (Brazelton, 1973; 1984), maternal responsiveness to crying was measured during observations at three months, and social support was determined during interviews at three months. Security of attachment was measured from videotapes of mother–infant interaction during Ainsworth's "strange situation" at one year (Ainsworth, Blehar, Waters and Wall, 1978). The strange situation involves a planned procedure which takes place in a playroom, involving the mother leaving her child alone, having a stranger enter the room, and then having the mother return. The baby's reactions to these events are recorded and used to assess security of attachment.

The most important finding from the study was that adequate social support was the best predictor of secure attachment, and that the effects of social support were most important for mothers with irritable babies. Low levels of social support were associated with insecure attachment between mother and child at one year of age, and this relationship held most strongly for mothers who had irritable babies in the early months. In other words, the situation of having an irritable baby, and low levels of social support, was the most likely predictor of insecure attachment or stress in the mother–child relationship at one year of age. Mothers who had irritable babies, but who also had adequate levels of social support, were much more likely to have a secure attachment with their child at one year. In this instance, the function of social support may have been to provide alternate responsive caretakers (spouse, grandparents, older siblings) to alleviate the potential pressure of high levels of responding from these mothers in the early months, and allow the relationship between child and mother to develop more slowly toward a secure attachment at one year.

Crockenberg's work points toward several potentially significant factors. Social support was clearly operative in conditions of relatively higher stress, in this instance, stress associated with having an irritable baby in the neonatal period. Further, what I will call the timing of social support, having adequate social support in the first three months, was influential in redressing a balance in the developing parent–infant relationship toward secure attachment at one year of age. From a developmental perspective, there may actually be a series of important phases in the developing parent–child relationship where the effects of social support are most necessary not only in helping to establish early patterns but also to help negotiate transitions potentiated by developmental changes in the baby's behavior patterns which create imbalances in the parent–child relationship.

In this study, social support appeared to mediate the event of having a temperamentally difficult infant, and therefore, leads one to question the importance of social support in early parenting with other populations of babies, such as premature or high risk infants, whose behavior patterns may be unpredictable or potentially disruptive. Even though this was a clinically normal population of babies, Crockenberg's research points to the need for listening to parents' perceptions of their babies' early patterns in the first months to identify those children who may be temperamentally difficult. Concurrently, the study points to the need to establish whether these parents feel they have adequate support from family and friends to meet the demands of early parenting.

Rather than see this in terms of a "deficit" model with health care professionals administering an objective measure of "parent perception of infant temperament" or "social network strength," I mean it more in terms of the attitude conveyed by "contextual assessment" (Fischer and Brodsky, 1978) whereby parents talk with someone else (parent, professional) in order to articulate their feelings in relation to their baby's behavior (Boukydis, 1985), and to assess the resources in their existing network. This contextual assessment typically occurs in informal contact between friends who are parents.

III Social support in one- versus two-parent families

Weinraub and Wolf (1983) studied social network, coping abilities, life stresses, and mother–child interaction with both single mothers having infants or pre-school children and married mothers and their children. Single parents were more socially isolated than married parents, had less stable social networks and experienced more stressful life changes. The single mothers reported having less emotional support, and less support for their roles as parents from their social network.

Increased availability of support and a reduction in life stresses increased the parenting effectiveness of both single and married mothers. Overall, in this study, there were no broad group differences between single versus married parents in the adequacy of the parent–child relationship. However, such factors as the extent of help with household chores, number of hours of employment, and number of social contacts had different impact on the ability of single and married women to be effective as parents. Optimal mother–child interaction in the single parent families was related to less stressful life events, reduced social contact, more parenting support, and less hours of maternal employment. Single parents who had few hours to themselves outside of work and time devoted to the pragmatics of running a household, had a fine balance between time with their children and time devoted to outside social contact. It appeared that single parents who had increased time devoted to social contact, had less time available with their children, and there was more stress in the parent–child relationship. Therefore, reduced social contact (as opposed to social support *per se*) was associated with better parenting for single parents. In interviews with the parents, single mothers confirmed this trade-off between time devoted to social contact and quality time with their children. They said that, for instance, while there are organizations for single adults, these organizations tend to focus on activities directed toward facilitating adult couple relationships and exclude the concerns of single parents with children. Many women would like to see organizations sensitive to the critical balance, which have more activities for single parents *with* their children. They also suggested telephone networks and informal structures which would enable single parents to discuss parenting activities with others.

The single parents with longer working hours tended to expect more mature functioning and place more controls on their children. At times this led to evidence of stress in the parent–child relationship especially when there was a clear mismatch between maternal expectations and the developmental capabilities of the child.

Optimal mother–child interaction in the two-parent families was associated with fewer stressful life events, satisfaction with emotional support and the availability of household help. For married women, but not for single mothers, increased availability of household help was associated with better parenting. Married women in this sample tended to go to work for less hours than their single counterparts, and spent more time in the home. Married women were more involved in balancing expectations about housework and actual division of household responsibilities between themselves and their spouses. Satisfaction with household help, which may also be an index of satisfaction with division of labor in the household, was related to more optimal parenting and less stress in the parent–child relationship. Single parents had only their own tolerances about adequacy of housework to consider. For married women, satisfaction with emotional support, as with availability of household help, was associated with optimal parenting. Both of these factors may be indirect indices of stress in the primary relationship, which involves a complex connection with stress in the parent–child relationship. Married women, who felt they had less emotional support, also tended to have more stress in their relationships with their children and gave evidence of less optimal interactions with their preschool children.

IV Social support for parents of term versus preterm infants

Crnic et al. (1983) examined the relationship between stress and social support on maternal attitudes and early mother–infant interactive behavior in mothers of healthy preterm and fullterm infants. All mothers were in intact two-parent families. At one month post discharge from hospital, Crnic and his colleagues interviewed mothers and assessed maternal life stress, social support (intimate, friendship, community), life satisfaction, and satisfaction with parenting. At four months they did interviews and observed mother–infant interaction in the home. They found few overall differences between mothers of preterm and fullterm infants. This lack of differences may have been a function of the health status of the preterm babies and support for early parenting provided in the hospital. Overall, both the mothers' perceived social support and life stress predicted their general life satisfaction. Mothers with low support and high stress have low life satisfaction ratings, while mothers with high support and high stress gave much higher ratings. In the latter instance, intimate support moderated the potentially disruptive effects of high stress. Again, mothers with greater social support and less stress reported more satisfaction with parenting, reported greater pleasure with their babies, and appeared more sensitive to their babies cues at four months of age.

Mothers with lower levels of stress had babies who appeared to be clearer in their interactive cues. Further, mothers with more intimate support had babies who appeared more responsive and were more emotionally involved. Generally, in this research, perceptions of adequate support in the primary relationship were most directly related to positive outcome, but there were instances where community support was influential, and may have compensated for disruption in the marital relationship. In terms of statistical models, there were several instances where social support had a main effect, for example, where high levels of support led to or predicted high levels of satisfaction with parenting or led to having highly responsive babies. Yet there were instances where social support had what is called a moderator effect; where, for example, in instances of high life stress, given that there were high levels of social support, this led to general life satisfaction. However, when there was high stress, with low social support, this led to, or predicted, lower levels of life satisfaction. Crnic and his colleagues went on to discuss our conceptualization of social support as a moderator. This perspective accounts for the previous work outlined by Crockenberg where social support was most predictive of secure attachment at one year of age in the instance where mothers had initially irritable babies.

V Social support for parents of twins

Glaser (1983, 1986) studied "metness of needs," spousal and social network support, and adjustment to mothering in mothers of twins. The general question addressed was whether the situation of parenting twins was demanding enough to call forth the need for specific help for specific problems over and above the general emotional support available from the mother's social network, or from her spouse. Glaser developed a "metness of need" scale covering instrumental, informational and appraisal-emotional needs to examine the independent effects of having or not having needs met, on maternal adjustment and depression at seven to nine months postpartum. Overall, Glaser found that women who had their needs met were better adjusted than women who did not receive the right amount of help for that need. Husbands were the most frequent helpers, and family were second most frequent helpers. Having a husband as one's "best helper" was linked to lower levels of depression and higher levels of comfort with mothering. Having a more extensive range of providers was positively associated with amount of help received. On a specific question related to who provided information about mothering twins, other mothers of twins were most frequently listed as providers of necessary information, and these mothers who had little contact with other mothers of twins had more problems with getting adequate information.

The critical comparison between previous measures used in research on social support (emotionally supportive spouse; social network extensivity and amount of contact with network) and the "metness of need" approach showed that the husband's emotional support was not as strong a predictor of comfort with mothering as any individual "metness of need" measure. Husband's emotional support was as powerful a predictor of level of depression as individual "metness of need" measures. Yet any two "metness of need" measures in combination were more than twice as powerful predictors of level of depression than was husband's emotional support. The husband was the most important provider of support, but having specific needs met eclipsed the importance of the emotional and instrumental help offered by the husband.

Further, the extent of the mothers's social network and amount of contact with network members had very little relationship to maternal adjustment or to amounts of help received. Whether or not mothers of twins had adequate help with housework was the most powerful predictor of level of reported depression. Mothers also expressed concern about having adequate child care resources, but overall there was more help available for child care than for housework. Obtaining adequate information about parenting twins was the second largest claim to inadequate help (housework was first) for the mothers of twins. With the relative infrequency of twin, or multiple births in the population, having contact with twin resources (other veteran mothers of twins) was seen as a crucial resource for addressing the particular needs of new mothers of twins.

VI Social support for parents of special needs infants

Dunst, Trivette, and Cross (1985) studied mothers' feelings about the importance of social support in 137 parents of mentally retarded, physically impaired, and developmentally at-risk infants and preschool children. Over time, mothers who felt that they had adequate social support from family and friends had a better sense of personal well-being, felt that their families were more cohesive, felt that they had better relationships with their children, had a better understanding of how to interact with their children, and felt that they had an adequate understanding of their children's behavior and development.

Themes in social support research and early parenting

The direction in recent research on social support and early parenting has led to an increasing need to understand parents' *internal appraisal* of the adequacy of support available to them in their friendship and familial networks. The movement in research on social support and stress has extended from purely objective counts of network members, and resources provided, to measures which take into account the mediation between objective factors and internal appraisal. This movement is not new in the philosophy of science and reminds one of the efforts to measure pain or stress, which began with external measures, took into account physiological correlates, and then had to balance these against the "subjective," or internal appraisal of pain or stress. Research efforts and clinical systems differ on how much they will: (1) take into account; (2) attempt to validate; or (3) help to articulate a person's appraisal of their situation. Further, at any given time in their lives, people differ in their ability to appraise the adequacy of their personal support networks. Being under either "acute" or "chronic" stress in itself may affect the ability to appraise one's situation as a parent. For instance, research on parenting of premature/high risk babies points to the "acute" stress which many parents feel after the baby is born. The baby is early, often with potentially serious illness, and violates a parent's expectations about the typical course of childbirth and early parenting (Freud, 1980; Nance, 1982; Harrison, 1983). The parents' network may be otherwise adequate for a child being born, but may be inadequate in some respects to meet the early unanticipated needs of parenting a premature/high risk baby. Further, parents under "chronic" stress from many different sources in their lives may also be unable to assess the adequacy of their personal networks to help with the demands of early parenting – when being a new parent is only one new demand being added to many other ongoing difficulties.

We must also be sensitive to the issue of the cost of social support. The next section will discuss research on the effects of parental partici-pation in parenting networks and parents' groups. While there are indi-cations of the benefits of participation, simply getting to a central meeting can be a major organizational task for people with a young baby. Actual participation in formal or informal meetings can be stressful for some people. Visits from friends or relatives, depending on the status of the parents' relationship with individuals in their network, can have elements of stress. Thus, as indicated before, more is not necessarily better when it comes to understanding social support, and there is a "cost factor" which is part of one's exchanges with one's personal and social network. Again, this points to the importance of an understanding of an individ-ual's estimation of the relative benefits and costs of getting help from their personal network to aid with early child rearing. When it comes to planning intentional structures to support early parenting, this "cost factor" and the need to understand a parent's understanding of the helpfulness of their social network is crucial. In the most basic sense, this means enlisting parents right from the start in planning. Formally, program planners call this a "needs assessment." Chapter 9 in this manual gives one example of what a needs assessment might look like. Taking the cost factor into account also involves providing options which people can tap when they want or are able to. The function of informal networks and formal professional services is not only to help parents obtain more resources, but help them to appraise their situation objectively in the first place.

The review of research on social support indicates that the adequacy of support effects different areas of functioning. Mothers of twins in Glaser's work (1986) indicated that overall they were much more likely to get help with child care than they were to get help with household chores. For some women getting help with child care may have been "helpful," but the overall level of demand of taking care of twins, especially in the first few months, may have been only slightly lessened.

Effects of parenting network participation on early parenting

The previous section reviewed some selected studies on the influence of informal network support for early parenting. There are situations where existing informal network support may appear inadequate for the demands of early parenting. In a simple sense, this means that we can look at ways either to strengthen the informal network (Cochran and Brassard, 1979), or to develop alternatives.

This section will provide a review of recent research on effects of participation in support networks in the early postpartum period. One purpose of this review is to illustrate the complexity of assessing the effects of network participation in the context of parents' lives. The studies selected are illustrative of the kinds of questions asked and exemplify the strategies which have been employed. A number of selected studies are presented in Table 1.1.

l Parenting groups and informal networks

In the study by McGuire and Gottlieb (1979), twenty-four couples participated in six weekly discussion sessions and were interviewed before and after the six week series. The groups had four to six couples each, and meetings were organized around discussion of topics related to general parenting concerns. As we can see from Table 1.1, the main findings revolved around group participants reporting that they had more frequent discussion with friends and family about child rearing issues, and uncovered more people to talk to in their social network about their feelings as parents. Group involvement allowed parents to discuss their concerns with other parents, and also, potentially to streng- then their own informal social networks around their ongoing child rearing concerns. Thus, provision of an initial alternative to the support in parents' informal networks eventually led to their being able to find, or develop, resources directed toward parenting concerns in their own informal networks. The mechanisms by which this took place are not clear, but were probably not a formal part of the operation of these groups. Thus, we can see that the unplanned for, or indirect effects of participation in a consciously conceived structure like an early parenting group, may lead to strengthening a parent's informal network. None of the studies reviewed in this section had a stated intention of developing

Table 1.1 Recent research on the effects of postnatal parent support groups

Study	Sample size	Population characteristics	Characteristics of group	Measures	Findings
McGuire and Gottlieb, 1979	N = 24 couples	–from physician's private practice –infant age 1–24 mo. X age = 14 mo. group X age = 11 mo. control –lower middle class –most parents attended prenatal classes	–random assignment to parent group vs control –weekly meetings – 6 wks –topical group discussion and readings (infant dev., nutrition, discipline)	Questionnaire before, and 5 wks after, intervention 9 variables 1. # of network members 2. # of available supports 3. frequency of supportive interaction previous 2 weeks 4. satisfaction with social support 5. social comparison with other parents 6. problem solving knowledge about parenting 7. parenting stress 8. perceived well-being 9. proxy measure of health status	–support group members discussed childrearing patterns with members of own social network more frequently than controls –support group members report an increase in number of people with whom they could discuss parenting concerns –main group function – chance to compare my experience as a parent with other parents –no differences in measures of stress, well-being, overall health status (however low pre-study levels of stress possible due to higher average age of infants)
Wandersman, Wandersman and Kahn, 1980	N = 41 parent group (18 fathers, 23 mothers) = 47 controls (23 fathers, 24 mothers)	–contacted at prepared childbirth class –primiparas –parental age = mid-20s –infant age Time 1 = 2½ mo. Time 2 = 8½ mo.	–Family Development Parenting Groups –6–10 wks each week, then 4 monthly meetings –focal topic – discuss and demonstrate new skills	*Time 1* 1. marital instrument – participation in household tasks 2. marital emotional – Spanier's Syadic Adjustment scale 3. network emotional – Newbrough – enough friends to help with problems *Time 2* 1. well-being (a) Wessman and Ricks's Personal Feelings scale (b) Dupuy – General Well-Being Schedule (fullness of life, energy, relaxation, health, positive mood) 2. marital interaction – Feldman - pos. and neg. marital interactions	–parenting group support and emotional marital support were found to be related to well-being, marital interaction, and parental competence for fathers –emotional, marital, and network support were positively related to well-being and marital interaction for mothers

Table 1.1 – continued

Study	Sample size	Population characteristics	Characteristics of group	Measures	Findings
Wandersman, 1980	N = 20 fathers (support group) = 27 fathers (control)	–contacted at prepared childbirth class –primiparas –fathers attended groups for both parents –middle class	–as in Wandersman et al, 1980 (above) –voluntary enrolment in parent group	3. Parenting Sense of Competence have necessary skills and rewarding 1. well-being 2. parental sense of competence 3. baby temperament (Carey) 4. father's participation (Vietze et al.) 5. parental attitudes (Cohler) 6. Dyadic Adjustment 7. positive and negative marital interaction 8. egalitarian ideology 9. husband help 10. social support –measures at 2–3 mo, 5–6 mo, 9–10 mo.	–general patterns of adjustment similar –parenting group fathers had lower feelings of relaxation and health, and more fussy moods in infants than controls –the quality of the marital relationship and attendance in parenting groups were associated with positive overall adjustment to baby at 9–10 months –father's initial dyadic adjustment and his participation in parenting groups predict only a small proportion of variance in later adjustment –fathers were positive about benefits of sharing concerns with other parents and watching their babies grow and play together
Cronenwett, 1980	N = 90	–women who had, or were participating in a post-partum support group started by the Lamaze Childbirth Assoc, Ann Arbor, MI –X̄ age 27 yrs, college graduate, econ. level	–initiated by leader who eventually withdrew –discussion of feelings, parenting and relationship issues –half the groups had babies present; half did not have babies present	–questionnaires sent to group participants	–80% felt their needs were met by group; helped to form lasting friendships (1) Discussion topics –problems – more personal discussion and less social discussion –0–6 months: discussions related to negative feelings about parenting –6 mos–1 yr: discussions related to returning to work –all ages: discussions related to labor/birth experience

Table 1.1 – continued

Study	Sample size	Population characteristics	Characteristics of group	Measures	Findings
Cronenwett, 1980 contd.		$15,000/yr, all married, and white; 30% returned to work while in the group; 73% primiparas, 85% vaginal births; 39% had participated in group previously	–none had spouses present –60% joined group when babies were 2–3 weeks old –67% met every 2 weeks; 33% met each week		–73% mentioned that recognition of universal nature of their feelings and their resultant feelings of reassurance of normality, 41% felt they learned not to doubt themselves, more self-confidence as parents *(2) Group effectiveness* –overall evaluations were positive, 77% who returned to work stayed in groups more than 1 yr, 85% who stayed at home were in groups less than 1 yr, group attendance was affected by presence of babies, less regular attendance in groups where babies were present –women who had more education tended to consider it a disadvantage to have babies present at meetings –sources of support (frequency of responses), friends and neighbors, pediatrician/nurse, post-partum support group, books, husband (no significance tests on relative importance) –most thought they learned more interpersonal openness, self-esteem, responsibility for self, acceptance of others, develop coping strategies –advantage/disadvantage to having baby present

Table 1.1 – continued

Study	Sample size	Population characteristics	Characteristics of group	Measures	Findings
Minde, Shosenberg, Thompson, Ripley and Burns, 1980	N = 29 families who had routine care (control) = 28 families who participated in self-help care program	–birthweight below 1,500 gms. –no physical abnormalities –singleton birth –at age 72 hrs. no serious complications	–once a week, range of involvement 7–12 weeks –10 parents –discussion of stresses, common problems of prematurity, dealings with the unit, development of premies	–observed parent–infant interaction during nursery visits and home visits 1–3 mos after discharge –1st interview 4–5 wks after birth, subjective experiences, backgrounds, attitude toward caretaking –2nd interview, discharge, attitude toward med/non-med care, amount of interaction with other parents, general caretaking competence –home visits, record sleep/feed patterns in previous 24 hrs, concerns about feeding, use of babysitters	–parents who participated in groups visited their baby in hospital more often than control parents –at discharge, group parents were more satisfied with medical/nursing care, and information they received; they learned from interactions with other parents, they had a better understanding of their baby's condition, they felt ready to care for their baby at home, and had a better knowledge of community resources. –during nursery visits after 3 wks, group parents were more active than control parents in touching their babies, looking en face, and talking to their babies –at home, group parents fed longer (2 mth visit), and used babysitters more liberally (3 mth visit), during feeds, they looked en face and talked to their infants more frequently at 1 mth, and talked to, looked at and touched their infants more often at 3 mths

a parent's existing network, but many studies showed that this took place during the course of a parent's involvement in a parenting network. Few groups consciously involve a member's family and friends in the activities that they provide. Both the influence of participation in a parenting group on the informal network, and the planning of parenting networks which consider ways to strengthen those informal ones already existing should be taken into consideration for the future development of such networks.

Reports of stress, general well-being and overall health status did not decrease in comparison with other parents who functioned as controls and who had similar characteristics to the parents who participated in the groups studied by McGuire and Gottlieb. The average age of children was 11–14 months at the time the study was conducted and there were relatively low levels of stress reported by group participants or control parents. Both sets of parents appeared to have adjusted satisfactorily to the demands of parenting in the early months, and the groups were not differentially instrumental in alleviating stress or adding to a sense of well-being.

II Different effects in group participants for mothers and fathers

The parenting groups studied by Wandersman (Wandersman, Wandersman and Kahn, 1980) involved parents with younger infants who met weekly for six to ten weeks and then once a month for four months. Assessment for group and control parents took place before and after involvement in the parenting group. Most noteworthy in this study was a differential effect in group participation for fathers and mothers. For fathers, it was group involvement which appeared to be most strongly related to later feelings of well-being, parenting competence and understanding in the marriage. Group participation for mothers, however, appeared to be less influential. For mothers, it was initial positive involvement in the marriage, and support from the social network which was positively related to later feelings of well-being and decreased reports of stress in the marital relationship.

Participation in these groups had a different effect for fathers compared with mothers. It appears that mothers' existing informal networks were adequate to support early parenting, while fathers found a supportive resource in these groups to enrich their responsibilities as parents. From McGuire and Gottlieb's study it was evident that participation in a group may indirectly affect relations in a parent's informal network. From this study, participation in a group may have different importance for different populations of parents (in this case, fathers versus mothers).

III Fathers' participation

Wandersman *et al.* (1980) did another study on the effects of fathers' participation in postpartum parenting groups for couples. Questionnaires were given to group and control fathers at two to three months. For both sets of fathers, the general patterns of adjustment were similar. The main positive finding was that the quality of the marital relationship and participation in parenting groups was related to fathers' positive overall adjustment to their baby at nine to ten months. Fathers who participated in the groups were positive about the overall benefits of being able to share concerns with other parents, being able to talk about their babies' development and compare with other children. Fathers who participated in groups, however, reported lower feelings of health and relaxation, and found their babies to be more difficult in temperament. Also, main analyses indicated that the initial status of the marital relationship and participation in the parenting group were relatively weak predictors of later adjustment.

IV Mothers who return to work

Cronenwett (1980) studied effects of participation by lay postpartum support groups initiated by a local childbirth education association. Women who returned to work during the first year tended to stay in the group longer than mothers who continued at home as primary caretaker of their baby. The groups appeared to be a central reference point and source of support for working mothers; while mothers who remained at home developed broader bases of informal support, in addition to the postpartum groups, as time went on. The benefits of group participation indicated by mothers included development of coping strategies, increases in self esteem, openness, and acceptance of the feelings of other parents. A majority of women felt their needs were met by the groups and that the groups helped them to meet other mothers with whom they initiated long-term friendships. Again, this study shows differential effects of participation for mothers who returned to work compared with mothers who stayed at home. Mothers, at home, were able to develop informal supports, while mothers who returned to work centered their developing base of support in these ongoing groups. As Wandersman (1982; 1986), in reviews on the effects of parents group participation has said; "parents and professionals must realistically analyze what kinds of programs can have what kinds of benefits (and costs) for what kinds of parents."

V Group participation for parents of preterm infants

The studies reviewed so far focused on groups dealing with general parenting concerns. There is one study on participation in parenting groups for parents with special concerns related to caring for babies born prematurely. Minde *et al.* (1980) studied the effects of participation in a hospital based self-help group for parents who had premature infants confined to a neonatal intensive care nursery. In this research, twenty-eight families met in groups of five to six parents each for seven to ten weeks with a veteran parent and a nurse coordinator. These families were compared with twenty-nine families whose babies were of similar characteristics and received routine care while in the hospital.

Parents who participated in the self-help groups visited their baby more often during hospitalization, appeared to show more optimal interaction with their baby during visits, and had more confidence and knowledge of resources at discharge. At three months post discharge, group participating parents were more concerned about issues related to their babies' development and showed more involvement with their babies during feeding. Not only did participation in the self-help group appear beneficial for parents during their babies' hospitalization, but participation helped parents become more capable in handling the transition when their baby went home.

Parent–professional relations in parenting organizations

The working philosophy in this manual involves an effort to encourage health service, and mental health professionals to move from a unidirectional to a collaborative model (Powell, 1984; Tyler, Pargament and Gatz, 1983) for providing resources to parents and infants. In the traditional unidirectional model, the professional is seen as an expert who provides necessary information, therapy, and/or resources, to a dependent population (Ayer, 1984). Inherent in this model is a conflict between the professional as expert and the need to foster independence and strengthen existing capabilities in parents. Heather Weiss addressed this issue in her introduction to "Programs to strengthen families":

> Balancing the authority and expertise of parents and program staff to implement a partnership model is not an easily accomplished process. It requires delicate balancing of not easily compatible views. Specifically, parents are seen as in need of assistance, on the one hand, but as "experts" on their children on the other. Program staff are seen as "experts" who have information parents need, but they are to provide it in a nonauthoritative way which does not encroach on parental expertise (Family Resource Coalition, 1983, p. 4).

With issues related to early parenting, professional involvement can extend beyond the role responsibilities and functional capabilities learned in traditional disciplines. In an article titled "Informal social support as an intervention" Dawson and colleagues concluded:

What we professionals are doing in many instances is responding to needs that are most usually met by persons in informal relationships with family members. This informal social support includes sharing of emotional burdens, advice, help in solving problems, and concrete, sometimes material assistance. Informal support is more flexible than are professional services in responding to the multiplicity of needs that families may present. Thus informal support can complement professional services (Dawson, Robinson and Johnson, 1982).

The intention of this book is to help professionals who work with parents to become agents of change – to develop parenting networks and strengthen informal networks. Garbarino (1980a), in an article on family stress and the prevention of child neglect and abuse, discussed ways to integrate formal and informal systems. These included collaborating with, or developing, self-help networks (Lieber and Baker, 1977), health, and home visitors (Garbarino, 1980b), family-centered childbirth (ibid.), mental health professionals as consultants to natural helping networks (Collins and Pancoast, 1976), and crisis teams to help disrupted families ride out periods of stress (McCleave-Kinney, et al., 1977). As the reader can see, the focus of this manual is a dual one, because it may be used not only by parents but by anyone interested in this task of strengthening informal social networks and resources for parents.

Results from early stimulation and intervention programs focusing on infant development are mixed. Evaluations based on brief, focused interventions in the early postnatal period do not often show significant long-term effects on intellectual or neuro-motor functioning with infants (Yang, 1979) and few studies of this type were designed to measure important concomitant changes in family functioning as a result of early intervention with babies, or with the parent–infant dyad.

Evaluations of early intervention efforts assume a scale which ranges from positive to benign effects. Little attention (or accurate empirical information) has been gathered or published about the potential detrimental effects on infant, or family functioning. In circumstances where there is labeled "psychosocial risk" the issue of possible harmful effects is of particular concern. The emphasis in this manual is to create options which allow for voluntary participation not to replace existing services, but to provide more options for parents, and to reduce possible coercion and selective non-participation by those otherwise in need but too threatened to partake of services.

Little attention has been given in the professional literature to the potential iatrogenic effects (Illich, 1976; Donzelot, 1979) of being labeled and treated as psychosocially at risk, and being subtly coerced (often in the face of few alternative resources) to participate in early treatment programs. For instance, in the past few years the media has given extensive attention to the problems of parenting with at-risk infants. Studies supposedly demonstrating a direct link (rather than a correlative association, subject to other factors than prematurity *per se*) between prematurity and child abuse have become well known. The event of having a premature infant is stressful. The emphasis on the importance of early bonding (Goldberg, 1983) leaves many parents of premature or high risk babies feeling guilty for having restricted early contact, or for having ambivalent feelings toward their babies. This amounts to a double burden: contending with the feelings inherent in the situation *and* having guilt for having ambivalent feelings. Coupled with the stress and uncertainty, parents are often concerned that their involvement with their baby is being watched, and are afraid that their parenting competence is being judged. The issue of care for premature infants is complex because there is a need for highly specialized professional treatment of babies. Further, the complexity of information about neonatal care, areas of uncertainty about treatment, and inter-professional tension, lead to extreme reticence about having non-professionals involved with parents of premature/high risk infants, especially during early hospitalization. In other writing (Boukydis, 1982, 1983), I have outlined the potential for collaboration between intensive care professionals and veteran parents. Even in this extreme situation, the model is to develop a collaboration between veteran parents and professionals, and to provide alternative voluntary resources for parents.

I Examples of parent–professional collaboration

Here are some ways in which professionals and parents have collaborated which have been described in writing on support for parents.

(A) Veteran parent or parent group participation as an extension of existing services
1 Parents as home visitors for new parents (Dawson *et al.*, 1982);
2 older women as home visitors for teenage mothers (Dawson *et al.*, 1982; Crockenberg, 1986);
3 parents (previously cited for abuse or neglect) as lay therapists in treatment of child abuse and neglect (Cohn and Miller, 1977);
4 participation in Parents Anonymous as part of multi-service treatment for child abuse following birth of premature/high risk baby (Nance, 1982; Harrison, 1983; Cherniss, 1986; Boukydis, 1982; 1984);
6 parents as mediators in family crisis work;
7 parents as teachers and organizers of early Head Start programs (Zigler and Berman, 1983);
8 parents as part of a support system for families with disabled infants (Davidson and Dosser, 1982).

(B) Parental involvement in innovative programs initiated by parents' organizations or parent–professional collaboration

1 Postpartum education and support groups (Honikman, this volume);
2 support for breast feeding;
3 support for fathers (Parke and Tinsley, 1986);
4 parent operated day care;
5 support groups for parents with disabled infants;
6 parents as instructors in a continuing education parent education programs (Ganong and Coleman, 1983);
7 support groups for parents with premature/high risk infants;
8 support groups for parents whose babies have died;
9 parenting stress hotlines;
10 parenting information and resource exchanges;
11 parents as home visitors;
12 parents as part of home visiting teams;
13 support groups for parents involved with abuse and neglect;
14 support groups for parents with twins/multiple births;
15 parental involvement in pre-post partum couples' groups (Cowan and Cowan, 1986);
16 comprehensive parent support systems (Badger and Goldman, 1986).

Research on involvement of veteran parents in providing services

The importance of self-help models

At the present time, research on participation of veteran parents in providing services to other parents, or on the influences of participation in some form of parenting network, are limited. The literature on social support indicates that friends, especially friends with children, and one's own parents, if they are available, are important "veteran parent" resources in parents' informal networks. If this is the case in the normal population, then one can imagine that parents in special circumstances may seek out other parents who have been through their situation previously, or who are currently coping with the problem (Ayer, 1984). Leiderman (1975) surveyed parents with babies in NICU's and asked parents what kind of help they needed and from whom – family, friends, nurses, doctors, social workers, and so on – they would most like to receive help. In this survey, the parents of intensive care babies chose other parents first, nursing staff second, doctors third, and then family, social workers and others. Parents were expressing a desire to discuss issues with other parents who had been through the same experience, to learn more effective ways of coping with the situation, and to have their current complex feelings validated. Another survey done by Neo-

Fight, a parents of prematures organization in Indiana, addressed the concerns of parents whose babies had been transported from a local hospital to a regional center for special care. Ninety-five per cent of the parents interviewed said that they would have liked to have had a visit from a veteran parent who previously had an intensive care baby at the time when they were confined to the local hospital and were unable to visit their child in the regional center.

The study reviewed previously by Glaser (1986) on mothers of twins showed the special emphasis these mothers placed on: (1) gaining information from other mothers of twins on how to handle the complexity of their lives; and (2) gaining personal validation for the feelings they were having during the first few months of twin parenthood.

A recent study by Ayer (1984) of mothers caring for severely mentally handicapped children at home, indicated that services tended to be determined by professional perspectives, and that many services were organized to substitute rather than reinforce mothers' caring capabilities. Mothers saw most services as too crisis oriented, and segmented; and many parents had turned, in increasing numbers over the past few years, to self-help groups to meet their needs.

I Parental involvement in early intervention

Several writers have pointed to the importance of parental involvement in early intervention projects as an important component in considering the long-term success of the program. In an instructive article on early childhood intervention, Zigler and Berman discussed the history of Head Start by showing how planners involved parents in planning and program operation:

> Head Start parents not only became involved in the daily activities of the program, but also they exercised real decision-making power in all planning and administrative aspects of their neighborhood centers. This was a major break from past practices in which educated and paid professionals dictated the operation of poverty programs to passive recipients (Zigler and Berman, 1983, p. 895).

This article on the evaluation of early intervention programs indicates that there may be a selective advantage to programs which focus on strengthening children's social competence, in part through strengthening family and familial support networks, rather than narrowly attending to the intellectual development of the child. Early research on Head Start programs indicated that rapid IQ gains in pre-schoolers were not maintained after entering grade school (Cicirelli, 1969). However, later research on a variety of Head Start programs, some of which involved parents and some of which did not, showed that long-term effects of preschool experience seemed to be most consistent when parents participate in shaping the educational process (Bronfenbrenner, 1975; Valentine and Stark, 1979; Darlington et al., 1980). In long-term evaluations, programs which involved parents in the preschool years had children who progressed through the grades with less failure, and who had less need for involvement with special education services. Children from Head Start programs which did not involve parents had a higher rate of failure in passing from one grade to the next, and were more involved with special services. What accounted for the differences? Zigler and Berman emphasize that parental involvement in early intervention helped to improve parents' own sense of competence and helped to develop informal networks between parents. Further, in areas where parents were involved in Head Start programs, people began to organize and to advocate for better resources for children and families in their neighborhoods. The family and neighborhood strengthening which took place continued to provide support for children as they progressed through grade school. However, in early intervention models focusing on intellectual stimulation of preschool children alone, parents and children were dependent on the services of the preschool program. Parents were not inspired to take charge of shaping their child's preschool education, remained isolated from each other, and did not organize to improve broader conditions affecting families in their neighborhoods. While children made considerable intellectual progress in preschool, the family and neighborhood climate had not changed to support children's progress in grade school.

II Parents as home visitors to new parents

Dawson, Robinson and Johnson (1982) described a program which used experienced mothers as home visitors to families with new babies. They described the functions of the home visitor:

> Since our approach is based on the conviction that the success of visiting depends in large measure on the extent to which the parents consider themselves valued as people, the visitor imparts her caring and desire for friendship through attentive listening, emotional sharing, and understanding of the parents' own concerns. Regular weekly visits and telephone accessibility demonstrate concretely the visitor's dependability and commitment. Complementing this emotional support, the visitor actively assists parents in augmenting their personal networks. To this end, the visitor aids parents in investigating sources of physical and material assistance, professional guidance, and social participation. In addition, the visitor may perform a variety of concrete tasks with or for the family in order to: (1) ensure proper and timely utilization of community resources; (2) reduce excessive family stress; and (3)

assure a family member's physical or mental well-being. This instrumental support often is provided through such activities as baby-sitting, transporting the child and mother to the clinic, or taking the family on outings (Dawson *et al.*, 1982, p. 2).

Research with control families who did not have home visitors in the first year shows in comparison a number of areas of improved functioning in the parent–infant relationship, parents' knowledge of child development, and parents' use of informal networks and community resources for parents who did have a home visitor. This program is similar to other programs which provide parent-to-parent match-ups or include parents on home visiting teams with public health nurses and child development specialists.

III Lay involvement in child abuse prevention and treatment

In an article on programing for responding to child abuse, Garbarino discusses the problems involved in early detection of families at risk for abuse and neglect (Garbarino, 1980a). One primary conclusion from his review is that we should concentrate our effort on preventive programs which reduce social isolation, build informal networks, and provide positive models for parenting.

In the area of serious parenting problems where there is referral to agencies dealing with child abuse or neglect, a national study done by Ann Cohn and her colleagues has shown that peer self-help (or involvement with "lay therapists" who were themselves previously cited for abuse or neglect) may be an integral part of the treatment process (Cohn and Miller, 1977). Cohn and her colleagues studied eleven child abuse and neglect demonstration projects in different parts of the United States. In projects which used lay therapists or referral to Parents Anonymous (PA: an extensive national self-help organization for parents dealing with potential, or actual, abuse and neglect) in combination with other services, clinical staff ratings of significant improvement of parents were significantly higher (52 per cent versus 39 per cent) than for parents involved in programs which did not include a lay therapist or PA component. Following treatment, the study suggest that there was less recurrence of abuse and neglect in programs which had the lay therapist or PA involvement.

Parents Anonymous contracted with Jean Baker of Behavior Associates (Lieber and Baker, 1977) to do a study of PA groups. Participation in PA was associated with a significant decline in physical and verbal abuse, an increase in parents' self esteem, a reduction in social isolation, and an increased knowledge of child development and child rearing options. The report contains material which is useful in estimating many factors leading to the successful operation of groups with different populations of parents. Parents from a broad range of economic and cultural backgrounds participate in Parents Anonymous, and a careful reading of the report may help to highlight which factors determine who will join and participate effectively. The studies by Cohn and Baker indicate the value of self-help networks in dealing with problems as severe as child abuse and neglect. It is often said that social isolation is a factor in abuse and neglect, and by providing relatively less threatening options isolated parents are more likely to participate either in a group or through telephone calls and home visits with a veteran parent.

IV Mutual aid networks for parents of premature/high risk babies

Deborah Cherniss (1986) recently completed a survey of sixty-three parenting organizations providing support to parents of premature and high risk babies. The functioning and organizational style of these groups varied considerably. So too did the type of collaboration between parents and perinatal professionals in operating these parenting networks. Cherniss' survey included the following information on parent–professional interaction in starting and running groups: 33 per cent of groups were based in the community, and 67 per cent were affiliated with one or more hospitals; parents began 44 per cent of groups alone, and 21 per cent of groups were initiated by a parent/professional team; social workers were more likely to begin groups on their own, while nurses were more likely to work with parents in starting groups.

Cherniss was able to examine important factors which contributed to the stability and survival of these groups. Those organizations which had stability, and had been operating successfully to benefit parents for two or more years, had a productive collaboration between veteran parents and perinatal professionals in operating the parenting organizations. These stable organizations also provided options for parents as their babies moved from hospital to home (parent-to-parent match-ups, regular meetings in the community, discussion groups, newsletters, telephone informational and counseling, contacts). Groups which were having problems were run by professionals or parents alone, and had fewer options for parent involvement. In the survey, the number one problem listed by most groups was reaching parents after their baby was discharged from hospital. This was thought to be compounded by parents being spread out over a large geographic area, having to commute too far to group meetings, and families being hit with financial burdens and child care concerns that made it difficult to attend formal meetings. This survey gives important detail on what accounts for an effective collaboration between parents and professionals, and also supports the notion of voluntary options where parents determine the time, and kinds of involvement that they deem useful in participating in a parenting network.

V Parents teaching parent education courses

A recent study by Ganong and Coleman (1983) compared the use of trained parent volunteers running parent education programs (called Parent–Child Interactive programs, at the University of Missouri extension services) with those run by professional staff. Ganong & Coleman evaluated both parent satisfactions and competence, and child gains (on the Cognitive and Perceptual Skills Test), and found no differences in measures in those groups run by trained volunteer parents versus professionals after the nine week series of parent education classes.

Conclusion

The previous section has reviewed studies in which parents and professionals have collaborated in providing services to new parents. At the present time, with major reductions in services which affect families, there is a need for creative, preventive options for new families, and advocacy for more changes at the level of social policy. In many cases, self-help, volunteer organizations are the only alternative to a drastic reduction in health, and mental health services. However, many health and mental health professionals find themselves in a bind. Along with a reduction of services in some areas comes increased pressure for longer hours of direct service. This leaves reduced time for being change agents. Many professionals were trained in the case worker, direct service model. It is hoped that the collaborative model implicit in this manual will give professionals new options for extending the effectiveness of their efforts. One need not take on the job of organizing and running some form of parenting organization alone. A true collaboration between a group of concerned parents and professionals leads to a feeling of efficacy for both groups. When people are engaged in a worthwhile effort with the non-hierarchical decision-making model evident in many volunteer organizations, they are able to put forth a concerted effort. With preventive options and network strengthening for parents, this means that professionals can concentrate their specific efforts toward people and families most in need of specialized services. The chapters in this book outline the skills and experience necessary to organize some form of parenting network in many different areas. There is evidence that a series of new professional domains (early intervention, parent education) is arising which touches on the concerns of families and early parenting. The history of the rise of professional interests (especially in fields of medicine) has brought with it the need to establish and justify an area of competence. This implies tension with existing established disciplines to prove the value of services offered, and a need to establish credibility with the public at large. Often, the new disciplines draw people who are establishing a career, or who are going through a transition in their career focus. These conditions can often lead to conflict with volunteer organizational efforts which touch on many of the same issues with early parenting, and child and family development. Again, the collaborative model in this manual is aimed at helping volunteer organizations which can creatively tap professional cooperation and expertise when necessary.

References

Ainsworth, M., Blehar, M., Waters, E. and Wall, S. (1978). *Patterns of Attachment.* Hillsdale, N.J.: Erlbaum.

Ayer, S. (1984). "Community care: Failure of professionals to meet family needs." *Child Care, Health and Development*, 10, 127–40.

Badger, E. and Goldman, B. (1986, in press). Program design of parent support systems as a function of population served: Some comparisons. In C. F. Z. Boukydis (Ed.), *Research on support for parents and infants in the postnatal period.* New York: Ablex, 1986.

Barrera, M. (1981). "Social support in the adjustment of pregnant adolescents" in B. Gottlieb (ed.), *Social networks and social support.* Beverly Hills: Sage.

Boukydis, C. F. Z. (1982). "Support groups for parents with premature infants in N.I.C.U.'s" in R. Marshall, C. Kasman, and L. Cape, (eds), *Coping with caring for sick newborns.* Philadelphia: Saunders.

Boukydis, C. F. Z. (1984). "N.I.C.U. support groups form in 1970's." *Support Lines*, 2(1), 1–4.

Boukydis, C. F. Z. (1985). "A theory of empathic relations between parents and infants: Insights from a client-centered/experiential perspective." *Focusing Folio*, 4(1), 3–28.

Boukydis, C. F. Z. (ed.) (1986). *Research on support for parents and infants in the postnatal period.* New York: Ablex.

Brazelton, T. (1973). *Neonatal behavioral assessment scale.* Philadelphia: Lippincott.

Brazelton, T. (1984). *Neonatal behavioral assessment scale, 2nd edn: Clinics in developmental medicine No. 88.* Philadelphia: Lippincott.

Bronfenbrenner, U. (1975). "Is early intervention effective?" in M. Guttentage and E. L. Struening (eds), *Handbook of evaluation research (Vol. 2).* Beverly Hills: Sage.

Cherniss, D. (1986). "Stability and growth in parent support services: A national study

of peer support for parents of preterm and high risk infants" in C. F. Z. Boukydis (ed.), *Research on support for parents and infants in the postnatal period.* New York: Ablex.

Cicirelli, V. (1969). *The impact of Head Start: An evaluation of the effects of Head Start on children's cognitive and affective development.* Washington, DC: National Bureau of Standards, Institute for Applied Technology.

Cochran, M. and Brassard, J. (1979). "Child development and personal social networks". *Child Development*, 50, 601–16.

Cohn, A. and Miller, M. (1977). "Evaluating new modes of treatment for child abusers and neglectors: The experience of federally funded demonstration projects in the USA." *Child Abuse and Neglect*, 1, 453–8.

Collins, A. and Pancoast, D. (1976). *Natural helping networks.* Washington, DC: National Association of Social Workers.

Cowan, C. and Cowan, P. (1986). "A preventive intervention for couples becoming parents" in C. F. Z. Boukydis (ed.), *Research on support for parents and infants in the postnatal period.* New York: Ablex.

Crnic, K., Greenberg, M., Ragozin, A., Robinson, M. and Basham, R. (1983). "Effects of stress and social support on mothers of premature and full-term infants." *Child Development*, 54, 209–17.

Crockenberg, S. (1981). "Infant irritability, mother responsiveness, and social support influences on the security of infant–mother attachment." *Child Development*, 52, 857–65.

Crockenberg, S. (1986). "Support for adolescent mothers during the postnatal period: Theory and practice" in C. F. Z. Boukydis (ed.), *Research on support for parents and infants in the postnatal period.* New York: Ablex, 1986.

Cronenwett, L. R. (1980). "Elements and

outcomes of a postpartum support group."
Research in Nursing and Health, 3,
33–41.

Darlington, R., Royce, J., Snipper, A.,
Murray, H. and Lazar, I. (1980).
"Preschool programs and later school
competence of children from low-income
families." *Science*, 208 (4440), 202–4.

Davidson, B. and Dosser, D. (1982). "A
support system for families with
developmentally disabled infants." *Family
Relations*, 31, 295–9.

Dawson, P., Robinson, J. and Johnson, C.
(1982). "Informal social support as an
intervention." *Zero to Three: Bulletin of
the National Center for Clinical Infant
Programs*, 3(2), 1–5.

Donzelot, J. (1979). *The policing of
families*. New York: Random House.

Dunst, C., Trivette, C. and Cross, A.
(1985). "Roles and support networks of
mothers of handicapped children" in R.
Fewell and P. Vadasy (eds), *Families of
handicapped children: Needs and supports
across the life-span*. Austin, TX: Pro-Ed
Publications.

Family Resource Coalition (1983).
*Programs to strengthen families: A
resource guide*. Family Resource Coalition,
230 N. Michigan Ave., Suite 1625,
Chicago, IL, 60601.

Fischer, C. and Brodsky, S. (1978). *Client
participation in human services: The
Prometheus principle*. New Brunswick,
NJ: Transaction.

Freud, W. (1980). "Notes on some
psychological aspects of neonatal
intensive care" in S. Greenspan and G.
Pollock (eds), *The course of life:
Psychoanalytic contributions toward
understanding personality development*.
Maryland: NIMH Publications, 257–69.

Ganong, L. and Coleman, M. (1983). "An
evaluation of the use of volunteers as
parent educators." *Family relations*, 32,
117–22.

Garbarino, J. (1980a). "What kind of
society permits child abuse?" *Infant
Mental Health Journal*, 1(4), 270–80.

Garbarino, J. (1980b). "Changing hospital
policies and practices concerning
childbirth." *American Journal of
Orthopsychiatry*, 50, 27–32.

Glaser, K. (1983). "Social support and
mother's adjustment to the birth of twins."
Unpublished doctoral dissertation,
University of Chicago.

Glaser, K. (1986). "A comparative study
of social support for new mothers of
twins" in C. F. Z. Boukydis (ed.), *Research

on support for parents and infants in the
postnatal period*. New York: Ablex.

Goldberg, S. (1983). "Parent–infant
bonding: Another look." *Child
Development*, 54, 1355–82.

Harrison, H. (1983). *The premature baby
book: A parent's guide to coping and
caring in the first years*. New York: St
Martin's Press.

Illich, I. (1976). *Medical nemesis*. London:
Marion Boyars.

Lieber, L. and Baker, J. (1977). "Parents
Anonymous – self-help treatment for
child abusing parents: A review and an
evaluation." *Child Abuse and Neglect*, 1,
133–48.

Liederman, P. H. (1975). "Discussion:
Parents of babies of very low birth
weight" in R. Porter and M. O'Connor
(eds), *Parent–infant interaction*. Ciba
Foundation Symposium, Vol. 33.

McCleave-Kinney, J., Madsen, R.,
Fleming, T. and Haapala, D. (1977).
"Homebuilders: Keeping families
together." *Journal of Consulting and
Clinical Psychology*, 45, 667–73.

McGuire, J. and Gottlieb, B. (1979).
"Social support groups among new
parents: An experimental study in primary
prevention." *Journal of Clinical Child
Psychology*, 8, 111–16.

Minde, K., Shosenberg, N., Marton, P.,
Thompson, J., Ripley, J. and Burns, S.
(1980). "Self-help groups in a premature
nursery – a controlled evaluation."
Journal of Pediatrics, 96(5), 933–40.

Nance, S. (1982). *Premature babies: A
handbook for parents*. New York: Arbor
House.

Nuckolls, C., Cassel, J. and Kaplan, B.
(1972). "Psychosocial assets, life crisis
and the prognosis of pregnancy." *Americal
Journal of Epidemiology*, 95, 431–41.

Norbeck, J. and Tilden, V. (1983). "Life
stress, social support, and emotional
disequilibrium in complications of
pregnancy: A prospective, multivariate
study." *Journal of Health and Social
Behavior*, 24, 30–46.

Parke, R. and Tinsley, B. (1986). "Fathers
as agents and recipients of support in the
postnatal period" in C. F. Z. Boukydis
(ed.) *Research on support for parents and
infants in the postnatal period*. New York:
Ablex.

Powell, D. (1984). "Professionals and
parent groups: What roles?" *Family
Resource Coalition Report*, 1, 6–7.

Tyler, F., Pargament, L. and Gatz, M.
(1983). "The resource collaborator role:

A model for interactions involving psychologists." *American Psychologist*, 388–98.

Valentine, J. and Stark, E. (1979). "The social context of parent involvement in Head Start" in E. Zigler and J. Valentine (eds), *Project Head Start: A legacy of the war on poverty*. New York: Free Press.

Wandersman, L. (1980). "The adjustment of fathers to their first baby." *Birth and the Family Journal*, 7(3), 155–62.

Wandersman, L. (1982). "An analysis of the effectiveness of parent–infant support groups." *Journal of Primary Prevention*, 3(2), 99–115.

Wandersman, L. (1986). "Parent–infant support groups: Matching programs to needs and strengths of families" in C. F. Z. Boukydis (ed.), *Research on support for parents and infants in the postnatal period*. New York: Ablex.

Wandersman, L., Wandersman, A. and

Kahn, S. (1980). "Social support in the transition to parenthood." *Journal of Community Psychology*, 198, 332–42.

Weinraub, M. and Wolf, B. (1983). "Effects of stress and social supports on mother–child interactions in single- and two-parent families." *Child Development*, 54, 1297–311.

Weiss, H. Introduction. In *Programs to strengthen families: A resource guide*. Family Resource Coalition, 230 N. Michigan Ave., Suite 1625, Chicago, IL 60601, 1983.

Yang, R. (1979). "Early infant assessment: An overview" in J. Osofsky (ed.), *Handbook of infant development*. New York: Wiley.

Zigler, E. and Berman, W. (1983). "Discerning the future of early childhood intervention." *American Psychologist*, 38, 894–906.

Issues in organizing and developing support networks and parenting organizations

CHAPTER 2

How to start a parents' organization

Jane Israel Honikman

Introduction

This chapter deals with the developmental process required to establish a parents' organization successfully. The following information reviews: (1) examples of possible organizers and settings; (2) personal qualifications for involvement in starting groups; (3) guidelines for each step and phase of the required stages; (4) references to successful groups; and (5) personal experiences with starting a parent support group.

During the 1970s, I was part of a committee which founded Postpartum Education for Parents (PEP) in Santa Barbara, California. PEP is a parent volunteer group which provides emotional support in a forum where parents grow in confidence as they pursue their own parenting techniques. Non-judgmental environments, both over the telephone and in a group setting, give parents the opportunity to share experiences with other parents.

Examples

The following examples of parents and professionals seeking advice are taken from my personal files:

- a Childbirth Education Association in Texas is interested in starting a discussion group for postpartum parents;
- a social worker in New Zealand wants to offer a telephone line for parents through Catholic Social Services;
- a former member of PEP moves to New Jersey and wants to found a group there;
- an RN in the Parent Education Department at a hospital in Michigan wants to reach more parents;
- a child care worker for an Indian tribe in Canada is interested in parent involvement;
- a parent reads an article in a popular magazine about groups and wants to start her own;
- a Health Education Coordinator at an overseas United States Air Force Base believes there is a need for parent groups at their clinic;

- a psychiatrist in Australia wants to investigate how postpartum groups may be integrated into a maternity ward;
- a MSW caseworker for the Lutheran Social Service of Iowa is developing a support program;
- two parents, a RN and a MSW, in California have just had their first babies and wish to organize themselves and other new parents;
- an administrator for Education Services in a Community Mental Health Center in Rhode Island is exploring developing a parents' program;
- a doctor in a pediatric practice in Colorado is interested in offering groups and telephone support for newly delivered parents.

Are you one of these individuals? Do you have a wish but need direction? This chapter is intended to answer the most commonly asked questions from parents and professionals: Where do I begin, how will I proceed, and with whom will I work? It is also hoped that you will find encouragement from these pages as you proceed with your efforts.

Personal qualifications

Are you committed?

Before you read any further in this chapter, ask yourself if you are qualified to organize a group. No matter who you are, a parent or a professional, the most important qualification needed to accomplish your goal is commitment. The best ideas cannot be turned into realities without accepting the full responsibility of binding oneself to each stage of the developmental process. Can you truly visualize yourself devoted to investigation, planning, and the implementation phases required to achieve success?

Do you have the time?

Recognition of the time required by the process is also critical. Pledging yourself to a goal is not enough without acknowledging how much time it will take. This task of designing and building a new organization or even modifying an existing one, will undoubtedly be an addition to your current schedule. Do you really have the time to stay committed? My research has shown that it can take anywhere from two months to three years to develop an organization to the point at which it becomes self-sufficient (Honikman, 1981).

Do you possess patience?

If you answered yes to the requirements of commitment and time, then the final question involves patience. Patience, as a qualification, is not to be understated or taken lightly. It requires perseverance to work through each stage of the organizing process. Even the best plans are subject to change, delay, and road blocks. The time factor alone may be the cause for unseen frustrations. While working with parents and professionals, one is bound to encounter personalities which require special attention. It is important to recognize that it is never easy to organize people, and it is usually impossible to please everyone. Being an effective leader requires a basic level of understanding and caring for other people and yourself. I believe the ability to organize and lead people is a combination of an "innate" personality trait and learned skills. Suggestions which may help include: (1) Know what your type of leadership style is and what effect it has on others; (2) understand what is important to your group and know what will motivate its members to stay involved; (3) express your own ideas and feelings effectively and listen well to others; (4) be sensitive to the needs of others (Lawson *et al.*, 1982). It is essential to possess the patience to handle all phases of the organizational process.

Guidelines for organizational development

The founders of PEP summarized their experiences in *A Guide For Establishing A Parent Support Program In Your Community* (Armstrong *et al.*, 1979). The intention was to inspire other people to start similar groups. The components of the developmental process outlined in the Guide are as follows:

A The idea stage
  1 Determine who, with whom, and where the group will organize.
B Investigation stage
  1 Explore what other groups exist both locally and around the country.
C Planning stage
  1 Assess the needs of the community.
  2 Establish your purpose, philosophy, goals, and objectives; determine what services will achieve your goal.
  3 Gather community support, encourage cooperation, avoid duplication of effort.
  4 Organize the group's internal structure or seek assimilation or association with an existing agency.
  5 Formalize a budget, seek funding, finalize status as a viable group.
  6 Recruit volunteers and/or hire staff.
  7 Provide training, and orientation to staff.
D Implementation stage
  1 Establish an advisory board of supportive community professionals.

    2 Begin publicity, and outreach to target population.
    3 Initiate operation and services.
E Evaluation stage
    1 Design internal and external processes for evaluation or seek
       outside designs for ongoing evaluation of services, staff, and
       volunteers.

A Idea stage

What do you want to accomplish?

Begin by daydreaming alone, or brainstorming with others about what
you would like to change or initiate for families in your community. Do
not attempt to analyze these thoughts. Let your mind wander freely.
Start by completing these types of sentences. "It would be wonderful if
. . ." or "If we could only have . . . here." Write down all the ideas that
follow. Do not eliminate even the craziest ones.

    As explained in the introduction, the PEP idea was to give parents
emotional support. We brainstormed what we would have loved to have
had available to us when our babies were born. We agreed that it would
have been wonderful to have had telephone contact with other parents
24 hours a day. A crisis telephone number or "hot line" had existed,
but none of us ever called it because it was associated with child abuse.
We wished for a "warm line" instead. In other words, we brainstormed
a telephone line which was not crisis oriented. A "warm line" would
bring parents together before any problem developed. It was a "crazy"
idea but exactly the concept we wished to pursue.

Who will work together?

Ask yourself "who am I?" Are you a parent, a volunteer, paid
professional, paraprofessional, or several of these? Search your mind
regarding who else might share your vision of the new idea. A close
friend, an acquaintance, a colleague, a professional are all good possibilities. Write down the names of all the people you would feel comfortable
approaching regarding your idea. Once again, do not analyze whether
or not they would have the time, only the mutual interest for the concept.

    My research indicates that those who determined the need for forming
a group usually became involved in establishing it. The backgrounds of
these people include medicine, education, psychology, sociology, philosophy, parenting, childbirth education, nursing, social work, counseling,
and religion. The PEP founders were all mothers working full time at
home, college graduates, and friends.

Where will the setting be?

Consider where you could work on your idea by asking "where do I currently spend my time?" At home, in an office, part-time, full-time, alone, or are you with other people. Could your ideas be explored in the setting of an existing agency, study group of a volunteer organization or both? List all possibilities regardless of whether or not you currently belong to a place or know someone else who does.

As members of a child study interest group of the Goleta Valley Branch of the American Association of University Women, the PEP setting was informal, part-time, and unstructured. We did most of our organizing at meetings in a local park with our children present and over the telephone.

My investigations of existing groups reveal that once a group is operational, its settings include homes, medical offices, hospitals, social agencies, schools and other community buildings.

The outcome of this stage is the determination of which individuals will work together as a core committee. Once this is established, whether it is a small or large group, you are ready to proceed to the next stage.

B Investigation stage

Experiences of other groups

After your idea or concept has been formulated and a core committee gathered, the next stage is the investigation. When the initial idea of PEP was being discussed during the mid-1970s, no one in our group had heard of existing programs. By chance, we noticed a brief description in *American Baby* magazine of a group called PACES in Chicago. They were our first contact with another group.

Finding other groups by chance is not good enough. The Guides we published and national publicity about PEP led me to conduct a study of the development and dynamics of postpartum support groups which was published in 1981. It was an attempt to gather data to serve as a tool in helping to form a national network of groups (Honikman, 1981).

In May 1981 a conference was convened in Chicago to form a coalition of parenting resources programs from Canada and the United States. For the first time, a unifying effort was underway to bring together the groups attempting to serve parents and their children (Callahan, 1981). The vision of Bernice Weissbourd, founder of the Family Focus in Evanston, Illinois has resulted in the formation of the Family Resource Coalition. Opportunities now exist to investigate what is being accomplished in other communities (Weissbourd, 1983).

During 1982–3, the Yale University Bush Center in collaboration with the Family Resource Coalition compiled information about innovative family support programs. They published a resource guide called *Programs to Strengthen Families*. The programs described in this chapter are selected from this guide (Zigler *et al.*, 1983).

C Planning stage

Confirmation of need

Reacting to an intuitive impulse that assumes that there is a population in need of the services your group wishes to supply, is not sufficient reason to develop a program. The success of a support group is generally proportional to documented need in your community. It is true that a "gut" or emotional reaction to any issue will provide a rallying cry for some, but there must be common sense, reason, practical approaches and endless patience.

Before a statement of purpose and specific objectives is written, the community's population needs to be asked if it agrees with your intentions. According to Florence G. Cassidy, "social need should be the determining factor in initiating, continuing, modifying, or terminating an organization (Cassidy, 1959). In formal terms, determining social need is accomplished through social surveys. Major types of surveys include written questionnaires and/or verbal interviews as research tools. Factual information, such as determining what agencies already provide existing services, is part of a needs assessment. In addition, the humanistic, emotional response to requests for information from the public is needed too. Questions which are related to opinions about wanting, needing, desiring a certain service are subject to the whims of the population you are surveying. The practical steps to consider before designing a needs assessment are: (1) Costs and who will pay; (2) length of time required; (3) consent of the agencies and individuals to be included; and (4) selection of who will conduct the study (Council of Jewish Welfare Federations and Welfare Funds, 1959).

PEP's founders devised a simple questionnaire and distributed it through obstetrical offices. This poll was not scientifically conducted, but the response was an overwhelming affirmation of our idea.

Referring to the examples given in my Introduction, all of these people are searching for ways to offer a new service to parents. From the childbirth educator, the case worker, the doctor, to the at-home parent, each has a hunch that they want to start something new. In each case, their ideas must be confirmed by a social survey. "Is there really a need for my new group?" Both factual data and consumer opinion need to be gathered and analyzed before proceeding. The manner in which you conduct your needs assessment will be determined by knowing who you are, your community, and the setting for your organization.

Putting an idea on paper

Good ideas are only the beginning. The need to articulate a specific statement of purpose or goal is as important as it is to be inspired, excited and enthusiastic over a concept.

For example, our efforts with PEP could not have proceeded beyond the "we need support" stage without a sentence stating our intent. We wrote "to ease the adjustment of the developing family immediately after the arrival of a baby." We covered several key points by those few words. For instance, the word "ease" does not sound as crisis related as the verb "to help." "Arrival" was selected instead of "birth" to include adoption and "developing" rather than "new" took PEP beyond the first-time-only families.

A few examples of the goals of other parents' organizations are as follows:

1   COPE (Coping With the Overall Pregnancy/Parenting Experience), Boston, MA states its goal as "to resolve the conflicts that arise in women and men during pregnancy and throughout their parenting lives."
2   Booth Parenting Program, based at a maternity hospital in Philadelphia, PA seeks "to facilitate optimal family relations from pregnancy through age three."
3   Family Support Services, Inc. in Denver, CO, an affiliation in a family practice residency, seeks to "reduce social isolation, and help meet the mother's need for emotional support" as well as "increase the family's participation in the community and encourage warm, stimulating interactions between infant and parent."
4   Parent Cooperative Preschool Program which is sponsored by a community college in Spokane, WA gives part of its goal as "to foster the development of parenting skills."

Means to the end

It is important to note that a goal does not include objectives. That is, there are no directions as to how a program will accomplish the purpose of the organization. Objectives are specific ways written separately in answer to the question "how will we achieve our goal?" Another way to identify objectives is to list the services your organization will provide the community.

For PEP, our objectives were to offer a forum for parents to meet other parents in parent discussion groups and to increase the confidence of parents over the warm line.

COPE offers counseling and education services through discussion groups for pregnant women and new mothers and individual counseling opportunities.

The Parenting Program at Booth Maternity Center's objectives of short-term counseling, telephone support and home visits meet their goal.

Family Support Services provides a lay home visitor program beginning with expectant parents.

The Parent Cooperative Preschool provides a "laboratory" preschool where parents can observe their own and other children, gather information, and become directly involved with their children's education.

Services

Public awareness and education have increased the numbers of parents' programs which currently serve our society today. The diversity of services offered in a multitude of settings reflects the unique qualities of each community. The list in the appendix shows the variety of resources which exist to serve parents (Honikman, 1981; Zigler et al., 1983).

The success of your organization is related to the quality of your services and why parents use them. Regular record keeping of participation and periodic evaluation of your services will help the organization's leaders determine if services are continuing to meet parents' needs.

For example, PEP conducts a yearly questionnaire of parents attending discussion groups. The majority of participants in 1982 and 1983 stated that the service met their reason for attending which was for friendship or social contact (PEP Board of Directors, 1983).

Community cooperation

Assuming that your committee's articulated idea has a clear focus, the next step is to gather community support and enthusiasm. At this point, we are speaking in terms of endorsement by individuals and agencies who agree that your efforts are worthy. A successful group will not be one which operates in a vacuum, ignoring the interests of the community's existing programs. Likewise, seeking endorsements confirms that you have progressed past the idea, investigation and affirmation stages of development. If there is going to be any duplication of services or any overlap of serving a select population, this step will uncover this potentially "dangerous" possibility.

I mention "danger" because of an experience the PEP founders encountered during our first search for funding. We had approached the local chapter of the March of Dimes but were refused any financial backing because one board member believed we were replicating the services offered by the La Leche League. Although this was not the case, a more thorough presentation explaining this issue may have prevented this misunderstanding.

PEP approached this phase of getting community support by requesting permission to use names of noted groups and individuals on our first brochure. We received endorsements from the Santa Barbara Pediatric Society, Santa Barbara Childbirth Educators, Santa Barbara County Mental Health Department as well as the local hospitals. Now that PEP is well known, we no longer list our supportors in the revised brochure.

The history of the Family Stress Center in Concord, CA shows a good understanding of this stage. Members of the Junior League of Oakland-East Bay conducted a survey of 120 children's service providers before forming a task force of more than thirty public and private professionals. They were well prepared to present their program to local politicians and the community at large.

In Milwaukee, WI four agencies cooperated in forming their Southside Wellness Project. This joint sponsorship is noteworthy since it serves a diverse community and mutual cooperation was essential to achieve their goal.

Another aspect of community cooperation is the importance of providing support to those who are dealing with this organizing. Your personal life is affected by the organizational process, and there is an element of stress which accompanies this work. If as a leader you begin to feel overwhelmed by the responsibilities, you should be able to ask for emotional as well as practical help from your community.

For example, the issue of providing child care during board meetings or training sessions may be resolved by asking for volunteers from your support community. PEP asked the Baby Sitting Cooperative of the Goleta Valley Branch of AAUW to do this during our first year. Subsequently, PEP started its own Baby Sitting Coop which provided this same help.

Assimilation or independence

Eventually your organization will need to discuss and decide upon its future course. Part of this question is determined by the formulation of an administrative framework. This process of writing an infra-structure will include formal by-laws and job descriptions. This is not easy and is a task often overlooked by people who are excited by a concept but feel burdened by such detail. By attempting to complete this step, you are now confronted by the issue of whether to organize as an independent, non-profit corporation or to seek assimilation into an existing agency. If it is difficult to design a formal administration perhaps autonomy is not appropriate for your group. It may prove better in the long run to hand over your concept to an appropriate group which can assume responsibility and continue your efforts. Other points to consider while deciding this issue include: (1)   The economic base of your community; (2)   the age structure of your population; (3)   its occupational distribution; (4)   the educational status; and (5)   its cultural heritage (Cassidy, 1959).

The PEP founders decided to establish PEP as an independent, non-profit corporation in 1978 after being a one year project funded by the Educational Foundation of the American Association of University Women. The PEP Articles of Incorporation formalized what had begun as an informal gathering of friends. It proved that an idea which is based upon a confirmed need, which has a well thought out purpose and is capable of structure can become an independent organization.

Monetary concerns

Funding is often the greatest challenge facing any group. According to Edward Zigler of the Yale Bush Center in Child Development and Social Policy: "Most programs are operating on a shoestring" (Zigler *et al.*, 1983). The money to operate a program may come from a variety of sources and, as with the funding for other social agencies, these purses are usually small. There are two broad categories of revenue: funding and fees. Types of funding included donations, both private and public, grants, government and foundations, and fundraising. Fees are generated by either fee for service or membership dues, both of which can be arranged on a sliding scale based on ability to pay.

The first step in dealing with this issue is the establishment of a realistic budget. After one is determined, a major question which must be asked is, "will our source of income be stable?" A sad fact is that funding can become such a problem that it drains energy from the intent of the organization.

In PEP's case, the program requires an annual budget of less than $3,000 since it operates without any paid staff or office space. The board of directors organizes an annual fundraising event rather than spending time and energy writing proposals year after year for grant support. The PEP Children's Clothing, Toy, and Equipment Sale has turned into a community service, generating goodwill for volunteers and consumers as well as revenue for operating PEP.

The following list compares nine organizations' services, staff, clients and their approximate budgets. These numbers show the wide range of options which exist for parents' groups. The factors which influence the size of a budget are: (1)   Type and size of staff; (2)   number and type of services; and (3)   place of operation.

1   PEP, California; 4 services, 0 paid staff, 50 volunteers, 1,500 families, $3,000 approximate budget.

2   831-BORN, Ohio; 9 services, 1 paid staff, 25 volunteers, 1,500 families, $2,000 approximate budget.
3   Parents After Childbirth Education, Ohio; 7 services, 5 paid staff, 6 volunteers, 200 families, $4,000 approximate budget.
4   New Parent Discussion Groups, British Columbia; 10 services, 3 paid staff, 20 volunteers, 200 families, $18,000 approximate budget.
5   The Children's Place, New Hampshire; 15 services, 4 part-time paid staff, 25+ volunteers, 350 families, $34,000 approximate budget.
6   Mother and Child Center, New York; 9 services, 8 paid staff, 6 volunteers, 85 families, $35,000 approximate budget.
7   Westmoreland Hospital, Pennsylvania; 12 services, 2.5 paid staff, 7 volunteers, 35 families, $41,000 approximate budget.
8   Parents Place, New York; 13 services, 14 part-time paid staff, 3 volunteers, 400 families, $94,000 approximate budget.
9   Family Stress Center, California; 11 services, 8 paid staff, 150+ volunteers, 400+ families, $200,000 approximate budget.

Who will run the program?

The final steps of the planning stage include the practical fundamentals of staffing the organization. At this point, the group organizers should be able to state what they want to do, for whom, and how. The next question is, "who will run our program?"

Professionals or non-professionals

The answer to this question needs to address the issues of paid and volunteer personnel and professionals and paraprofessional staff. The core committee has been dealing with this indirectly throughout the organizational process depending upon their own status and the setting of the group. Certainly, the formalization of the budget is a direct confrontation with these concerns.

For PEP, this question was less complicated than for most founders of a parents' group. As volunteers from the outset, we knew that our program's goals and services would remain staffed by volunteers. There was never any question of paying any staff person, professional or otherwise. Our low budget dictated this requirement.

Douglas Powell wrote, "One of the most difficult issues in organizing a parents support group pertains to the role of the professional" (1984). The PEP founders decided to utilize professionals in our community as resource people. An advisory board was formed prior to the onset of services. Then, as now, eight professionals are included: An accountant, nurse practitioner, RN, pediatrician, obstetrican, childbirth educator, attorney, and marriage and family counselor. Their role is to provide the board of directors with encouragement, feedback and expertise without a fee. They attend formal meetings held quarterly as well as speak at PEP training and in-service sessions. PEP volunteers feel free to contact these professionals whenever a need arises.

The staffing of an organization is important, but my experience has been that the status of the staff members is not a problem so long as they are caring, non-judgmental people. In my opinion, those who are best qualified to assist parents are other parents who feel comfortable and accepting of themselves in their own parenting role.

Training

The training component is a critical segment of the organization. Among the four founders of PEP was one parent who had had some experience training others in her job. Judy Mrstik wrote "A Leaders' Guide for Training Volunteers in Parent Support Services" to complement the other two PEP publications. Based upon the PEP philosophy that there are many ways to parent, the essence of PEP's training is recognition that volunteers do not possess all the answers. Learning to guide parents as they seek self-confidence during the early months of parenting is the key point of PEP training.

I believe firmly that any parents' organization, whether staffed by professionals or not, volunteer or paid, must be trained in basic communication skills and group dynamics. Critical to these is the fine art of active listening. It is important tto remember that these skills need to be enhanced, supported and continued for all staff members throughout their involvement with parents. Initial training is only a first step. Ongoing in-service training is a must (Honikman, 1982).

Equally important to training is staff support. People giving emotional support need support themselves. In the formal setting of an agency, staff support may be taken for granted. In a volunteer setting, staff support is often overlooked. The PEP board of directors provides regular linkage among its volunteers with a telephone call from a board member to several volunteers. Job satisfaction is discussed along with whatever may be on the volunteer's mind relating to PEP and their personal life. Other ways this has been done at PEP include: (1) Social gatherings with family members; (2) in-service meetings for volunteers only; and (3) a monthly *News Notes* which highlights one volunteer's background along with organizational news.

D Implementation stage

Projecting your group's image to the public

Now that your parents' organization has been carefully planned, it is ready to show itself to the community.

This phase must include some type of public relations campaign in order to reach the target population. Publicity for the public at large is important as well. People can learn about your services through the use of the media, paid advertisements or news releases, an organized speakers bureau or informal telephone contact, through professional referral or word of mouth, and with brochures, newsletters or pamphlets.

The organization we originally contacted in Chicago called PACES has a newsletter called *The Pacesetter* as part of their public relations efforts. Their founders point out, "The public memory is short. Only by constantly appearing in the news can a group hope to attain significant recognition" (Mason *et al.*, 1979).

PEP's experiences indicate the need to reach out to parents before the arrival of the child. This is done through a service called Baby Basics which is a monthly infant care class. We provide hands-on demonstrations for parents-to-be as well as discussing the emotional changes which happen in a family after the baby's arrival. Since PEP sponsors this, our volunteers speak about our other services thus promoting the services our organization offers families. Another outreach service is the Postpartum Telephone Call made to parents who have asked for a volunteer to call seven to 14 days after the birth. This is another opportunity for the PEP parent to invite the new parent to call the Warm Line at any time and to join a parent discussion group.

Beyond the local level, there is value in joining a national organization in order to receive support, achieve recognition and further the cause of your group. There are a variety of professional associations with which to become affiliated depending upon the focus of your organization. For example, PACES in Chicago belongs to the International Childbirth Education Association. Parents Place in San Francisco is affiliated with the Jewish Family and Children's Services. PEP has become a member of the Chicago-based Family Resource Coalition. This Coalition is a national grassroots network of individuals and organizations promoting the development of prevention-oriented, community-based programs to strengthen families. They have a listing of members if you are searching for contacts.

A parents' organization must possess and project an atmosphere of openness in order for participants in a program to feel comfortable. Whether in person or over the telephone, a friendly, warm personality will enable parents to feel at ease; at the same time, it is important to be businesslike and professional.

PEP requires that the following points be made at the beginning of a new discussion group or during the course of one-to-one support:

1 a review of the philosophy and purpose of PEP;
2 PEP volunteers are not experts and the sharing of ideas will come from participating parents;

3   all PEP conversations and discussions are held in strict confidence;
4   PEP does not endorse any products or make referrals to professionals;
5   participants are requested not to mention the names of physicians, hospitals or other related places or people.

These last two points are particularly important in order to maintain the support of the community as well as to avoid any legal problems.

Addressing parent's issues

Parents experiencing life with a newborn are very likely to be concerned with a specific range of issues. The following topics are derived from PEP conversations and discussions of parents participating in the PEP program.

Typical topics

Childbirth experience; lack of sleep; reality versus expectation of what it would be like bringing a baby home; feeding schedules; breastfeeding; bottlefeeding; crying baby; should I let the baby cry?; illness; relations within the family unit; mother–baby, father–baby, mother–father; establishing closeness as a couple; time together; communications; sexual relations; leaving the baby with others; traveling with baby; mother's diet; relations with the family, in-laws; how to deal with advice from others and books; relationship and communication with the doctor; meeting baby's needs versus spoiling; infant development; parents have needs too; finding time for oneself; mother returning to work; feelings and problems; childcare; solid foods; sleep problems; safety; babyproofing; siblings; discipline; weaning; community resources; when to have another child.

Each one of these topics has many books written about it covering a wide range of opinions and research. My favorite ones happen to be those I used when my children were born, probably out of an emotional attachment to the time they "saved me." My experience with parents has been that they find favorites as well either through friends, family or off the book or library shelf. The resources which "work wonders" are those which make the reader, listener or viewer feel strong and confident.

Balancing format and flow

While it is true that most issues and questions from parents are predictable, it is important to allow a parent a chance to gain self-confidence at his and her own rate.

It can happen that a support giver will take over a situation as the expert. This can occur particularly while a parent feels inadequate and vulnerable. The key is to remain available and supportive. This can be done by asking a parent what has been tried and by providing suggestions such as "this has worked for me" or "sometimes I find ... is helpful." By allowing the parent to explore alternatives, confidence will grow. The process is very much one of trial and error since all situations and their participants are unique.

It is important to remember that the essence of support gives people the ability to grow as individuals and the opportunity to learn from experience.

There are times when a parent seeks out more individual contact time with a PEP volunteer. PEP policy leaves the decision up to each person as to how much time and energy to devote to certain situations. For example, one of the calls I received on the Warm Line was from a nursing mother who needed assistance in person rather than over the telephone. I found several volunteers who were willing to go to the caller's home and give support. If a parent's demands become excessive, then a professional from the PEP Advisory Board is called to assist the volunteer in dealing with the situation.

E Evaluation stage

Taking the time to set up a process for evaluating one's program is often overlooked by organizers. In formal settings some type of evaluation is usually included because it is requested by an outside funding source. "Evaluation is a central concern because the development of family programs has by and large outstripped the capacity to evaluate their effectiveness" (Zigler *et al.*, 1983). There needs to be an accumulation of data to show that programs work. Without facts and figures and documented opinions it is difficult to justify one's existence.

PEP has been evaluated annually since 1978. As part of the first year grant from the American Association of University Women, an outside evaluation committee surveyed volunteers and parents involved in PEP. Questionnaires covered participants' satisfaction with the structure and type of services provided. The results of this process, now conducted by the board of directors, are published as part of the PEP Annual Reports.

Methods of evaluation include observation, interview, questionnaire and examination of records and other appropriate written materials. The Yale University/Family Resource Coalition's *Programs to Strengthen Families* Guide includes an evaluation component with each organizational description. Dr Heather B. Weiss states:

> The value of these programs will be more fully documented and understood when sensitive and systematic evaluation strategies are

developed that are more capable of measuring what the programs do. Such evaluations will go beyond the simple question of what works, to a more differentiated set of questions: what works for whom, when, how and why? (Weiss, 1983).

Conclusions

In this chapter, I have attempted to present a guide or outline for starting a parents' organization. I have received requests for this formula from hundreds of people in as many different situations. As often as I would have liked to wave a magic wand and give them simple answers, this task can rarely be simplified.

My first recommendation to all individuals and groups is that they join the Family Resource Coalition. As members they will be part of the network promoting and exchanging information and resources which promote the development of community-based programs. The Coalition maintains a clearinghouse of information and programs involved with families in the United States and Canada. Its members are available to offer assistance to those outside of North America as well. There is no reason to work in isolation or to reinvent the wheel. Furthermore, there is strength in numbers.

There is one aspect of the process which would make the creation of groups much easier. If professionals and parents could communicate with one another about the importance of parents sharing with other parents, then a giant step in creating new services for families could be achieved. Perhaps this is an issue which should be addressed at informal forums or formal conferences.

There appear to be three levels of involvement or activity within and between organizations. The first is parent to parent, next is family with family, and the third is group to group. Visualizing each level reveals the ripple effect which occurs when people support people. Parents need not feel alone and isolated, families can share their strengths with each other and organizers of groups can help spread their expertise. Professionals will learn from parents and parents will gain insights from professionals. The word networking is often used to describe this partnership. There are now connections between people which may not have existed before parents' groups became established.

Our backgrounds may be diverse, the settings may vary, and the names of the groups may differ, but the message is the same. People are organizing parents' groups because they care about themselves, other families, their communities and our society. They are committed to making a difference and a positive statement. It is my hope that this book will help all who wish to continue to work together in an effort to establish parents' organizations.

Appendix

General services

advocacy	childbirth education classes	childcare
counseling	community bulletin board	intervention
drop-in center	health care and education	discussion groups
hot line	infant care classes	home visitors
lectures/workshops	information and referral	library/toy lending
newsletter	networking	respite care
social activities	postpartum phone calls	skills/goods exchange
warm line	technical assistance	transportation

Special circumstance support service offered by PEP volunteers

adoption	allergies	delayed parenthood
birth defects	bottle feeding	breastfeeding
cesarean birth	colic	hernias
home delivery	hospitalization	infant death
jaundice	miscarriage	single parent
teenage parenthood	working mother	

References

Armstrong, J., Edmondson, J., Honikman, J., and Mrstik, J. (1979). *A Guide for Establishing A Parent Support Program In Your Community*. Postpartum Education for Parents, 927 Kellogg Avenue, Santa Barbara, CA 93111, pp. iii, 65, 79, 80.

Callahan, B. (1981). "Family Focus Conference: Highlights." Personal notes, on file with J. Honikman, 927 N. Kellogg Avenue, Santa Barbara, CA 93111.

Cassidy, Florence G. (1959). "Principles of Community Organization" in A. Dunham and E. B. Harper (eds), *Community Organization In Action, Basic Literature and Critical Comments*, Associated Press, New York.

Council of Jewish Welfare Federations and Welfare Funds (1959). "Social Surveys" in A. Dunham and E. B. Harper (eds), *Community Organization In Action, Basic Literature and Critical Comments*, Associated Press, New York.

Honikman, J. (1981). *A study of the dynamics and development of Postpartum Support Groups*. 927 Kellogg Avenue, Santa Barbara, CA 93111, pp. 75–85.

Honikman, J. (1982). "PEP Volunteers Assist Parents In Santa Barbara." *Family Resource Coalition Report*. Vol. 1, no. 4, 230 N. Michigan Avenue, Chicago, IL 60601.

Lawson, L. G., Donant, F. D., and Lawson, J. D. (1982). *Lead On!* Impact Publishers, PO Box 20852, San Luis Obispo, CA 53220.

Mason, D., Jensen, G., and Ryzewics, C. (1979). *How To Grow A Parents Group*. International Childbirth Education Association, Inc., Milwaukee, WI.

Mrstik, J. (1979). *A Leaders Guide For Training Volunteers in Parent Support Programs*. Postpartum Education for Parents, 927 Kellogg Avenue, Santa Barbara, CA 93111.

PEP Board of Directors (1983). *6th Annual Report*. April.

Powell, D. (1984). "Professionals and Parent Groups: What Roles?" in *Family Resource Coalition Report*. Vol. 3, no. 1.

Weiss, H. (1983). "Introduction" in *Programs To Strengthen Families: A Resource Guide*. Family Resource Coalition, 230 N. Michigan Avenue, Chicago, IL 60601.

Weissbourd, B. (1983). "The Family Support Movement: Greater Than The Sum of Its Parts." *Zero to Three*. National Center for Clinical Infant Programs, 733 15th Street N. W., Suite 912, Washington D.C. 20005. Vol. 4, no. 1.

Zigler, E., Weiss, H., Kagan, S. L. (1983). *Programs To Strengthen Families*. Yale University and The Family Resource Coalition, 230 N. Michigan Avenue, Chicago, IL 60601.

CHAPTER 3

Peer support for parents of preterm infants

Linda Gilkerson and Stephanie Porter

I Parent experiences and needs

Three years ago I couldn't imagine ever thinking about this again.

Bobby will be three on July 4. He came out with a big blast. It was very unexpected. He was at 29 weeks gestation.

Up until then, I had the most perfect pregnancy that anyone could ever want. I wasn't sick one day. I was doing all of the right things, eating the right foods, exercising.

All of a sudden I felt contractions. It took me a while to realize what was happening. I called the doctor and he sent me to the hospital. Thank God for the hospital. They couldn't stop my contractions after a whole day of giving me Terbutiline and they decided this child wants to come.

On July 4th he showed up, I didn't even have the opportunity to see him in the delivery room because he was so sick. My husband was right there with us. They held him up and said "Here he is" and then dashed him to the intensive care unit. At that point, I really didn't feel like a mother. I felt like this really didn't happen to me. My husband had left to follow the baby. I had no idea what his complications were. All I knew was that I wouldn't see him until the next day.

My husband returned when I was in my room. He said things would be fine. They told us we'd have to wait a 72 hour period to see if he'd do well. We still had no feelings that we were parents. This was a very odd time for us. We were almost in shock. I could almost feel as if this wasn't my child.

I went to see the baby the next day. I looked at this puny little boy who was filled with all kinds of monitors and was black and blue from the bad delivery. I asked myself where is that pink little chubby little baby that we were supposed to have? I had no feeling, no bonding whatsoever. My husband had more of a bond with our son than I did. I felt I'm not a mother yet.

It wasn't until the following night until about 2.30 am that I had a horrible feeling that I should call the special care nursery. They said: "We had just gotten in touch with your husband. We were about to call you – Bobby is not doing well." We both got to the SCN at about the same time. They had been bagging him for three hours and they felt he wasn't responding at all. I think they were giving us some time to say good-bye. At that point I realized: "My God I'm a mother . . . I haven't held my baby yet." The doctor said, "Touch him, feel him, tell him you love him. Let him know you are here because they know your voice." We did this for about 10 minutes. My husband stayed with the doctors and I had left the room. My parents were in the waiting room. It was the first time I cried. I hadn't even held my baby. I didn't know what it was like to hold a baby.

Fifteen minutes later my husband and the doctor came out and said, "Bobby's responding now. He's back on the respirator. He still has a long way to go but we've gotten by a very crucial point." They had lost him and brought him back. The doctor said, "We think he's going to stay where he is for awhile. I've seen it many times; the parents give those children their survival. They give them that fight. But what kind of support do parents need to sustain them during the long haul ahead?"

(The above parent experience was taken from taped transcripts from *The Preterm Infant Course*, Wheelock College, Boston, MA, 1984.)

When the pregnant couple's anticipated birth plan is disrupted by a premature birth or other complications, families feel a sense of loss, guilt, and fear of being out of control. While in the neonatal intensive care unit (NICU) most families receive a great deal of support from their primary nurse or the staff nurse most directly involved. Others may feel closer to another staff member (neonatologist, social worker, etc.) and rely on him or her for information as well as support.

The emotional upheaval felt by parents has prompted many special care nurseries to offer time for families to come together to share experiences and ask questions. There are a variety of methods that facilitate this interaction among parents. The most common strategy is a parent group. For some people there is a certain stigma attached to participation in a support group. Support groups occasionally conjure up images of sharing, opening up, exposing oneself. When facing a life and death crisis, some families tend to feel extremely vulnerable. Regaining and maintaining a sense of control can be very important. For these families, a group session or educational meeting providing information works best. The premise is information. The outcome is also support from professionals as well as other parents.

The education meeting may also include a night when parents of former NICU babies come and share their experiences. A graduate parent night provides new families with a renewed sense of hope and gives them a realistic picture of the future. Many new families find great strength in seeing those parents who have, in their words, "made it."

Many NICU's are showing the latest films on premature baby development and the impact of the experience on the families. During this time families have the opportunity to have their emotions validated and learn more about their new baby. Alternate resources – a suggested reading list, lending library, or recent articles file – may also be available for those who desire additional information.

Sources of support after discharge from the NICU or community hospital nursery include the family physician or pediatrician, community health nurses, infant follow-up clinics, and early intervention programs. While each of these services offers valuable care from professionals, typically parent-to-parent or peer support is not included.

In NICU families there is a great feeling of uncertainty about the present and the future. Many families who leave the NICU remember these feelings vividly and often offer to provide peer support to other premature parents while their baby is hospitalized. This parent-to-parent support may happen informally through parents, staff members, or may be a more formalized community program. The support may also be provided through a parent visitation program where veteran parents come to the NICU and talk with those new families experiencing the crisis. The earliest interaction between parents may take place when the mother is experiencing a high-risk pregnancy and subsequently premature birth. She may be on bedrest in a hospital or at home. This is a time when many families need additional support and resources. A parent-to-parent program implemented at this early stage may help to alleviate some of the frustrations and anxiety faced by the parents.

In summary, parents need to choose the appropriate type of personal support available. Each parent will differ in his or her coping strategies; we need not judge the style in which parents handle their crisis. We need only to make available an array of services including professional and peer support opportunities during and after hospitalization.

II Design of a peer support program

As shown in the previous section, the organized support for parents during the post-NICU phase is typically from professionals in health care and developmental programs. Ongoing contact, or even sporadic contact, with other families who have experienced the ups and downs of the NICU drops off dramatically after discharge. A parent commented:

> The premature birth of a child is a frightening and confusing thing for us. And in spite of the exceptional care and attention that these children and their parents receive from the physicians and nurses in

the NICUs, we still feel the need to communicate with other parents who have been down this road before.

Another parent expressed the need in this way: "For the first two years or so, you wonder with a premie if they will walk, if they have CP or eye problems or other problems. I wish we had other parents to talk with!" Upsets and stresses are part of having a very sick newborn. Sharing concerns with other parents can provide reassurance that one's feelings and experiences are not "crazy" but normal within the context of the situation.

In this section we present the strategies used by Project Welcome, a federally funded Handicapped Children's Early Education Program Project, to develop a parent-run peer support program for families after discharge. In the following section, we describe how the peer support program has made the transition from being one component of the federally funded demonstration project to an independent, non-profit community-based parent organization.

A Leadership

1 *Parent coordinator.* The responsibility for developing any parent support program should be assigned to an individual or to a team of co-leaders. We believe that the parent coordinator(s) should be the parent(s) of a premature infant. This will ensure first-hand familiarity with the experiences, needs and issues to be addressed by any activities planned for parents. Peer leadership encourages a two-way flow of support and information; thus the program can be shaped by both parent participants and the leadership.

2 *Parent council.* A parent council may be established to advise, steer and support the parent coordinator. An effective working council should be of moderate size. For example, a group size of 10–12 members generally assures that about five members will participate regularly and actively; the participation of the others will be variable. Members should represent a variety of experiences, e.g., short and long NICU stays, babies in for acute and observational hospitalizations, mothers and fathers, parents of children with and without special needs. Names of prospective council members may be suggested by NICU staff, other professionals and/or other parents.

Members of the council can work with the coordinator(s) to obtain and review information about other premie groups and decide which support services should be offered. Other council activities may include suggesting topics for monthly meetings, writing the newsletter or other written products, coordinating social activities, making presentations and eventually assuming leadership roles.

B Collaboration with the NICU

If you are working closely with a hospital, and particularly with the NICU, it is extremely important as a preliminary step to establish a trusting relationship with the NICU. The NICU staff feels a sense of responsibility toward the families they serve. They need opportunities to tell what they believe their families need and to discuss the advantages and disadvantages of the various program formats the group is considering.

NICU's have established patterns of working with parents. Initially, therefore, it may be less threatening to provide community programs to discharged parents than to implement a new in-hospital program. Planning a high-quality education program that proves its effectiveness in the community will make it easier later on to implement support programs for in-hospital families. Families who participate in a program are likely to communicate their positive feelings to hospital staff.

It is important to be patient during the planning time. We all want the best support for families with premies and are eager to provide needed services. Collaborating with the NICU helps assure easier access to parents and more appropriate program offerings.

C Recruitment

Once a decision is reached on the types of parent programs to be offered, plans for recruitment should begin. Recruitment methods will differ from one community to another and will depend on the nature of the programs offered. Some of the suggestions that follow may prove useful.

Permission slips may be filled in by families who are interested in obtaining information from the parent support group. Parents may find these in an admission or discharge packet, in the parent room, or may be given them by one of the nurses. The use of the permission slips eliminates the use of hospital mailing lists which reach many parents who are either uninterested or who may have had a child who died. This system also insures confidentiality for families.

Pediatricians, VNA's, community hospitals and early intervention programs may be sent a flyer, describing the groups, which they can post on their parent resource board. These programs may have lists of parents who might be interested in the specific activities you are planning. The coordinator should plan a system for maintaining an updated mailing list of e.g., parents, agencies, health professionals.

Direct mail can be supplemented by announcements in the local newspaper's calendar of events, or by public service announcements on local television and radio stations. Once the program is underway, of course, satisfied parents will spread the word.

A final word: Do not expect 100 per cent response to even the most exciting program planned. Parents of premature infants (like all parents) have many interests, commitments, and constraints on their time. A positive response rate of 10 per cent should be considered excellent. The opportunity to participate should be considered the primary goal, not the numbers of participants.

D Program options

Families need an enormous amount of support as they go through the experience of having a premature baby. This support can take many forms, including telephone support, education, informal and formal small groups, socially-oriented groups and access to other resources. Because parents have different needs at different stages, it is important to try to offer parent support in different formats, so that parents can choose what works best for them.

In this section we describe strategies for initiating a parent education group and a telephone support program. Additional options for parent support are also presented.

1 Parent education group

The NICU experience can be a devastating time for families. During the first year, both in the NICU and after discharge, parents may not be ready to share their feelings and experiences. An education series, offering families an opportunity to learn about their babies, may be the most attractive program for parents at this stage. The primary goal of the series should be to provide parents with specific information regarding their premature infant. In the process of obtaining this important information, parents share their experiences with one another and accomplish the ultimate goal of the program: support.

The series may be presented in a variety of formats: monthly session, a time-limited mini-series of four weekly sessions, or once every few weeks or months. Topics may be presented by both parents and professionals. The combination of professional information and parental experiences is very helpful for parents to hear. The education series can also be opened to both professionals and parents. Professionals who attend may find that communicating with these families gives them new perspectives on other families they serve as well as alternative ideas for providing support.

The education series may also be offered to parents only. At these meetings, the parents may feel freer to talk about NICU feelings and experiences, about experiences with community programs, or to discuss feelings about their child. Parents know intuitively that each mother and father wants the best for their child and loves their child deeply, even though they may need to share how upset, confused, angry, or frustrated they are. This type of acceptance can be harder to feel – even though it may be there – with professionals in the audience.

To announce the education series, families may be sent a letter introducing the program, explaining how their name was obtained if permission slips were not used, giving directions to the meeting place, and enclosing a stamped postcard that can be returned to the parent coordinator to request announcements of upcoming events.

Since many families find it difficult to return to the NICU or hospital environment after discharge, it is recommended that the education series meet in a non-hospital environment. A school or church hall, library, or a parent's home may be suitable. Many families will bring their babies so the environment should be suitable and comfortable for the baby as well as for adults.

On arriving, parents should be met by group leader(s) and/or parent council members and should be introduced to each other as they arrive. Many families arrive early and enjoy setting up seats, offering coffee and refreshments to others, as well as putting up signs to direct other parents to the meeting place.

The agenda for a typical group meeting follows:

- *Introduction* by parent coordinator of self and members of parent council. Parents attending need not introduce themselves, although the parent's name and age of child may be helpful for a guest speaker. (5 minutes)
- *An overview* of the program and brief description of plans for future meetings. (5 minutes)
- *Presentation* by guest speakers (guest speakers include parents and professionals) followed by a question/answer session. Usually in a first meeting, parents will be reluctant to speak out. (30 minutes)
- *Coffee break* with refreshments supplied by parents. This is the time that parents will talk with one another. Exchanging ideas, information and experiences is crucial in helping parents of children who have been in NICU. (20 minutes)
- *Question/answer session.* (5 minutes)
- *Summary* by parent coordinator (5 minutes)
  Evaluations should be given to and collected from families after each meeting to receive feedback regarding content.
- *Informal goodbyes.* (10 minutes)

Topics suggested by families who utilized the Project WELCOME parents groups include: growth and development of the premature infant; family experiences during infancy; toddlerhood and preschool years; developmental concerns; rehospitalization; childhood nutrition; common premie medical conditions; causes of prematurity; early intervention programs; and making choices about child care.

No single program is going to meet the needs of every parent. Parents will choose those topics that are of most interest to them. Some families will attend only one session because that topic is of interest; others will participate regularly because they need the continued support these groups can provide. A mixture of participants with different goals may facilitate individual support. Families will naturally match themselves with others whom they find interesting and supportive.

Some participants in an education series may suggest the creation of special topic groups. These are short-term groups, comprised of smaller numbers of parents who request support and information around a very specific common issue. Possible topics for these groups include: toddlers; fathers; breastfeeding; going home; premies with cerebral palsy, single parenting; and twins.

2 Telephone support programs

Parents, both in the NICU and at home after discharge, are often confronted with a sense of emotional and physical isolation. At times they feel they are the only parents dealing with a particular problem of prematurity. They are unaware of other parents who have experienced the same problem and the same sense of isolation. They may be depleted of energy and unable to reach out. Even for those who know about existing support groups, the physical and emotional demands of their child may inhibit their attendance at educational meetings or special topic gatherings. A telephone support system can be designed to help these families while in the NICU or after discharge. The goal of a parent-to-parent program is to enhance and complement the availability of support provided in the NICU and offer support after discharge as needed. Parent-to-parent volunteers, or outreach parents, are parents who have had a child in the NICU, who have been trained, and are available to provide support to others in a similar situation.

Many questions arise in the planning phase for this program: Who will be outreach parents? What kind of preparation should outreach parents have? What will outreach parents say? Will outreach parents give medical advice? Who will support the outreach parents?

Parents who are interested in participating as an outreach parent are identified in several ways: they may offer their services to the NICU staff who refer them to the program; they may be recruited from the group membership; or they may respond to requests for outreach parents in a parent newsletter. Parents who are active in other parent activities are likely to participate as outreach parents. A formal screening process may be established, or rapport can be gained with prospective outreach parents through other group activities. The latter process tends to be more pleasant for both parties. If a parent volunteers who is unknown to NICU staff or the parent coordinator, that person may be encouraged to participate in the training session. This is a way of becoming familiar with the person's abilities, intentions and capabilities. NICU staff (and the parent coordinator) generally feel more comfortable referring families to people they know personally.

Once a group of interested parents is identified, a training program will be provided. Such a program should be a collaboration between parents and professionals where emotional as well as practical issues can be addressed. The training sessions are invaluable to all and tend to allay the legitimate concerns of the NICU staff. For those parents who may not be known to the staff, the training sessions provide some evidence of their capabilities and desire to be an outreach parent.

Sample agendas for two training sessions, with a summary of each topic, are included in Appendices A and B, pp. 70–81. Discussion topics include emotional and physical aspects of third trimester for full-term and preterm pregnancies; stress and coping in families; parent experiences in labor and delivery, NICU, and going home; parent questions after discharge; peer counseling; and support after death of a baby.

Parents should be asked to evaluate the outreach parent training sessions at the end of the program. Professionals may also be invited to attend as consultants and to provide their perspectives on the effectiveness of the program. Continued evaluation and feedback will allow for changes to increase the program's effectiveness.

When the program is in operation, trained mothers and fathers will be available to speak with parents of special care infants. There are various ways that referrals may be made. Each program should develop the referral procedure that best meets the needs of staff and parents. Typically, we have found that parents prefer to be called by an outreach parent rather than making the call themselves. The following procedures have been implemented successfully:

(1) A letter may be posted in the NICU in an easily visible location or in the parent's room on the bulletin board, explaining the availability of the parent-to-parent program. New parents, if interested, can fill in their name, telephone number, and other pertinent information on a form provided and leave it in a designated place. The parent coordinator can then review outreach parent forms, make an appropriate match, and ask the outreach parent to call the new parent.

(2) The medical or nursing staff may inform parents of the program. If the parents are interested, they may fill in an information form, or a staff member may call the parent coordinator, providing appropriate information about the parent's needs. The parent coordinator then makes the appropriate match. In certain instances, the medical or nursing staff may make the appropriate match by utilizing families known to them or by using the list of trained outreach parents. Keep in mind that it is not important who makes the referral or who gives the names out; it is important that parents receive the support.

(3) A new parent may call the parent program and request to talk

with an outreach parent. Parents are given the choice of either calling or being called by an outreach parent.

(4) Premies range typically from 24 weeks, to 37 weeks gestational age. Some premies have complications, while others have minimal or few medical problems. Making appropriate parent matches depends on the parent's needs at a given time. Some families need to talk with parents who have undergone a surgical procedure, while others want to talk about their premie in an early intervention program. It is important to listen to what parents say they need, rather than only to what we think they need.

(5) After the training session, continued support for outreach parents needs to be built in to any telephone support program. This can be accomplished in various ways. For example, after outreach parents make their first call, they can be contacted by the parent coordinator. In this way, they receive support and encouragement, and the parent coordinator has the reassurance of knowing how the call went. A periodic outreach parent support group meeting can provide parents with another source of support. This meeting can be used to share experiences of the parent-to-parent calls. Names and personal information about new parents are kept confidential. Program changes and future planning can also be a focus of this meeting. Finally, outreach parents can receive regularly updated lists of resources available to them. This list may include professionals who are available to answer questions or provide support.

3 Additional parent activities

A strong parent program provides multiple options for parents. The following is an introductory description to alternative activities which can supplement group and individual support.

For those families who do not participate in other program activities, a newsletter may provide useful information. Before writing a newsletter, it is helpful to review newsletters from other premie parent programs. Interested parents may volunteer to write the newsletter. Parents who attend the education meetings can take notes and summarize information for the newsletters. Parents may volunteer to write about their experiences on a specific topic, e.g., twins, breastfeeding, toilet training. A newsletter is also a way of sharing information about new articles, books, community resources, etc.

Parents often enjoy getting together socially. Refreshments may be contributed by parents or obtained as donations from various cookie, ice cream, and juice companies. This latter method also increases community awareness of the parent support program. Clowns, Santa Claus, magicians, bubbles, and balloons add to the enjoyment of spring picnics and holiday parties. If social events are held at the hospital, the hospital staff can also enjoy the festivities.

Fundraising is a parent-led activity which may help to provide equipment for the NICU or transportation money for parents for visits to the NICU. Fundraising can also be used to provide salary support to the parent coordinator or supplies for the program. Many groups have undertaken fundraising activities with great success.

There are many articles written about prematurity. Parents, hospital staff, and others who discover appropriate articles can contribute them to a resource file. A parent volunteer may take on the responsibility of maintaining the file. Recent additions to the file can be mentioned in the newsletter or brought to the attention of outreach parents or participants in an education series.

There are many agencies, services, and products appropriate for parents of premies today. Flyers describing those services can be collected and made available at any meeting for parents. For example, parents can be reminded of hearing screening programs or local parenting programs. Flyers on infant development and medical conditions can also be distributed. Descriptions of clothing, car seat and toy exchanges are also useful – especially when these exchanges are parent-generated projects.

III Evolution of the Project WELCOME Program

The original goal of Project WELCOME was to have the parent group maintain its viability through other funding sources after three years of federal support. During the first three years of the Project, the parent group provided the parent activities outlined in the preceding section of this chapter. Salary support was provided for the parent coordinator and services of a secretary were available from Project WELCOME. When Project WELCOME became an Outreach Project in the fourth year, the project could provide salary support (four hours/week) for the parent coordinator to consult with the parent group regarding leadership development. The parent coordinator's direct service and leadership functions now needed to shift to parents in the community. Thus, a new model for peer leadership and group organization was developed.

The new model began with recruitment of a parent from each of the three hospitals to serve as a parent representative for that NICU. Previously, the parent coordinator had been the contact person for all three nurseries. Since each hospital differed not only in size but in the level of care given to babies, it was important that each hospital be represented by a parent who had had a baby cared for in that unit. Names for potential parent representatives were obtained by the nurses on the units. The parent representatives are available to the unit to do inservice programs regarding parent support, visit with parents, supply the hospital with brochures and make referrals to the parent-to-parent program, educational services, and other resources. The parent representatives met with the parent coordinator frequently to acquaint them with the program. An informal training was also provided as needed in the areas of preterm infant development, premie medical conditions and other topics requested by the representatives. The training was provided by professionals and by the parent coordinator.

The parent representative model is working at this point in two out of three of the hospitals and is being initiated at the third. While one hospital prefers the parents to actively participate on the unit doing visiting, another prefers telephone check-ins along with occasional visits to the NICU. Other responsibilities of the representatives include notifying staff of any recent articles or resources for families.

As the Project WELCOME model changed, the Advisory Board felt a name change was appropriate; "NICU: Parent Support" was adopted. To further validate the program, it was felt that the group should incorporate and obtain tax-exempt status. The Advisory Board recommended a lawyer who had had two premature births. The services of the lawyer and her firm have been donated until the group is financially independent. Articles of organization and by-laws (Appendix B, p. 72) were written incorporating the goals and objectives of NICU: Parent Support. A Board of Directors and Officers of the Corporation were chosen. All of the steps leading to obtaining incorporation, and tax-exempt status were easily completed with the help of legal counsel.

With incorporation and tax-exempt status, NICU: Parent Support Inc. has begun fundraising. Obtaining this status made a profound impact on those who have supported this group. It has truly validated the program and made the Board of Directors look at the group with a sense of renewed energy.

When the officers were decided for the corporation, the parent coordinator decided to become vice president while offering the position of president to another parent who had been enthusiastic, competent and sincerely interested in the program. Having consistent leadership promotes stability and offers insight into the program. New leadership provides enthusiasm, new strength and fresh ideas.

This has been the first step in the continuing growth of NICU: Parent Support, Inc. With continued support from parents and professionals, it is our hope to become a self-sustaining community-based program, therefore fulfiling the original goals of Project WELCOME.

Appendix A

Outreach parent training session (1)

Topic: Explanation of parent-to-parent program
Leader: parent coordinator
Handouts: • any recent material on parent groups or premies;
          • outreach parent information sheet;

- requirements for participation in outreach parent program;
- bereavement packet.

Topic: Contrasting full-term vs high-risk pregnancy
Leader: RN or parent

This session deals with the emotional and physical aspects of the last trimester of pregnancy for full term and preterm parents. Parents review the expectations of their pregnancy and birth as well as their actual experience.

Topic: How it feels to have a premie
Leader: Social worker or parent

The format varies with individual speakers. This is a time for parents to share the emotional aspects of having a premie. From the time the child is delivered to the present, parents need to express their feelings of confusion, anger, relief, happiness, etc. Parents are made more sensitive to the wide range of emotions their peers may be experiencing, as well as receiving support for the issues current for them.

Topic: The most frequently asked questions after discharge
Leader: Community or NICU RN or parent coordinator

Many parents make frequent calls to the NICU after discharge. With the parent-to-parent network outreach parents may be asked to help find people with answers to questions regarding premies in car seats, medications, sleeping, feeding, visitors, oxygen, premie clothing and diapers.

Topic: Peer counseling
Leader: Individual with skills in this area or outreach parent

Part one of this session offers parents a theoretical view of how we cope with emotional pain and how we utilize supports in a safe environment. Part two deals with an outreach parent's suggestions on what to say after saying "hello."

Parent-to-parent training session (2)

Topic: Guidelines for outreach parents
Leader: Outreach parent and professional

Practical advice on making outreach telephone calls is given – e.g., length of call, frequency, ending calls, accepting and/or rejecting calls from program coordinator, getting support after a call.

Topic: Stress and family relationships
Leader: Social worker
    Understanding stress in today's family is discussed including issues for
    fathers, mothers, single parents and working parents.

Topic: Stress and coping of families in the NICU
Leader: Social worker or NICU nurse and outreach parent
    Many aspects of the NICU are stressful. This session deals with the
    unique situations faced by NICU families. Discussion may include
    transport, siblings and juggling schedules for the family. Validating
    each person's crisis is essential in this discussion.

Topic: Stress and coping by families after discharge (including community
    hospital)
Leader: Community hospital RN, community agency personnel (may
include EI, VNA, etc.).
    Transition is always a difficult time. Focus is on some changes being
    made in communities to accommodate premie families. Discussion on
    ways parents may help ease the transition for others.

Topic: What happens if the child dies?
Leader: Social worker or RN and outreach parent
    Many NICU families fear their child may die or have a child who
    died. Explanation of our feelings and any personal experiences are
    shared. Ideas about what to say and do, and what might be helpful
    are presented.

Appendix B By-laws of NICU: Parent Support, Inc.*

Article I – The Corporation

    1. *Name.* The name by which the Corporation shall be known as
is NICU: PARENT SUPPORT, INC. (which shall hereinafter be
referred to as the "Corporation").
    2. *Purpose.* The Corporation is a nonprofit organization
incorporated under the Chapter 180 of the Massachusetts General
Laws and is formed for the purposes enumerated in its Articles of
Organization, as they may be amended from time to time.

Article II – Membership

    1. *Members.* The Members shall consist of those persons named
as Directors in the Articles of Organization, and such other persons

*Prepared by Hale and Dorr, Counselors at Law, Boston, Massachusetts.

(including individuals, corporations and unincorporated associations) elected as Members by vote of Members representing a majority of all votes which all Members are entitled to cast.

2. *Rights and Obligations of Members.* The Members shall have the right to vote for the election of Directors. Except as otherwise limited by the Articles or By-Laws of the Corporation, they shall have such additional rights, including (without limitation) the right to make, amend and repeal By-Laws and to authorize an amendment or restatement of the Articles of Organization and to authorize a consolidation or merger, as are conferred upon the Members by statute.

3. *Termination of Membership.* (a) Any Member may resign from the Corporation upon 30 days' prior written notice to the Board of Directors or to the Clerk of the Corporation. (b) Membership in the Corporation may be terminated at any time and for any reason by a two-thirds (2/3) vote of the Members.

Article III – Meetings of Corporation Members

1. *Annual Meetings.* An Annual Meeting of the Members shall be held on the second Wednesday in November at a time and place to be determined by the Board of Directors and stated in the notice of the meeting. If no Annual Meeting is held in accordance with the foregoing provision, a special meeting may be held in lieu thereof and any action taken at such meeting shall have the same effect as if taken at the Annual Meeting.

2. *Special Meetings.* Special meetings of the Members may be called by the President, or by any three (3) Directors, and shall be called by the Clerk, or in the case of death, absence, incapacity, or refusal of the Clerk, by any other officer, upon written application of three or more Members stating the time, place and purpose of the meeting.

3. *Notice of Meetings.* A written notice of every meeting of Members stating the place, day and hour thereof, and the purpose for which the meeting is called shall be given by the Clerk or other person calling the meeting at least seven days before the meeting to each Member. Notice is deemed given when deposited in the mail, postage paid and properly addressed to the Members at the Member's address as it appears in the records of the Corporation. No notice of the time, place, or purpose of any regular or special meeting of the Members shall be required if every Member is present.

4. *Waiver of Notice.* Whenever notice of a meeting is required to be given a Member under any provision of the Articles of Organization or By-Laws of the Corporation, a written waiver thereof, executed before or after the meeting by such Member, or

his or her attorney thereunto duly authorized, shall be deemed equivalent to such notice.

5. *Quorum of Members.* A quorum for the transaction of business at any meeting of the Members shall be the number of Members representing a majority of all votes which all Members are entitled to cast, represented either in person or by proxy. When a quorum is present, any matter to be acted upon by the Members shall be decided by a majority of the votes cast by the Members unless otherwise provided by law, these By-Laws or the Corporation's Articles of Organization.

6. *Adjournments* Any meeting of the Members may be adjourned to any other time and to any other place permitted by these By-Laws by the Members present or represented at the meeting, although less than a quorum, or by any officer entitled to preside or to act as Clerk of such meeting, if no Member is present or represented. It shall not be necessary to notify any Member of any adjournment. Any business which could have been transacted at any meeting of the Members as originally called may be transacted at an adjournment thereof.

7. *Voting and Proxies.* Each Member shall have one vote in any matter of the Corporation during any such meeting. A simple majority of the total votes present and voting at the meeting shall decide any question presented except as hereinafter provided. All Members may vote either in person or by written proxy dated not more than six months before the meeting named therein. Proxies shall be filed with the Clerk of the meeting, or of any adjournment thereof, before being voted. Except as otherwise limited therein, proxies shall entitle the persons named therein to vote at any adjournment of such meeting, but shall not be valid after final adjournment of such meeting. Proxies need not be sealed or attested and a proxy purported to be executed by or on behalf of a Member entitled to vote shall be deemed valid unless challenged at or prior to its exercise.

8. *Action of Members Without a Meeting.* Any action required or permitted to be taken at any meeting of the Members may be taken without a meeting if all Members consent to the action in writing and the written consents are filed with the records of the meetings of Members. Such consent shall be treated for all purposes as a vote at a meeting.

Article IV – Board of Directors

1. *Powers.* The Directors may exercise all the powers of the Corporation except such as are required by law or the Articles of

Organization or the By-Laws to be otherwise exercised. The Directors shall have the general direction, control, and management of the activities of the Corporation. Except as otherwise provided by the By-Laws, the Directors shall have the power to purchase, lease, and sell such property, and to make such contracts and agreements as it deems advantageous. They may determine their own compensation and duties in addition to those prescribed by the By-Laws, of all officers, agents, and employees of the Corporation. In the event of a vacancy in the Board of Directors, the remaining Directors, except as otherwise provided by law, may exercise the power of the full Board until the vacancy is filled.

2. *Composition.* The Board of Directors shall consist of seventeen (17) Directors. The initial Directors shall be those persons named in the Articles of Organization. Directors shall serve for a term of one (1) year or, if longer, until their successors are elected and qualified. A Director may resign by delivering his or her resignation in writing to the other Directors or to the Clerk of the Corporation.

3. *Removal.* A Director may be removed from office at any time (a) with or without cause, by vote of a majority of the Members or (b) for cause, by vote of two-thirds of the Board of Directors. A Director may be removed for cause only if notice of such action shall have been given to all of the Directors or the Members, as the case may be, prior to the meeting at which such action is to be taken and if the Director so to be removed shall have been given reasonable notice and opportunity to be heard before the body proposing to remove him or her.

4. *Vacancies.* Any vacancy in the Board of Directors, unless and until filled by the Members, may be filled by vote of a majority of the remaining Directors present at a meeting of Directors at which a quorum is present or by appointment of all of the Directors if less than a quorum shall remain in office.

5. *Enlargement of the Board.* The number of the Board of Directors may be increased or decreased at any annual or special meeting by vote of Members representing a majority of all votes which all Members are entitled to cast or by vote of a majority of the Directors present at any meeting of Directors at which a quorum is present or by appointment by all of the Directors if less than a quorum shall remain in office.

6. *Regular Meetings of the Board of Directors.* The Board of Directors shall hold a regular meeting each year for the election of officers as soon as practicable after final adjournment of the Annual Meeting of the Members. At the Annual Meeting of the Board of Directors, it shall establish a schedule of regular meetings, to be held at least quarterly. Regular meetings of the Board of Directors, including the first Meeting following the Annual Meeting of the

Members, may be held without notice if the time and place of such meetings are fixed in the By-Laws or by the Board of Directors. Notice of the time and place of regular meetings, if required, shall be given by the Clerk. Notice may be given orally, by telephone, telegraph or in writing; and notice given in time to enable the Directors to attend, or in any case notice sent by mail or telegraph to a Director's usual or last known place of business or residence, at least three days before the meeting shall be sufficient. Regular meetings of the Board shall be open to the public unless the Board votes to hold a closed session.

7. *Special Meetings of the Board of Directors*. Special meetings of the Board of Directors may be called on written notice stating the exact time, date, and place thereof and delivered in person at least 48 hours prior to such meeting and signed by the President or any three (3) Directors. At Special Meetings only the business specified in the notice shall be transacted. Special Meetings of the Board shall be open to the public unless the Board votes to hold a closed session.

8. *Waiver of Notice*. Notice of a meeting need not be given to any Director, if a written waiver of notice, executed by him or her before or after the meeting, is filed with the records of the meeting, or to any Director who attends the meeting without protesting prior thereto or at its commencement the lack of notice to him or her.

9. *Quorum*. At any meeting of the Board of Directors, a majority of the Directors then in office shall constitute a quorum. A lesser number than a quorum may adjourn any meeting from time to time without further notice. Each Director shall have one (1) vote. If a quorum is present, a majority of the Directors present may take any action on behalf of the Board of Directors, including the election of officers, except to the extent that a larger number is required by law, the By-Laws or the Articles of Organization of the Corporation.

10. *Executive and Other Committees*. The Directors may elect an Executive Committee from their number, at any regular or special meeting of the Directors, provided that the President and the Treasurer or Assistant Treasurer of the Corporation shall, for their respective terms of office, be members of any Executive Committee and shall be entitled to vote equally with the other members of such Executive Committee.

In the absence of the Clerk from any meeting, a temporary clerk shall be appointed by the meeting.

11. *Removal and Vacancies*. Once a Director has been elected to the Board of Directors, that Director can be removed prior to the end of his or her normal term of office only for cause, by a vote of

two-thirds of the present and voting membership at a Special Meeting called for that purpose under Article III, Section 2.

The Board of Directors can remove a Director only for cause by a vote of two-thirds of the Directors at a Special Meeting called for that purpose under Article IV, Section 7. Failure of a Director to attend three (3) consecutive meetings of the Board shall constitute a resignation by the Director unless an appropriate and timely response is received by the Clerk of the Corporation from the Director upon notification of his or her absences.

When a vacancy occurs on the Board of Directors, through resignation or involuntary removal, the new Director selected to fill the unexpired term shall be elected by the Board of Directors or if any institutional representative, shall be appointed by the appropriate institution.

12. *Action of Board of Directors Without a Meeting.* Any action required or permitted to be taken at any meeting of the Board of Directors may be taken without a meeting, if all the Directors consent to the action in writing and the written consents are filed with the records of the meetings of the Board of Directors. Such consents shall be treated for all purposes as a vote at a meeting.

13. *Compensation.* Directors shall receive no compensation for performance of their duties as Directors of the Corporation.

Article V – Officers

1. *Enumeration.* The officers of the Corporation shall consist of a President, who shall also be the Chairperson of the Board of Directors, a Vice-President, a Clerk and a Treasurer, each of whom shall be a member of the Board of Directors. Such other officers and assistant officers as may be deemed necessary may be elected or appointed by the Board of Directors. Any two (2) or more offices may be held by the same person, except the offices of President and Clerk or President and Treasurer.

2. *Election.* The President, Vice-President, Treasurer, and Clerk shall be elected annually by a simple majority of the Board of Directors at their first meeting following the Annual Meeting of the Members. Other officers may be appointed by the Directors at such meeting or at any other meeting.

4. *Tenure.* Except as otherwise provided by law, by the Articles of Organization or by these By-Laws, the President, Treasurer and Clerk shall hold office until the first meeting of the Board of Directors following the Annual Meeting of Members and thereafter until his or her successor is chosen and qualified; and all other officers shall hold office until the first meeting of the Board of Directors following the Annual Meeting of Members, unless a different term is specified

in the vote choosing or appointing them. Any officer may resign by delivering his or her written resignation to the Corporation at its principal office or to the President or Clerk and such resignation shall be effective upon receipt unless it is specified to be effective at some other time or upon the happening of some other event.

5. *Removal.* The Board of Directors may remove any officer with or without cause by a vote of a majority of the entire number of Directors then in office, provided that an officer may be removed for cause only after reasonable notice and opportunity to be heard by the Board of Directors prior to action thereon.

6. *Vacancy.* A vacancy in any office may be filled for the unexpired balance of the term by vote of a majority of the Directors present at any meeting of Directors at which a quorum is present or by appointment by all of the Directors if less than a quorum shall remain in office.

7. *President.* The President shall be the chief operating officer and the chief executive officer of the Corporation. The President shall, subject to the direction of the Directors, have general supervision and control of the business of the Corporation. The President shall, when present, preside at all meetings of the Directors and shall have such other powers and duties as may be vested in him or her by the Board of Directors. At the Annual Meeting the President shall submit a report of the Operations of the Corporation for such year and a statement of its affairs, and shall from time to time report to the Board all matters within his or her knowledge which the interests of the Corporation may require to be brought to its notice.

8. *Vice President.* The Vice President shall, in the absence or disability of the President, perform the duties and exercise the powers of the President and shall perform such other duties and shall have such other powers as the Directors may from time to time prescribe.

9. *Treasurer.* The Treasurer shall, subject to the direction of the Directors, have general charge of the financial affairs of the Corporation, including its long-range financial planning, and shall cause to be kept accurate books of account. The Treasurer shall prepare a yearly report on the financial status of the Corporation to be delivered at the Annual Meeting.

10. *Clerk.* The Clerk shall be a resident of the Commonwealth of Massachusetts, unless the Corporation has designated a resident agent in the manner provided by law. The Clerk shall attend all meetings of the Members and the Board of Directors, and shall record upon the record book of the Corporation minutes of the proceedings at such meetings. He or she shall have custody of the record books of the Corporation and shall have such other powers

and shall perform such other duties as the Directors may from time to time prescribe.

In the absence of the Clerk from any meeting, a temporary clerk shall be appointed by the meeting.

11. *Committees.* Chairpersons of Standing Committees shall be appointed by the President of the Board of Directors from the Board of Directors. Ad hoc committees may be established by the President as necessary.

12. *Other Powers and Duties.* Each officer shall, subject to these By-Laws, have in addition to the duties and powers specifically set forth in these By-Laws, such duties and powers as are customarily incident to his or her office, and such duties and powers as the Directors may from time to time designate.

13. *Compensation.* Officers shall receive no compensation for performance of their duties as Officers of the Corporation.

Article VI – Miscellaneous Provisions

1. *Fiscal Year.* Except as otherwise determined by the Directors, the fiscal year of the Corporation shall begin on November 1 and end on October 31.

2. *Seal.* Subject to change by the Directors, the Corporation shall have a seal which shall bear its name, the word, "Massachusetts," and the year of its incorporation, and such other device or inscription as the Directors may determine.

3. *Execution of Instruments.* All checks, deeds, leases, transfers, contracts, bonds, notes and other obligations authorized to be executed by an officer of the Corporation in its behalf shall be signed by the President or the Treasurer except as the Directors may generally or in particular cases otherwise determine.

4. *Corporate Records.* The original, or attested copies, of the Articles of Organization, By-Laws and records of all meetings of the Members shall be kept in Massachusetts at the principal office of the Corporation, or at an office of the Corporation's Clerk or resident agent. Said copies and records need not all be kept in the same office. They shall be available at all reasonable times to the inspection of any Member for any proper purpose, but not to secure a list of Members for a purpose other than in the interest of the applicant, as a Member, relative to the affairs of the Corporation.

5. *Evidence of Authority.* A certificate by the Clerk, or a temporary Clerk, as to any action taken by the Members, Board of Directors or any officer or representative of the Corporation shall as to all persons who rely thereon in good faith be conclusive evidence of such action.

6. *Articles of Organization.* All references in these By-Laws to the

Articles of Organization shall be deemed to refer to the Articles of Organization of the Corporation, as amended and in effect from time to time.

7. *Transactions with Interested Parties.* In the absence of fraud, no contract or other transaction between this Corporation and any other corporation or any firm, association, partnership or person shall be affected or invalidated by the fact that any Director or officer of this corporation is pecuniarily or otherwise interested in or is a director, member or officer of such other corporation or of such firm, association or partnership or is a party to or is pecuniarily or otherwise interested in such contract or other transaction or is in any way connected with any person or persons, firm, association, partnership, or corporation pecuniarily or otherwise interested therein; provided that the fact that he individually or as a director, member or officer of such corporation, firm, association or partnership is such a party or is so interested shall be disclosed to or shall have been known by the Board of Directors or a majority of such members thereof as shall be present at a meeting of the Board of Directors at which action upon any such contract or transaction shall be taken; any Director may be counted in determining the existence of a quorum and may vote at any meeting of the Board of Directors for the purpose of authorizing any such contract or transaction with like force and effect as if he were not so interested, or were not a director, member or officer of such other corporation, firm, association or partnership, provided that any vote with respect to such contract or transaction must be adopted by a majority of the Directors then in office who have no interest in such contract or transaction.

8. *Tax Exemption.* It is intended that the Corporation be treated as an organization described in Section 501(c)(3) of the Internal Revenue Code of 1954, as amended, and notice shall be given to the Secretary of the Treasury or his delegate as provided in Section 508(a) of said Code. Notwithstanding any other provision in these By-Laws to the contrary, for so long as the Corporation constitutes a private foundation as defined under Section 509 of said Code, all requirements and prohibitions described in Section 508(e)(1) of said Code are incorporated herein by reference and hereby made applicable to the Corporation; and, without limitation of the foregoing, the Corporation shall act or refrain from acting so as not to subject itself to the taxes imposed by the following sections of the Code, to wit: 4941 (relating to taxes on self-dealing), 4942 (relating to taxes on failure to distribute income), 4943 (relating to taxes on excess business holdings), 4944 (relating to taxes on investments which jeopardize charitable purpose), and 4945 (relating to taxable expenditures).

Article VII – Indemnification

The Members shall indemnify and hold the Directors harmless in accordance with the provisions set forth in the Articles of Organization.

Article VIII – Dissolution

In the event of the termination, dissolution or winding up of this Corporation in any manner or for any reason whatsoever, its remaining assets, if any, shall be distributed in accordance with the provisions set forth in the Articles of Organization.

Article IX – Amendments

These By-Laws may be amended by the affirmative majority of the votes cast by Members of the Corporation attending any meeting of Members at which a quorum is present, provided that the substance of any proposed amendment is stated in the notice of such meeting. If authorized by the Articles of Organization, the Directors, by a majority of their number then in office, may also make, amend or repeal these By-Laws, in whole or in part, except with respect to (a) the provisions of these By-Laws governing (i) the removal of Directors, (ii) the indemnification of Directors and (iii) the amendment of these By-Laws and (b) any provisions of these By-Laws which by law, the Articles of Organization or these By-Laws, requires action by the Members.

No later than the time of giving notice of the meeting of Members next following the making, amending or repealing by the Directors of any By-Law, notice thereof stating the substance of such change shall be given to all Members, and any By-Law adopted by the Directors may be amended or repealed by the Members.

Any By-Law adopted by the Directors may be amended or appealed by the Members entitled to vote on amending the By-Laws.

A true record.

CHAPTER 4

Support networks for fathering in the postnatal period

Carolyn Mebert and Michael Kalinowski

I History

In order to understand what we know about how the roles of fathers may have changed over time, it is necessary to look at the history of child, or developmental psychology because the information we have about fathers comes primarily from that field. As a field of "scientific" inquiry, child psychology is relatively new. Published accounts of systematic observations of children only began appearing with regularity in the late 1800s and the first scholarly journal in the US devoted specifically to child development was founded in 1891 (*The Pedagogical Seminary*). It was only with the advent of child psychology as a scholarly discipline that researchers began looking at the myriad factors that might contribute to the development of individuals from infancy (or even conception to adulthood. These early investigations, and most current studies, were guided by particular theoretical or philosophical views on the nature of people and of development. Though some of the still predominant philosophies of development maintain that most of the psychological nature of human beings is biologically determined, early in the twentieth century a very strong environmentalist contingent became prominent in US psychology. With this increasing emphasis on the contribution of environmental factors to development, the nature of parent–child relations, and the ways in which parents affect their children became important topics of study. For understanding the role of fathers in particular, it is somewhat unfortunate that this enterprise was undertaken at a time when mothers were children's primary caretakers. Thus, it was to mothers that psychologists went to find out about parental attitudes and behaviors and parent–child relations. In most of the research published on parents and child-rearing practices through the 1960s, the word parent is almost fully synonymous with mother, and the major image we get of the father is of a shadowy figure with a paycheck, who also happens to be a fairly good disciplinarian primarily because he is a novel figure in his child's environment.

That this may not be the role fathers have always played is revealed in some recent historical essays. John Demos (1983), for example, has sketched out an interesting picture of fatherhood from colonial times to the present. The view he presents of the colonial father is of an individual who was warm and affectionate and served quite a variety of functions in the lives of his children: guidance counselor, benefactor, moral overseer, psychologist, model, progenitor, companion, and caregiver. In Demos's words, colonial fatherhood was an *"active, encompassing fatherhood woven into the whole fabric of domestic and productive life" (ibid.* p. 164). A major task of childrearing in colonial times was producing morally upstanding and rational adults. Mothers, being prone to emotional excesses, were in need of protection themselves and simply did not have the strength of character necessary for raising proper citizens. The tasks of fathers and the importance of fathers within the family system was clear. This view is further reflected in common law which maintained that a man's wife and children were his property to be cared for. In the case of divorce, children, with very rare exceptions, were placed in the custody of their father.

The nineteenth century was a time of major social and economic change in this country. As society changed, so did the roles of fathers and mothers. The basic softness and emotionality of women were now seen as making them particularly well suited to the task of nurturing and otherwise caring for and, by mid-century, even teaching children (e.g., Scarr, 1984). Men were working away from their homes in increasing numbers and spending increasing amounts of time away from their children. The roles of fathers changed as the "fabric of domestic and productive life" came to look more and more like a patchwork quilt. The father of the middle to late nineteenth century may have been much like the "traditional" (Fein, 1978) father of the twentieth century: first and foremost he was provider, then part-time playmate, disciplinarian, audience, and moral support for the mother (Demos, 1983). The primacy of mothers in childrearing was seen also in changes in the legal system, most notably in the "tender years doctrine" which resulted in mothers obtaining custody of children following divorce unless declared unfit by the court (Leupnitz, 1982).

As the roles of family members did not change much from the mid-nineteenth century to the mid-twentieth century (at least in the middle class and except during wartime), it was from this type of family situation (father as breadwinner, mother as childrearer) that most of our information on the importance of mothers and fathers in children's development came. What did change, though, was that a body of scientifically collected data was accumulating to substantiate the necessity of the typical division of family labor. Earlier workers in the "child study movement," following from the findings presented in baby biographies (written mostly by fathers) had been describing perceptual development (Preyer, 1895), intellectual processes (Binet and Simon, 1972), play and emotions (Hall, 1923), and neuromotor development (Gesell, 1929) in children. With the rising interest in psychoanalytic theory and behavioral interpretations of it, considerable intellectual energies were being devoted to proving, for example, that infants needed to develop a strong, *specific*, and secure attachment to their mothers in order to develop into psychologically healthy adults. Children were observed in orphanages, and baby monkeys were raised with wire surrogates in order to determine the effects of "maternal deprivation" (e.g., Spitz and Wolf, 1946; Harlow, 1958, respectively); mothers and their children were observed interacting in laboratories or in their homes (e.g., Sears, Whiting, et al., 1953); mothers were interviewed about their childrearing practices (Sears, Maccoby, and Levin, 1957); and so on. A picture developed of the mother–child relationship as central and the father–child relationship, by default, as virtually non-existent. As Bowlby explained it:

> In the young child's eyes, father plays second fiddle. . . . Nevertheless . . . fathers have their uses even in infancy. Not only do they provide for their wives to enable them to devote themselves unrestrictedly to the care of the infant and toddler, but, by providing love and companionship, they support the mother emotionally and help her maintain that harmonious contented mood in the atmosphere of which her infant thrives (Bowlby, 1953, p. 15).

Little attention was paid to the fact that the children in orphanages and the monkeys in their cages were suffering from deprivations other than maternal and that fathers might have filled some of the void in their lives. Further, in this "traditional perspective" (Fein, 1978), little attempt was apparently made to obtain information about fathers from the fathers themselves. For Sears and colleagues this was simply "not feasible," and besides, their work was done for mothers: "If a mother knows the effect of a particular [childrearing] practice, she can decide whether to use it or not" (Sears *et al.*, 1957, p. 11). The scientific community seemed to be so entrenched in the implicitly held or explicitly stated notion that parenting required a "maternal instinct" inherent in women that fatherhood, for psychological purposes, did not exist. The issue of competence vs performance in parenting was confused, with the common assumption being that because fathers did not do much in the way of child care, they *could not* do much. (It should be pointed out that this situation was not entirely advantageous for women. Being seen as primarily responsible for children's psychological and physical well-being also meant being blamed when something went wrong.)

The end of the "traditional perspective" on fatherhood and the emergence of the "modern perspective" (Fein, 1978) was brought about, in part, by research findings that indicated that paternal absence could have detrimental effects on children (e.g., Hetherington, 1966; Lynn and Sawry, 1959; Mischel, 1961; etc.). Though many of these early studies of paternal absence were flawed (e.g., they often confounded paternal absence with economic conditions and maternal attitudes) and thus their conclusions are sometimes questionable, they did, at least, point out the very strong possibility that if fathers can produce problems in children when they are not in the home, then maybe fathers do contribute something positive when they are present. Research on the effects of paternal absence continues, but it has broadened in perspective: included now in such studies are factors like reason for father's absence, age of child when father left, sex of child (initially only boys were studied), mothers' behavior and attitudes, and so on. Though the research is becoming more comprehensive, it is difficult to make any general statements about the effects of father's absence since effects vary with age, sex, race, socioeconomic status, and availability of other men in the environment (Parke, 1981). The father did, however, emerge from this research as more than just the paycheck-carrying disciplinarian. He is now seen as an important figure in children's emotional, intellectual, and social development, particularly in his likely affects on achievement motivation, moral reasoning and behavior, and sex roles (Fein, 1978).

Since the early paternal absence studies were published, more and more researchers have been directing their efforts toward describing the experiences, behaviors, and effects of fathers in intact homes. (One cannot help but wonder if this is a reflection of the researchers' involvement with their own children – many researchers are male.) Much of this research focuses on the infancy period, and an increasing amount involves expectant fathers. These studies are part of what Fein (1978) has termed the "emergent perspective" on fathering and are very likely a by-product of an emergent perspective on sex-role stereotypes, economic opportunities, and divisions of labor in the workplace and in the home. The father who is becoming known through this research has a variety of skills and experiences heretofore unrecognized or overlooked: he experiences pregnancy in some way -- through physical symptoms, life crises, and/or developmental progression; he can nurture and otherwise care for children (even infants, and do it quite well); he can be as good a "house husband" as many women are housewives. The emerging father can do everything (except be pregnant, deliver, and nurse a baby) his wife does, he just does not do it as often as she. And, once again, we can see the changing view of fathers reflected in the law: joint custody statutes are now in effect in over thirty states in the US. This could be seen as indicating that the legal system is recognizing fathers as able caregivers, but joint custody could also be seen as a superficial accession to men's rights as parents. In many states the statute refers only to legal custody; physical custody still goes to mothers more frequently than to fathers.

II Information about fathers and suggestions concerning support needs from the emergent perspective

The work reported here must be considered within the context of the changing social climate that brought the research questions to the fore. Furthermore, it must be understood that the results are for groups within which there is usually quite a bit of variability and from which generalizations to the whole population cannot always be made. For example, it may well be that fathers who are willing to have their experiences while expecting a baby, or their interactions with their children, scrutinized by researchers are different in some ways from fathers who, for whatever reason, do not participate in such research.

A The expectant father

Support needs: dealing with stress, frustration (sexual and otherwise), understanding symptoms, pressure to perform in some expected or idealized manner, disappointment when things do not go as planned.

The months of expectant fatherhood can be viewed as a developmental stage during which there are certain tasks to be accomplished or conflicts to be resolved (Barnhill, Rubenstein, and Rocklin, 1979). One of the major tasks during this stage is redefining roles and relationships within and outside the family. In part this involves moving from being the child of one's parents to being the parent of one's child, but it includes changes in the marital relationship and, possibly, changes in work activities as well. As more information becomes available about the roles fathers can and often do play in pregnancy and childrearing, and as more options become available to fathers, more decisions must be made by prospective fathers. Many decisions concern the degree of involvement the father will have in his wife's pregnancy and his child's birth and rearing.

Beginning at a very concrete level, the prospective father typically has a choice of participating in prenatal visits to the obstetrician, childbirth education classes, and labor and delivery. Although we know of no effects of fathers' attendance at prenatal checkups, participation in childbirth classes and labor and delivery do seem to be beneficial, not just for the father, but for the mother and baby as well. When fathers attend prepared childbirth classes, they learn what their wives will be experiencing and how they can help. They also have the opportunity to talk with other men who are in the same, or a similar, situation. When fathers attend labor and delivery, mothers are more likely to experience less pain and anxiety, somewhat shorter labors, and greater pleasure at the birth (Entwisle and Doering, 1981; Hennenborn and Cogan, 1975). There is also the suggestion in the literature that fathers who participate in delivery find it a "peak" experience and may become more involved with or "attached" to their babies (Parke, 1981). However, paternal involvement in all of this may not be right for all men. As Bittman and Zalk (1978) point out, a father's decision about what to do during labor and delivery must be based on a realistic assessment of his ability to handle all that is involved (e.g., seeing his wife in pain, providing support, cooperating with birth attendants) and his reasons for considering participating in the first place (e.g., the pressure that comes from the "everyone is doing it so I should" view is probably not the best reason). These authors do suggest that for fathers who have not made the decision about labor and delivery, participation in childbirth education classes might be useful. In our research (Mebert and Kalinowski, 1984) we have found that early in pregnancy many men were uncertain or ambivalent about being present for their child's birth, citing squeamishness, having never even been in a hospital, lack of tolerance for anyone's pain, and so on as reasons. Toward the end of their wives' pregnancies, however, most had decided they would be present, though for a few it was because their wives really wanted it. At three months postpartum, all of the fathers seen to date reported being present and most found the birth a very positive experience, using words like "awesome," "miracle," "unbelievable," to describe it. Mothers found the fathers more helpful during labor and delivery than the fathers thought they were themselves, and fathers found the childbirth classes more useful than the mothers did.

Some men, even if they attend prenatal classes, practice breathing exercises religiously, and are fully prepared for their child's birth, yet are barred from the delivery because of the need for an "emergency" (or unplanned) cesarean. Although some research on cesarean deliveries indicates that women's experiences are more positive when their husbands are present (Cranley, Hedahl and Pegg, 1983), many hospitals still exclude fathers if the surgery is unscheduled (some ban fathers from the operating room whether or not the cesarean is scheduled). For these men a variety of feelings may accompany their child's birth: they may be worried about their wives, disappointed in their wives and/or themselves (for not being able to do things "right"), perhaps guilty – feeling that they were not supportive enough, frustrated at their inability to be present at the birth, and so on (Pedersen, Zaslow, Cain, and Anderson, 1981). It is probably helpful for men in this situation to focus more on the infant than on what the infant's birth was like, understanding that a good relationship with the child is not dependent upon being present at his or her birth. What little research there is dealing with the effects of cesarean birth on fathers indicates that "cesarean fathers" engage in more caregiving activities with their infants, but less play than do "vaginal fathers" (Pedersen et al., 1981), or that while "cesarean fathers" may do more caregiving, they do so only for the first few months, after which there are no differences between fathers whose babies were born by cesarean and those whose babies were delivered vaginally (Hwang, 1984). Though fathers of cesarean babies may do more caregiving, it is not clear whether they find this pleasurable or burdensome. Many childbirth educators offer special classes for couples anticipating a cesarean delivery and these can be particularly useful when they cover not only the details of surgical delivery but what to expect in the aftermath as well. There are available several books and a national organization (C-SEC, Inc., Waltham, MA, see page 189) that provide information, both supportive and technical, about cesarean deliveries.

Another side of the cesarean experience that has come out in our research is the jealousy that some women experience because their husbands were the first to hold and feed the baby. Some women become concerned that their husbands have "bonded" with the baby while they, off in the recovery room, have missed out on those first important minutes or hours of their babies' lives. These feelings could lead to some tensions within the family. However, as a number of researchers have pointed out recently, the phenomenon of immediate postpartum bonding is highly questionable (Chess and Thomas, 1982; Goldberg, 1983). Although popularized versions of the bonding research would lead one to belive that contact with an infant immediately after birth guarantees the formation of a strong emotional attachment to and healthy development of the baby, there is no good evidence that this is the case. Similarly, separation from the baby in the initial postpartum period does not necessarily have deleterious effects on all involved. We have found in our work that many parents report feeling no particularly strong bond or emotional attachment to their infant right after birth, but a consistently stronger attachment is reported in the follow-up interviews over the infant's first year. As with most relationships, the parent–infant attachment is not set at the first encounter, rather it grows and strengthens with time.

Conscious decisions involving participation in pregnancy and birth are just part of what makes up the stage of expectant fatherhood. There are other features of the experience that may be less consciously motivated. For example, some men go through what has been termed the "couvade syndrome." They have an increase in unpleasant physical symptoms, some of which mimic the symptoms of pregnancy e.g., nausea, vomiting, fatigue, backache, weight gain (Lamb and Lipkin, 1982; Liebenberg, 1969; Munroe and Munroe, 1971). The appearance of these symptoms in expectant fathers is thought to have some psychological base: anxiety, pregnancy envy, acceptance of fatherhood, resistance to fatherhood, etc. (Enzig, 1980). There is little or no indication that this syndrome is abnormal and, in fact, Munroe and Munroe (1971) provide evidence that men who experience somatic symptoms during their wives' pregnancies are subsequently more involved in childcare, suggesting that this type of psychological involvement in pregnancy might help prepare some men for the nurturing aspect of fatherhood.

While the couvade syndrome may be one way men deal with conflicts arising during pregnancy, Gelles (1975) has reported another, more troubling way. In a study of family violence, Gelles found cases of wife abuse occurring or increasing during pregnancy in 10 per cent of his sample. He suspects that the incidence may actually be higher in the population and suggests that some men may engage in physical violence toward their pregnant wives out of frustration (sexual or other), anxiety, jealousy, in order (consciously or not) to produce a miscarriage, or because their wives seem vulnerable and are thus seen as easy targets. Whatever the case, Gelles's work as well as other recent work on family violence indicate that some men have a very difficult time dealing with the changes that come with impending parenthood. The difficulty may be more pronounced when the pregnancy was not planned and the man cannot accept the fact of it, when the partners are very young and/or unmarried, and when social supports are not available in the couple's environment (Straus, Gelles, and Steinmetz, 1980).

The psychoanalytic literature is replete with theoretical accounts of men's psychological integration of parenthood during pregnancy and postpartum. Work from this perspective indicates that pregnancy may lead to increased dependency and childlike behavior in some men. This regression, however, is in the service of the ego, and is an important component of the developmental transition from child to parent. That is, the regression men may experience during their wives' pregnancies provides them with the opportunity to re-evaluate their relationships with their own parents, working out residual conflicts they may have with their parents (particularly their fathers), and eventually adopting a parenting role for themselves (e.g., Grossman, Eichler, and Winickoff, 1980, ch. 7).

Benedek (1970), in her discussion of the "psychobiology" of fatherhood makes a distinction between *fatherhood* as a situation that results from the expression of a biological, instinctual drive for survival enabling a man, finally, to compete on equal ground with his own father, and *fatherliness*. Fatherliness is the empathic responses a man displays toward children and the emotional interactions and warm, loving relationship he develops with his own children. Benedek makes a strong case for the importance of an adequate role model in the form of his own father for a man's development of fatherliness. This is a rather hard line approach in its almost fully all-or-none stance: only if a man had a nurturing father can he develop the fatherliness Benedek describes. Men who put work ahead of their families, who take the role of physical, economic provider as primary most likely had fathers who did the same and will produce sons who will continue in the tradition – fathers all, but not fatherly fathers, and thus, not complete. Although her's is an extreme position, Benedek does touch on two very important and inter-related issues: the importance of role models and the distinction between, as one of our subjects put it "being a father and being a daddy." The father (several times over) in our study was asked what being a father meant to him. In his response he noted, much as Benedek and others have, that any man can be a father, but it takes special effort and work and a different kind of caring to be a daddy. He and many of the emergent fathers of today are working at being daddies without benefit of the multitude and varieties of role models available to mothers.

B Fathers and infants

Support Needs: learning how to care for infants, adjusting to changing demands on time, adjusting to changes in household routines, adjusting to changes in marital relationship.

At this point it is tempting simply to catalogue all of the abilities fathers have been found to possess and exhibit in interactions with their infants. It is sufficient to say that all of the caregiving abilities typically thought of as part of the maternal role are present in fathers, though fathers may not display them with quite the same frequency as mothers (Parke, 1981). For men who are willing and able to take the time and effort to learn how to handle babies, few problems are encountered in childcare activities and much pleasure may be derived from them. Most women probably do have more experience handling infants and may, therefore, seem more adept and efficient in childcare routines than men, but most men are capable of learning these new behaviors.

In this regard, however, some conflicts may arise when men hold traditional views about the division of household responsibilities. The belief that one cannot perform certain functions may lead to an unwill-ingness even to attempt performance. In many cases the belief that men are incapable of infant and child care stems from a confusion of biological sex and sex roles (Frodi, 1980). Western society maintains such strong and pervasive sex role stereotypes that it is very difficult to get beyond them to find out if there are any biological limitations on the behaviors of which each sex is capable. Although flexibility in sex roles is increasing and there is greater overlap in the activities in which men and women engage, old traditions die hard. In multigenerational social contexts (such as exist in most workplaces), older views may hold sway largely because old and authority are likely to be highly correlated. Thus, many "emergent" fathers may find themselves in the position of wanting to be more involved with their infants but are reinforced by their colleagues and superiors for placing other considerations, i.e., work, first. This is apparently the situation that exists in Sweden where fathers, by law, are given the same opportunity as mothers to take paid leave from work for some months after the birth of a child. The opportunity exists, but very few men have taken it, apparently for fear of being penalized or being seen as mavericks (Lamb and Levine, 1983). It does seem that a number of long-held views and prejudices will have to be dispelled before there is truly equal parental opportunity for men and women.

In cases of two career households problems can arise with the birth of an infant as attempts are made to arrive at an equitable division of household and childcare responsibilities. An important factor influencing the resolution or avoidance of such conflicts is the degree of congruence between parents' attitudes towards women's roles and the mother's employment status (Stuckey, McGhee, and Bell, 1982). If the mother works and the father thinks she should not, there are likely to be problems as there will be if the mother works and *she* thinks she should not. In any event, even when the mother works and both she and her husband agree she should, the mother typically still bears the major responsibility for childcare. This is somewhat unfortunate in that some of the other problems to be mentioned below could be alleviated if a more equal distribution of responsibility could be effected.

As more mothers join the workforce, more attention must be paid to the issue of childcare alternatives. Very rarely are fathers mentioned in this context. A review of the day care literature published since 1978 revealed that when "parents" were questioned about their child's day care experience or when parent–child relations were studied in day care children, the parent in question was always the mother (Mebert, 1984). This could be due to a bias on the part of the researchers, but it may also indicate that mothers are the parents most involved in their child's day care experience. Although they may not do it much, fathers can participate in their child's alternate care arrangements by dropping the child off, picking the child up, and becoming involved in the governance of parent-run centers. The latter may be particularly beneficial to fathers as it gives them the chance to meet the parents of their children's peers and discuss mutual concerns, as well as enabling them to have some say in the care their children receive.

Marital relations are very likely to be affected by the birth of a child. Although many couples report being more satisfied in their marriage and closer to each other following the birth of their babies, some couples experience difficulty adjusting to their new situation. Grossman *et al.* (1980) and Shereshefsky and Yarrow (1973) have identified some of the problems and concerns that can affect a marriage during the first year postpartum: changes in the frequency of sexual activity, fatigue, financial problems, job related issues, decrease in time spent doing things as a couple, and so on. Interestingly, the primary association Grossman and her colleagues found between the actual birth and subsequent parental relations was in cases in which complications of labor and delivery had occurred. In such situations the relationship was better, presumably because the men had been more involved with their infants and more responsive to their wives right from the start.

Finally, a not uncommon problem many men face during their child's infancy is being jealous of the amount of attention the infant receives from its mother (Bittman and Zalk, 1978; Grossman *et al.*, 1980). Certainly some of that attention had been directed toward the husband before the baby came and it is hard to give up a good thing, even for a good cause. In this as in other potential problem situations, fathers can facilitate a resolution by becoming more equal partners in the sharing of childcare responsibilities. If father and mother share the tasks involved in caring for a baby, then presumably they will have more time to spend together and the parental fatigue that usually accompanies the first year postpartum will be more evenly distributed.

Although we do focus here on sharing infant care, we also recognize that some people find very young babies quite uninteresting. People in our sample have told us that they just try to get through the rather unsatisfying first few months of their infants' lives because they know it will all get better when the baby starts to crawl or starts to walk or starts to talk. Finding pre-mobile or pre-verbal infants dull does not seem to be uncommon for mothers *or* fathers, but it may interfere more with fathers' interactions with babies because fathers' play tends to be more activity oriented.

Infants have a remarkably varied set of competencies, even from the first days of life. Though some of these are not immediately obvious and crying and wetting tend to be more salient, taking the time to learn about what his infant can do and how responsive the infant is to environmental stimulation can help a father develop a sense of competence as a parent and an appreciation of all the changes that go into producing the "more interesting" walking, talking toddler. He may also get to see how much he contributes to those changes.

The documentation of problems and conflicts some fathers experience as they make the transition to parenthood has made evident the need for supportive services for these men. The next section of this chapter provides a review of a selection of existing services and offers suggestions for the development and evaluation of programs for fathers.

III Analysis of existing networks

Programs for fathers in the postnatal period have only recently become available, most having been established since 1978. We have identified forty-three; undoubtedly there are many others. We have also found thirty-nine books for fathers which include at least one chapter on birth and the neonatal period. A review of these, however, is beyond the scope of this chapter. Some of the programs evolved naturally out of Lamaze or other childbirth classes; a few developed in reaction to those parent–infant groups where parent meant mother; others were created because fathers wanted to share their experiences and help other men. The focus of these programs for new fathers ranges from infant massage to the place of the new father in the nuclear age. Klinman and Kohl (1984) offer the best resource guide to these programs. Several others are listed in Payne (1984).

A Peer support networks

One might think men would want to share the birth experience and postnatal concerns with their close male friends. However, as Miller (1983) notes, deep friendship between adult men is quite rare in our society. Levinson *et al.* (1978) found that while a man may have a wide social network, in general close friendship with a man is rarely experienced by American men.

Men are, of course confirmed in fatherhood by their peers. However, this is often limited as well as short lived.

> My newspaper associates, most of them fathers themselves, briefly increased my feeling of self-esteem. I still do not know whether the mild ovation they gave me when I reported for work the night after your birth was due merely to friendship, or to the heathen glee chilled bathers feel when they see an innocent about to dive into their icy pool, or only to the prospect of wassail the newly-made father is expected, by tradition, to provide. The handwringing and the back pounding made me feel momentarily that I had accomplished a noteworthy feat of strength or skill, and two weeks later, even the heartiest of my congratulators had forgotten that you existed (Van de Water, 1939).

Recently there has been an increasing number of informal peer support networks developed for fathering in the postnatal period. Occasionally these informal groups have remained together up to seven years (Karagianis, 1984). Often they have not met with much success, some feeling men tend only to group in crises or sports. Stein (1982) provides valuable information on setting up and sustaining men's groups, including those for fathers.

B Small center-based networks

Several small, center-based programs have been established to provide discussion groups for new fathers. Some also have places for new fathers to drop in, libraries, telephone help lines, and consultation and referral services. One of the oldest is Rick Porter's Center for Fathers in Transition (#8, 2121 Ocean Ave, Santa Monica, CA 90405) which opened in

1975 and now offers an extended Lamaze class geared to new fathers. Neighborhood Support Services for Infants (38 Union Square, Somerville, MA 02143) started in 1976. Historically they have served primarily single parent families (Payne, 1984), but are now addressing needs of new fathers. The California Parenting Institute (342 Keller Street, Pentaluma, CA 94952) began a "Father and Infant Group" in 1980. The First Time Fathers Group (3 Old Causeway Road, Bedford, MA 01730) provides new fathers with an opportunity to share their experiences. It has been in operation since 1982.

Examples of other similar small center-based programs include the Father's Center in Ardmore, PA (Family Resource Coalition Report, 1984); the Parents of Young Children Group in LaGrange, IL; For Dads Only in Baton Rouge, LA; the Fathers Group in San Francisco, CA; the "Fathers Committee" of The Parents Division of the American Society for Psychoprophylaxis in Obstetrics of Kenmore, NY; and the "Booth Buddies" of the Booth Maternity Center of Philadelphia, PA. Klinman and Kohl (1984) provide good thumbnail sketches of many of these center-based programs serving new fathers.

C Large scale efforts

The largest attempt to support fathers of very young children was the federal Parent and Child Center (PCC) initiative. Forty centers were organized and funded between 1968 and 1970 to provide comprehensive services for economically disadvantaged families which had one or more children from birth to three (Johnson, 1973). Thirty-three of these centers remain. The program was designed to involve fathers as well as mothers, to assist parents to become more effective, and to improve the overall developmental progress of children. These PCCs, as they came to be called, had a positive effect on the lives of hundreds of families and continue to serve 3,500 children (Zigler, Kagan, and Klugman, 1983). They have, however, been plagued with serious economic, political, logistical and programmatic problems from their inception (Kalinowski, 1976). As a large-scale intervention effort they have had, at best, mediocre results where fathers are concerned (Goslin, 1974; Holmes, 1973; Kerschner, 1970).

A much smaller and more organized federal effort, the Parent Child Development Centers (Goslin, 1974; Robinson, 1975) were organized from the beginning with systematic research and evaluation goals as paramount considerations in program design and implementation. Initially, only three centers were designated with replication the eventual goal. These have now been integrated within the PCC network.

The Minnesota Early Learning Design (MELD) (123 E. Grant St, Minneapolis, MN 55403) provides information and support to first time parents in small, long-term support groups incorporating a peer self-help approach. Groups are organized during pregnancy so that babies of participating parents are born within three or four months of each other. The programs operate at twenty-five locations in fourteen states. According to Payne (1984) 40 per cent of the group members are fathers.

In 1974 Sweden introduced a radical new policy under the terms of which fathers as well as mothers could share seven months of paid leave around the time of a child's birth (Kamerman and Kahn, 1981). Employers were also required to allow fathers ten days of paid sick leave when a child was born. This was the first nation to have officially attempted to increase paternal involvement during the postnatal period. However, as discussed earlier in this chapter, despite a nationwide advertising campaign, and several modifications of the program designed to maximize its usefulness, the results have been very disappointing (Lamb and Levine, 1983). In the US few businesses and universities allow fathers paternity leave.

D Hospital-based programs

The Parenting Center at Children's Hospital (200 Henry Clay Ave, New Orleans, LA 70118) was established in 1980 by volunteers from the Junior League, which provided the initial financial support. In 1982 the hospital agreed to become the permanent funding source. This center provides a supportive environment and serves as a resource center for parents. Approximately one half of those attending open classes at night are fathers. The Center also has "Fathers Only" programs and a small Saturday "drop-in" program for fathers.

In Philadelphia, the Parenting Program at Booth Maternity Center (City Line and Overbrook Aves, Philadelphia, PA 19131) opened in 1977 and offers workshops, discussion sessions and playgroups targeted to new fathers (Payne, 1984). There is one father's class as part of the Infant Care Program at Evanston Hospital (2650 Ridge Ave, Evanston, IL 60201) in which fathers learn to bathe and diaper babies and discuss being new fathers. Klinman and Kohl (1984) review several other hospital-based programs including: The Family Birth Center of Mills Memorial Hospital in San Mateo, CA, which offers weekend "Parent Support Groups" conducted by a pediatrician and nurse practitioner; "The Art and Science of Fathering" is part of an evening program targeted to new fathers offered by North Colorado Medical Center, and Aims Community College of Greeley, CO; St John's Hospital of St Paul, MN has a short course "For a Father and His Baby" as does the Mount Sinai Medical Center of Milwaukee, WI. In Jeanette, PA, the Monsour Medical Center includes a "Fathering Module" as one of their eight prepared childbirth education classes.

E University-based programs

The Fatherhood Project of the Center for Parent Involvement at The School of Education at Boston University (604 Commonwealth Ave, Boston, MA 02215) is offering a "Parent Education for Fathers" course designed to improve fathers' relationships with children and a "Special Discussion Group for Fathers" designed for men who find themselves in the position of becoming new fathers under compromised circumstances.

Robert Zavala has taught "Child Development from a Male Perspective" in the Los Medanos Community College Child Development Program (2700 E. LeLand, Pittsburg, CA 94565) since 1974. College courses for fathers are also available at Napa Valley College, the University of North Dakota, and the University of Akron, while Seattle Central Community College and Washington State University offer short courses for new fathers (Klinman and Kohl, 1984).

The Department of Family and Consumer Studies at the University of New Hampshire (Durham, NH 03824) operates a small research library on fathers, and The Fatherhood Project at the Bank Street College of Education (610 W. 112th St, New York, NY 10025) has a national clearinghouse on fatherhood.

F Programs for new teenage fathers

Teenage fathers face several stressors in the early postpartum period (Elster and Panzarine, 1982) and have specific emotional and health educational needs (Elster and Panzarine, 1980). The degree to which these stressors are managed and needs are met will influence the parental behavior of both the teenage father and his partner (Elster and Lamb, 1982; Parke, Power, and Fisher, 1980).

The largest initiative to encourage paternal involvement in new adolescent fathers is a Ford Foundation funded experiment in eight US communities, coordinated by Bank Street College. One service, the Portland Fatherhood Project (2041 New Everett, Portland, OR 97209) represents a cooperative effort between the National Council of Jewish Women Insights and the Boys and Girls Aid Society. The project concentrates first on baby care – feeding, diapering, and how to play with an infant (*Life*, 1984), and includes home visits, educational and employment assistance, and couples groups. Another service, the Teen Indian Parents Program (3045 Park Ave, Minneapolis, MN 55407) has local funding provided by the Minneapolis Foundation, and offers fathers advice on nutrition, child abuse, parenting skills, and a range of other services (*Newsweek*, 1983). The other Ford programs include the Fatherhood Program in St Paul, MN; Teenage Pregnancy and Parenting Fatherhood Project of San Francisco; Teen Fatherhood Project, Bridgeport, CT; Teen Father Component of Jefferson County Public Schools, Louisville, KY; Teen Father Collaboration in New York; YWCA Fathers Outreach Component of Dutchess County, Poughkeepsie, NY; and the Teen Fathers Program at the Medical College of Pennsylvania, Philadelphia, PA.

Other programs for new teenage fathers (see Klinman and Kohl, 1984) include Our Place, a Family Focus program, Evanston, IL; the Teen Father Groups of the Family Planning Services of Central Massachusetts in Worcester, MA; The Door: A Center of Alternatives in New York City which runs a Young Fathers Group; and The Teen Father Program – A Family Service in Cleveland, OH.

IV Recommendations

A Planning programs

There are increasing empirical, theoretical, and practical data available to those interested in providing support to fathers during the postnatal period. A careful review of this information is recommended prior to further development of support services.

A large percentage of projects is directed by fathers or includes fathers in important roles. This helps establish credibility. However, whether to target postnatal support exclusively to fathers is somewhat debatable (Stein, 1982), given attendance figures for programs including only fathers. Programs which involve fathers and mothers as teachers and participants would appear to fare best.

Developing programs to attract and keep new fathers appears not to be an easy task. Programs for fathers which have focused on skill training or are geared toward particular groups, such as fathers whose wives are interested in returning to work, have sometimes met with more initial success. Some programs have also found initial success with recreational or social themes. Careful consideration should be given to the initial and continuing focus of these programs in order to capture and hold the attention of targeted fathers.

Flexibility may be very important in establishing programs for fathers. For example, if it is decided that a discussion group for fathers of newborns seems a reasonable choice, consideration should be given to the number of sessions. It might make more sense in some situations to offer two different six week programs or three four-week modules rather than a single twelve week session in order to encourage continuous involvement even for relatively short periods of time.

If there is sufficient rationale for providing technical or material support to fathers of newborns, one might argue that the hospital is the more appropriate place than the pediatrician's office because fathers may be most open to supportive services near the time of their child's birth. This is not necessarily to suggest that physicians are not appropriate for providing support in changing, bathing, or interacting with the newborn, or considering the changes fatherhood brings to men.

In more general terms, the workplace, public libraries, and video and audiotape should be further explored, perhaps backed up with telephone helplines for referrals to individual father advocates or professionals as appropriate. An important principle to consider is the delivery of support in the most natural, nonthreatening and potentially most effective manner. It is our opinion that a community supported combination of cost-effective support systems is likely to provide greater and more thorough support than most isolated centers or discussion groups, however well meaning or well funded.

B Implementing programs

One of the biggest problems with providing services to fathers is the packaging and marketing of them to attract fathers and to sustain their involvement over a reasonable period of time. A large number of programs contacted mentioned this was one of their serious concerns. While organizers are convinced of the need for support services, it is not yet the case that fathers themselves perceive the need for organized support after birth. The fathers in our study, for example, had not expressed any need for formal support services; most preferred to seek advice from colleagues and relatives when necessary.

It would appear that an ideal audience to target for postnatal services might be fathers already enroled in childbirth classes. Expanding those prenatal classes to better serve the needs of fathers and then extending a variety of support systems to them after the birth of the child appears to be a sound strategy. Providing written or audiocassette information through obstetrical offices, especially where support staff are committed enough to the concept to advocate the service is also recommended. The maternity ward or birthing center is a third alternative for marketing different support services for fathers since most fathers now participate in births. Many programs for fathers have required a consistent and continual recruitment effort, even after the program has been in operation for some time.

The authors suggest establishing the broadest possible community support prior to opening a service, covening an advisory committee of a broad spectrum of respected fathers to further establish credibility, and obtaining feedback from participants.

Our own experience has been that a gradual "phase in" of whatever services are provided may be ultimately most successful. We would further advise delaying public relations for other than recruitment purposes until the services are ready for public scrutiny. Also, it would appear that many successful programs have made significant adaptations in their services in order to respond to unanticipated needs of fathers.

A number of successful programs are component parts of hospitals, universities or social service agencies which have made significant financial and other commitments to these postnatal programs. Where institutional commitments have not been explicit, unwitting subsidization of time, space, and materials may occur.

General information on fundraising for those without substantive experience in this area is available from Finn (1982). Specialized information is also available on basic fundraising strategies (Pendleton, 1981; Taylor, 1981; Thrift, 1984), writing proposals (Lefferts, 1978; White, 1975), and approaching corporations (Hillman, 1979) and foundations (Kurzig, 1980).

Evaluative data on postnatal programs for fathers are conspicuous by their absence. This makes it difficult to adapt existing programs to better meet the needs of fathers and increases the likelihood that new program initiators will repeat the mistakes of the pioneers. It is beyond the scope of this chapter to address other than the need for regular recorded participant evaluations of services and occasional external reviews. Among the possibilities for further assistance in this area include Guba (1981), Kosecoff and Fink (1982), Rossi and Freeman (1982), and Wolf (1984).

Acknowledgment

Work by Mebert and Kalinowski (1984) reported in this chapter was supported in part by a NIH Biomedical Research grant administered through the University of New Hampshire and by a grant from the New Hampshire Agricultural Experiment Station.

References

Barnhill, L., Rubenstein, G., and Rocklin, N. (1979). "From generation to generation: Fathers-to-be in transition." *Family Coordinator*, 229–35.

Benedek, T. (1970). "Fatherhood and providing" in E. J. Anthony and T. Benedek (eds) *Parenthood: Its psychology and psychopathology*. Boston: Little, Brown.

Binet, A. and Simon, T. (1972). "The development of the Binet-Simon scale (1905–1908)" in W. Dennis (ed.) *Historical readings in developmental psychology*. NY: Appleton-Century-Crofts.

Bittman, S. and Zalk, S. R. (1978). *Expectant fathers*. NY: Hawthorn Books.

Bowlby, J. (1953). *Child care and the growth of love*. Middlesex, England: Penguin Books.

"Bringing up teenage fathers." *Life*, June 1984, 96–100.

"A chance for young fathers." *Newsweek*, October 24, 1983, 11.

Chess, S. and Thomas, A. (1982). "Infant bonding: Mystique and reality." *American Journal of Orthopsychiatry*, 52, 213–22.

Cranley, M. S., Hedahl, K. J., and Pegg, S. H. (1983). "Women's perceptions of vaginal and cesarean deliveries." *Nursing Research*, 32, 10–15.

Demos, J. (1983). "The changing faces of fatherhood: A new exploration in family history" in L. F. S. Kessel and A. W. Siegel (eds) *The child and other cultural inventions*. NY: Praeger.

Elster, A. and Panzarine, S. (1980). "Unwed teenage fathers: Emotional and health educational needs." *Journal of*

Adolescent Health Care, 1, 116–20.
Elster, A. and Panzarine, S. (1982).
"Teenage fathers." *Clinical Pediatrics,*
22, 700–3.
Elster, A. and Lamb, M. (1982).
"Adolescent fathers: A group potentially
at risk for parenting failure." *Infant
Mental Health Journal, 3*, 148–55.
Entwisle, D. R. and Doering, S. G. (1981).
The first birth: A family turning point.
Baltimore, Md.: Johns Hopkins University
Press.
Enzig, J. E. (1980). "The child within: A
study of expectant fatherhood." *Smith
College Studies in Social Work, 50,*
117–64.
Family Resource Center Coalition Report,
1984, 3, 1.
Fein, R. (1978). "Research on fathering:
Social policy and an emergent perspective."
Journal of Social Issues, 34, 122–35.
Finn, M. (1982). *Fundraising for early
childhood programs: Getting started and
getting results.* Washington, DC: National
Association for the Education of Young
Children.
Frodi, A. M. (1980). "Paternal-baby
responsiveness and involvement." *Infant
Mental Health Journal, 1*, 150–60.
Gelles, R. J. (1975). "Violence and
pregnancy: A note on the extent of the
problem and needed services." *Family
Coordinator, 25*, 81–6.
Gesell, A. L. (1929). "Maturation and
infant behavior patterns." *Psychological
Review, 36*, 307–19.
Goldberg, S. (1983). "Parent–infant
bonding: Another look." *Child
Development, 54*, 1355–82.
Goslin, D. (1974). *Children under three
and their families: Implications of the
Parent and Child Centers and the Parent
Child Development Centers for the design
of future programs.* Washington, DC:
Department of Health, Education and
Welfare.
Grossman, F. K., Eichler, L. S., and
Winickoff, S. A. (1980). *Pregnancy, birth
and parenthood.* San Francisco: Jossey-
Bass.
Guba, E. (1981). *Effective evaluation.* San
Francisco: Jossey-Bass.
Hall, G. S. (1923). *Life and confessions of
a psychologist.* NY: D. Appleton and Co.
Harlow, H. F. (1958). "The nature of
love." *American Psychologist, 13,*
673–85.
Hennenborn, W. J. and Cogan, R. (1975).
"The effect of husband participation in
reported pain and probability of

medication during labor and birth."
Journal of Psychosomatic Research, 19,
215–22.
Hetherington, E. M. (1966). "Effects of
paternal absence on sex-typed behaviors
in negro and white preadolescent males."
*Journal of Personality and Social
Psychology, 4*, 87–91.
Hillman, H. (1979). *The art of winning
corporate grants.* NY: Vanguard Press.
Holmes, M. (1973). *The impact of Head
Start Parent–Child Center Programs on
parents.* Washington, DC: Department of
Health, Education and Welfare.
Hwang, C. P. (1984). "Vaginal vs.
cesarean delivery in a Swedish sample:
Effects on father- and mother-infant
interaction at 3 and 8 months." Paper
presented at the International Conference
on Infant Studies, NY, NY, April.
Johnson, R. (1973). "Parent and child
centers: Early intervention." *Head Start
Newsletter, 6*(9), 3.
Kalinowski, M. (1976). "A developmental
model of education for parents of children
up to three years of age." Doctoral
dissertation, University of Massachusetts.
Dissertation Abstracts International, 37,
239.
Kamerman, S. B. and Kahn, A. J. (1981).
*Child care, family benefits, and working
parents.* NY: Columbia University Press.
Karagianis, M. (1984). "A modern father
image." *Boston Globe Magazine,* 17
June, 10.
Kirschner Associates (1970). *A national
survey of the Parent–Child Center
Program.* Washington, DC: Department of
Health, Education and Welfare.
Klinman, D. and Kohl, R. (1984).
*Fatherhood U.S.A.: The first national
guide to programs, services and resources
for and about fathers.* NY: Garland.
Kosecoff, J. and Fink, A. (1982).
*Evaluation basics: A practitioner's
manual.* Beverly Hills, CA: Sage.
Kurzig, C. M. (1980). "Foundation
fundamentals: A guide to grantseekers."
NY: Foundation Center.
Lamb, G. S. and Lipkin, M. (1982).
"Somatic symptoms of expectant
fathers." *Maternal Child Nursing, 7,*
110–15.
Lamb, M. E. and Levine, J. (1983). "The
Swedish Parental Insurance Policy: An
experiment in social engineering" in M. E.
Lamb and A. Sagi (eds) *Fatherhood and
family policy.* Hillsdale, NJ: Lawrence
Erlbaum Associates.
Lefferts, R. (1978). *Getting a grant: How*

to write successful grant proposals. Englewood Cliffs, NJ: Prentice-Hall.

Leupnitz, D. A. (1982). Child custody. Lexington, MA: Lexington Books.

Levinson, D. J., Darrow, C. N., Klein, E. B., Levinson, M. H., and McKee, B. (1978). The seasons of a man's life. NY: Ballantine.

Liebenberg, B. (1969). "Expectant fathers." Child and Family, 8, 264–7.

Lynn, D. B. and Sawrey, W. L. (1959). "The effects of father-absence on Norwegian boys and girls." Journal of Abnormal and Social Psychology, 59, 258–62.

Mebert, C. J. (1984). "The effects of day care on children and families." Paper presented at the New England Association for the Education of Young Children Conference, Manchester, NH, April.

Mebert, C. J. and Kalinowski, M. (1984). "Possible influences of prenatal and birth-related variables on parents' perceptions of infant temperament." Paper presented at the International Conference on Infant Studies, NY, April.

Miller, S. (1983). Men and friendship. Boston: Houghton Mifflin.

Mischel, W. (1961). "Father-absence and delay of gratification: Cross-cultural comparisons." Journal of Abnormal and Social Psychology, 62, 116–24.

Munroe, R. L. and Munroe, R. H. (1971). "Male pregnancy symptoms and cross-sex identity in three societies." Journal of Social Psychology, 84, 11–25.

Parke, R. (1981). Fathers. Cambridge, MA: Harvard University Press.

Parke, R., Power, T., and Fisher, T. (1980). "The adolescent father's impact on the mother and the child." Journal of Social Issues, 50, 971–5.

Payne, C. (ed.) (1984). Programs to strengthen families: A resource guide. Chicago: Family Resource Coalition.

Pedersen, F. A., Zaslow, M. J., Cain, R. L., and Anderson, B. J. (1981). "Cesarean childbirth: Psychological implications for mothers and fathers." Infant Mental Health Journal, 2, 257–63.

Pendleton, N. (1981). "Fund raising: A guide for non-profit organizations." Englewood Cliffs, NJ: Prentice-Hall.

Preyer, W. (1895). The mind of the child. NY: Appleton & Co.

Robinson, M. (1975). "Three models for

parent education: The Parent–Child Development Centers." Paper presented at the meeting of the Society for Research in Child Development, Denver, CO, April.

Rossi, P. and Freeman, H. (1982). Evaluation: A systematic approach. Beverly Hills, CA: Sage.

Scarr, S. (1984). Mother care, other care. NY: Basic Books.

Sears, R. R., Maccoby, E. E., and Levin, H. (1957). Patterns of child rearing. Evanston, IL: Row, Peterson & Co.

Sears, R. R., Whiting, J. W. M., Nowlis, V., and Sears, P. S. (1953). "Some childrearing antecedents of aggression and dependency in young children." Genetic Psychology Monographs, 47, 135–234.

Shereshefsky, P. M. and Yarrow, L. J. (1973). Psychological aspects of a first pregnancy and early postnatal adaptation. NY: Raven Press.

Spitz, R. and Wolf, K. M. (1946). "The smiling response: A contribution to the ontogenesis of social relations." Genetic Psychology Monographs, 34, 57–125.

Stein, T. (1982). "Men's groups" in K. Solomon and N. Levy (eds) Men in transition. NY: Plenum.

Straus, M. A., Gelles, R. J., and Steinmetz, S. K. (1980). Behind closed doors: Violence in the American family. NY: Anchor Books.

Stuckey, M. F., McGhee, P. E., and Bell, N. J. (1982). "Parent–child interaction: the influence of maternal employment." Developmental Psychology, 18, 635–44.

Taylor, B. P. (1981). Guide to successful fund raising (2nd edn) NJ: Groupwork Today, Inc.

Thrift, C. S. (1984). "Families and the education of young children." Paper presented at the New England Association for the Education of Young Children Conference, Manchester, NH, April.

Van de Water, F. (1939). Fathers are funny. NY: John Day Co.

White, V. (1975). Grants: How to find out about them and what to do next. New York: Plenum.

Wolf, R. (1984). Evaluations in education: Foundations of competency assessment and program review. NY: Praeger.

Zigler, E. F., Kagan, S. L., and Klugman, E. (eds) (1983). Children, families and government. Cambridge University Press.

PART 3

Skills for improved functioning

CHAPTER 5

Fund raising and networking for parenting organizations

Maureen Lynch and Page Talbott Gould

Introduction

As the authors of this chapter we feel that we have no great wisdom about fund raising. It is a challenging and unpredictable activity. And if it were not for some turns of good fortune, we would probably be reading this chapter rather than writing it. Since we are writing it, perhaps we can pass on some of the things we have learned so that you will not have to learn them at the expense of your program.

It is very easy for those of us in community non-profit organizations to develop a sort of surly self-righteousness about fund raising. We are doing good work, we think, so why do we also have to become experts in marketing, proposal writing and corporate giving. Those requirements set up by funding sources are just hoops for us to jump through. Anyway, most of the money just goes to already funded non-profits: the rich just get richer. Because it is so time-consuming, it is very easy to find yourself resenting fund raising as well as the people from whom you are required to make requests. To think more positively, remind yourself why you are so concerned about your program – why the need is so tremendous, what you plan to do in the coming year, how this will affect specific peoples' lives. Once you have yourself re-focused it will be much easier to do your job. After all, the people you will be contacting have only a limited amount of money to donate. Their concern is that they give it to groups which are commited and capable, so that their funding choices will turn out to have been wise ones. It is your job to let them know that you will make them look good if they support you. Your own natural enthusiasm, coupled with a well-prepared presentation, should be allowed to carry you along. Hopefully, it will also carry along a funding source.

In this chapter we will be discussing onetime, versus ongoing donations; various funding sources such as in-kind contributions, donations, benefits, product development, grants and membership dues; developing a budget; obtaining seed money; writing grants; and giving presentations.

Getting started

Developing a budget

One of the first things you should do is to develop a budget. Then, prioritize the categories relevant to the budget. In other words: of all the expenses, what is the most critical? Perhaps the group is willing to absorb the expense of postage, xeroxing and telephone calls, but definitely needs funds for a scholarship program. You can prioritize expenses by looking at two things: a prioritized list of services, and expenses of those services. Sometimes the "line" expenses will surprise you. More specifically, you will sometimes discover that the organization actually translates to very little in monetary terms. However, by covering that expense (and not expecting volunteers to pay for it), you have greatly increased the morale of the group and gained much needed momentum. In prioritizing the budget lines, you need to be sensitive to such issues.

Some community organizations, which have been operating for years, thrive without ever having a budget. They have committed volunteers, always seem to scrape together donations, and are blissfully fiscally illiterate. But the day comes when the present group of volunteers gives its last collective sigh, and there are no others waiting in the wings. A budget allows you to approach local industry and civic organizations about donations for specific projects or for operating expenses, thereby hopefully staving off the day when all of the volunteers feel overpowered and end up quitting.

When you make up your budget remember to be true to the character of your organization. There are so many different formats that a group can take and still be a healthy organization. You may find that the area of spending that is particularly stressing your group covers telephone and postage. Your volunteers are willing to continue at a steady pace, but really need to have their telephone bills reimbursed. Or maybe that is not even an issue for you. Instead, your organization needs help with printing expenses. The point here is to evaluate your needs. In doing this you may want to look around you – Compassionate Friends operates very differently from the March of Dimes, both of which are very different from the Rotary International. Read annual reports, talk to people about the choices they made, learn from others' mistakes. Some of the things you will be looking at include make up of the board – some expect a minimum annual donation. What types of priorities have the various groups established in developing their budgets? Every policy decision has tremendous impact on the organization. Though it is exhausting to constantly be scraping about for money to cover expenses, a certain group cohesiveness often forms during these lean periods. By looking at how other organizations have evolved, you will develop a clearer idea of the direction you want to take.

Initial donations

When you start, be flexible. So many people seem to feel that all their problems would be solved if they had a $200,000 government grant; and, unfortunately, that is all they can think of. There are so many ways to acquire funds. Sometimes an affiliation with an institution will be more fruitful than a one shot donation. Such an affiliation (e.g., with a university, hospital, church, corporation) could provide free office space, telephone, xeroxing, secretarial support, etc. So when you begin to think of seed money, allow yourself to imagine as many different ways of obtaining it as possible.

Some granting agencies, individuals, or corporations are willing to help a group get underway; others are more interested in providing large grants after a group is established. Nevertheless, an ability to demonstrate other ongoing sources of income is frequently critical to a successful grant proposal. Following, then, are suggestions about possible sources of ongoing support. Not only is such support critical to the operation of parent groups, but the presence of such fixed income allows those in the organization to concentrate their efforts on services rather than on fund raising.

A large initial grant from a local hospital or national organization can serve as an endowment fund for a smaller organization which can then use the income (usually 6 per cent–10 per cent) for operating expenses. An initial grant of $50,000 for example, could yield from $3,000–$5,000 annually, ample funds for many groups whose principle expenses are telephone, duplicating, printing and postage.

In communities where the service of a parent group will primarily benefit one hospital or school, approaching that institution with a proposal for an endowment fund may be met with considerable interest. If that institution could convince a benefactor of the benefit of such a group they could then oversee the establishment of such a fund. The future of the group would be financially secure without an annual search for operating expenses.

While a hospital or school may be the most obvious administrator of such a fund, a community organization may also be interested in assuming the responsibility of raising an initial fund of this sort. Civic groups such as Rotary Club, Junior League, and Kiwanis have helped support parent groups in various communities. If the establishment of a permanent endowment fund is not feasible, then an annual request for funding to such a group might be another possibility. Once a parent support group has proved its resourcefulness, effectiveness, and importance to the community, many local philanthropic organizations are happy to lend their support. Be sure to find out when the organization in question plans its projects for the coming year; their normal range of grants; and how presentations or applications should be made. Are decisions based on a site visit, lunch with group leaders, or do they require a more formal presentation at their office? What content of a written grant proposal do they require – number of people served, budget justification, volunteer training? Many inexperienced fund raisers think it is somehow cheating to ask these types of questions. However, funding sources appreciate being able to inform applicants about preferred procedures.

In some communities, parent groups have become closely allied with civic organizations which can be pointed to with pride as a source of funding. In return, members of the group should participate in fundraising events sponsored by the host organization whenever possible as a show of thanks and mutual support. Parent group members might, for example, become involved with the Mothers' March for the March of Dimes, or help run the annual barbecue of the Rotary Club.

Maintaining financial support

Product development

The development of products requires considerable advance planning and some financial investment. An advantage of creating innovative products is the availability of an ongoing source of income with the potential for continued growth of customers and products. The disadvantage of producing and marketing a group's own products, of course, is that the group must necessarily assume a certain amount of financial risk in the course of developing the product. Yet enterprise in the nonprofit sector has become increasingly popular.

It is daunting to realize that 90–95 per cent of all small businesses fail. They usually fail for one of three reasons: poor planning, insufficient capital, or bad management. Your business cannot afford to fail because such a failure would reflect on the reputation of the organization and its leaders, its position in the community, and its relationship with funders. Also, failure would use up limited financial resources. The bottom line is that the business is not important, the non-profit organization sponsoring it is. For that reason it is even more important for entrepreneurs in the non-profit sector to educate themselves about business venture approaches.

It is thought that successful entrepreneurs have three qualities: persistence; the ability to learn from mistakes; and the capacity to take moderate risks. Laura Landy, president of Business Strategy Associates in New York City has become a pioneer in helping community organizations form business ventures. Armed with a Master's degree in Business

Administration, and a keen social conscience, she has managed to transform well-meaning but naive non-profit leaders into successful entrepreneurs. Landy has said that, "Most entrepreneurs start with a business plan; when this should actually be one of the last steps. A cautious, prudent planning process can reduce failure substantially." Such a process includes looking at the program and its environment, the proposed business and its fit with the non-profit organization, and a feasibility study. "Staying closer to your non-profit base," says Landy, "tends to lower risk and give greater control without necessarily lowering the return." For example, see the Product Development Matrix (Fig. 5.1).

Product Market	NOW	NEW
NOW	Market 1. penetration	Product 3. development
NEW	Market 2. expansion	Diversification 4.

1. = Least risk; 4. = Most risk

Figure 5.1 Product Development Matrix

It might be possible to find a corporation or business to underwrite the start-up costs of production, thus relieving the group of short-term financial liability. In some cases, it might also make sense to find buyers before beginning production.

The cost of the products will vary according to whether their sale will be viewed primarily as a service or as a significant source of income. Some groups, for example, have developed literature which they are happy to share with other groups. These initial groups only wish to recoup the cost of printing and postage. Alternatively, a group which has developed its own training manual may see the distribution of the manual as a viable source of income for the organization, and will price it accordingly.

Other products which have been developed successfully by parent groups include clothing and patterns for children with special needs, greeting cards, films and slide tapes. Methods of marketing such products vary from low key advertising in professional journals to mass mailings to parents and professionals alike. Needless to say, the more extensive the advertising, the more expensive the project. Most important, remember to look into the tax regulations for business ventures of non-profits. In the United States for instance there is a distinction drawn between related and unrelated income.

Before launching into the development of a product, it is crucial to perform some kind of market survey. This can be as simple as contacting members of other support groups nationwide to find out if others are already producing such items, or it can entail a comprehensive question-naire sent to a broad sample of parents and professionals selected randomly from communities across the country. Whatever your method of conducting a survey, be sure to do some homework first. Yours may be a brilliant idea, but someone else may have already thought of it. Maybe you can help make the existing product available in your community, or perhaps your idea differs sufficiently from the existing one to make your product viable. Avoid putting yourself in the position of being the last one to know about an existing product or service.

Service development

One service which has been a source of income to some parent support groups is the provision of education programs for hospital staff. Programs on a variety of topics for professionals can serve as a way of updating hospital personnel about services offered by the group as well as sharing information on the latest techniques related to such areas as breastfeeding, transition from hospital to home, parenting the sick infant or child. Staff members meet volunteers from the support group, are reassured by their level of competence, and have a renewed interest in referring their patients to the group.

Most hospital nursing departments have a budget which includes honoraria for those conducting in-service training. This amount can vary from $25 to $100 per program. In the case of a group which serves a number of hospitals via regular in-service programs (held once or twice a year), such sessions can prove to be a valuable source of ongoing income in addition to spreading good will and information.

Dues

Another potential source of ongoing income for a group of any size is annual dues, either in the form of membership payment or as a paid subscription to a newsletter. In the latter case, the cost of the subscription would exceed the cost of publishing and mailing the newsletter. Outside funding sources such as grant-giving agencies and private corporations and foundations look hard at an organization's willingness to solicit its own membership for financial contributions. After all, if one's own constituency is not willing to lend support, why should anyone else?

Clearly, the resources of families that have incurred tremendous medical bills during the hospitalization of a child, for example, are already over-taxed. But a $5 membership is a minimal contribution which represents a commitment to the organization more than financial hardship for the family. Most support group membership dues are low ($5–$10) with the opportunity for those with greater monetary resources to make additional contributions.

Most groups offer their services free of charge to families during a crisis period. Solicitation of membership fees is delayed until several months after the initial contact is made. In other instances, membership information is included in the brochure describing the group's services, with the added comment that support and information is available free of charge, leaving the contribution strictly voluntary.

It is important that groups charging dues or subscription fees keep accurate records of this income and send renewal notices when appropriate. These records will be extremely valuable when it comes time to working on a grant proposal or the upcoming year's budget.

Other donations

In addition to the immediate families served by parent support groups, others who have been influenced by contact with the group are potential sources of financial support. Extended family members such as grandparents are often extremely grateful for support received. Less burdened by parenting-related bills, these family members might well be interested in subscribing to a newsletter or in making a direct contribution to the group.

The professionals who have benefited from the services of the support group might also be interested in making a contribution. Doctors, nurses, social workers, individually or through their department, should be asked to subscribe to the newsletter or join the group as dues-paying members. Again, the fee charged may be minimal, but the implication of support for the group in the community can be invaluable.

Separate lists of parents, other family members and professionals should be accurately maintained so that the numbers of members and/or subscriptions from each group can be tallied easily. Once or twice a year these lists should be updated, while new members should be solicited on an ongoing basis. Such solicitation might be in the form of a questionnaire to graduate parents asking those who have already weathered a crisis for information about their experience, suggestions about ongoing programs, how the group has helped the family, and additional names of interested families. Volunteer opportunities within the group can also be identified.

Publicity

Another way of generating financial support for the organization as well as interest in its programs is publicity, in the form of newspaper stories, television or radio interviews or public service announcements. Sometimes local hospitals or schools served by the group will help generate media coverage of events or projects. Having the backing of such an institution can give the group credibility in the community.

Stories can focus on individual families (of particular interest to local papers), on fund raising activities, or on educational programs. Human interest stories about families with medical problems are often popular with the press. These stories can serve as lead-ins to information about the group and can serve as a direct or indirect request for donations. Be sure to include the address of the group in the story as well as the name of a contact person.

Try to establish individual and personal contacts with members of the media. Suggest a meeting, bring pictures, clippings, brochures and possible story ideas. Make it easy for the reporter to follow up on the story by giving names, addresses and telephone numbers. One successful story can lead to another, so continue to feed ideas to your contacts.

Benefits and fund raisers

Once you have identified and established regular sources of income, your group might want to investigate running a benefit program to fund a special project. Some fund raising projects prove to be so successful that they become annual events which can then be counted on as a regular source of income. The scope of such projects depends on the amount of volunteer time available to launch them, on support from the community, and on the overall energy available from everyone in the group.

Why not think big? Sometimes the amount of time spent planning a small project – a bake sale, for example – can equal that for an even larger event. If you have found a good location, time, and a large group of workers to run the bake sale, consider including a swap shop of baby clothes, a craft fair featuring hand-made items, and an information sharing table. Publicity for your event is key, so be sure to involve your media contacts. Post notices with area merchants where possible, and give your event sufficient advance notice to be able to run an article about it in your newsletter. Finally, mail information to television and radio stations for public service announcements.

Other fund raising events that have proved successful for parent support groups include seminars on topics relating to the group's special concerns, auctions, dinner/dances, theatre benefits, and trips to amusement parks. Most non-profit as well as profit-making entertainment facilities offer promotional "packages" for non-profit organizations. The advantage of a fundraiser of this kind is that the event is created and planned for you. The disadvantage is that you must guarantee a large attendance in order to make the fund raising financially worthwhile to your group.

Be sure to allow ample time for planning any fund raising event. Few good projects can succeed with only one or two months' notice. The larger the scope of the event, the greater the lead time needed. Some groups find that within weeks of the completion of one annual fund raiser, they have to begin planning the following year's event.

Other sources of support

The three remaining sources of support are corporations, foundations, and governments. We have grouped them together since they all tend to require the presentation of a grant proposal. However, they are very different, both in requirements and in interests. It is generally true that what they will require of you in writing is the least for corporations (1–3 pages), middling for foundations (3–7 pages), and extensive for government (20 or more pages for a federal grant).

For tax and public relations reasons, corporations regularly make donations. There are more corporate philanthropic programs now than there were ten years ago, and they have become much more professional. This change has produced corporate giving departments that appear similar to private foundations. But it is important to remember that they are corporations with different goals and intentions than foundations. It has become accepted to say that 2–5 per cent of pre-taxed income of corporations goes for philanthropic causes. In reality corporations first compute existing commitments such as scholarships for employees' children and multi-year funding to community organizations, then they allocate the balance to new projects. The funded projects are almost always related to the nature of the company.

Keep in mind that budgets are prepared four to six months before the allocation period. It is important to determine who has control over the department. It either resides with the corporate giving staff or with the chief executive officer of the company. If it is with the latter there is a certain amount of unpredictability and favoritism. This is fine if you are one of the chairman's pet projects; but if you are not, it can be very frustrating trying to figure out how to break in. Of course, seldom is it this black and white, but nevertheless it does help to know the procedure for making decisions and the amount of autonomy the department has.

You need to become very sophisticated about corporations – understand their inner workings, be polished about presentations, and look on the staff member as your ally to be involved early in the application process. But perhaps even more important, do not look upon the corporation as your savior. With all the mergers and divestitures taking place, corporations are in a tremendous flux. As they close down branch offices and move into new ventures, this will have a tremendous influence on their giving patterns.

Many fund raisers say that during the first year or two you should not expect to raise much money, perhaps only small gifts of $100 or $500. They feel that mostly you will be developing relationships. During this period you may be more successful requesting an in-kind donation such as the printing of your newsletter or the volunteering of an employee to set up your books or serve on your board. Regardless of the outcome, do not forget to apply the criticism you receive not as a personal affront but as a lesson to be learned before approaching other corporations.

You may decide to approach a specific company because it produces a product related to the concern of the group, because it has a commitment to local needs, or because you know someone in the company. In order to find out about the company, you can get a copy of their annual report and talk to the individual in charge of corporate giving. During your conversation, be considerate about time. Usually this position is held by an employee who has many other responsibilities. Simply introduce yourself, and find out the schedule, and procedure for applying. Usually, annual reports will tell you to whom money was donated and how much they received. Ask for any information not in the report during your conversation. It would also be helpful to know in which areas they are interested in giving money – for example, general operating expenses, purchase of a computer, or expenses for members to attend volunteer management workshops. Though this is important to know, be cheered by the thought that there can always be a first time for previously unthought of donations. This is where your enthusiasm comes in. Gerber Baby Foods had never funded an intensive care nursery until they were convinced by a committed doctor and nurse. Now the Gerber Unit of Butterworth Hospital in Grand Rapids, Michigan is a source of continuing pride to the company.

Foundations are another possible source of support. There are 22,000 private foundations in America, and thousands more in other countries. Some of them are company foundations, others are small family foundations developed mostly for tax reasons, and others such as the Robert Wood Johnson Foundation, the second largest foundation with assets of $1.2 billion, is a little of both. Though approaching companies is so individualized that you appear to be on your own, the effort of foundation fund raising involves access to an excellent resource. It is appropriately enough named The Foundation Center (with regional offices in several cities in the United States). The Foundation Center provides excellent services such as The Foundation Directory, which lists foundations by state, areas of interest, and range of giving, as well as indicating addresses and telephone numbers. Frequently, foundation boards meet quarterly to review proposals. It is important to remember that due to initial letters of introduction, site visits and other procedures, eight or twelve months usually pass before a donation is received.

It is encouraging to note that foundations are taking more of an interest in community based organizations. "The foundations field is not dominated by a few foundations the way it used to be," says James A. Joseph, President of the Council on Foundations. "Issues no longer seem to lend themselves to individual solutions. Needs have multiplied, and while Ford was once a giant, it is now small potatoes in terms of human needs. So foundations, especially those further down the list from Ford and Johnson, have decided to work closer to home, to pour their efforts into a small number of specific programs in particular areas of the country."

Recently state and federal grants have been cut back drastically. However, there are still targeted areas that may fit your project. A Boston parent organization recently received a three year federal grant. Exploring this area, despite the tremendous paperwork involved, may be productive for you. For sources of state funding contact your state funding representative. For federal sources you can review the Federal Register. Since an annual subscription to the Federal Register is $300, you may want to review one at the library. If you have not done so by now, this is a good time to become friends with your area's university "development officer," the individual in charge of fund raising for the university. Also, talk to people in your community who have received government grants, and review samples of grant proposals. Feel free to call grant officers at the various government funding sources. It is perfectly fair to ask them for recommendations about whether your project fits upcoming targeted areas. There are many fine books available which outline the writing of grant proposals. The Grantsmanship Center has an excellent checklist that is very helpful in developing a proposal (address in the reference section).

Limitations on space have prevented us from describing other material we usually cover in workshops. Remember, your program deserves support. All you need to learn is how to present your program to obtain the financial support you need. Presenting your program in a good light is nothing mystical or exotic, it is just a skill. And like any skill, it can be learned; it just takes practice. Because there are so many opportunities for raising funds for parent groups, it is extremely important that members of the group discuss their options annually. Such a discussion provides an opportunity to review the group's goals, needs and interests. Moreover, it will serve the function of generating excitement for the coming year. At this meeting the members can brainstorm and will, no doubt, come up with ideas to their liking. With enthusiasm and commitment to the projects, members of the group will have little trouble identifying and tapping ongoing sources of financial support.

Further reading and useful contacts

Catalog of Federal Domestic Assistance and the *Federal Register* are both available from the Superintendent of Documents, US Government Printing Office, Washington, DC 20402.

Enterprise in the Nonprofit Sector, available on written application to Partners for Livable Places, 1429 21st Street NW, Washington, DC 2036. Phone: (202) 887–5990.

The *Foundation Directory*, *Corporation Foundation Profiles*, and the *Foundation Grants Index Annual* are all available from The Foundation Center, 79 Fifth Avenue, New York, NY 10003. Their toll-free number is (800) 424-9836.

Thomas Ferrence specializes in strategic planning, organization and board development. He is the founder and director of a unique program based at the business school of Columbia University: The Institute for Not For Profit Management, Columbia University, 212 Uris Hall, New York, NY 10016.

Giving and Getting, Chemical Bank study of corporate philanthropy, 1983–8. It is available from The Not For Profit Group, 1212 Avenue of the Americas, New York, NY 10036.

Laura Landy is a specialist in business ventures for non-profits, she is president of Business Strategy Associates, 110 West 71st St, New York, NY 10023.

Management Control in Nonprofit Organizations (1984) by R. N. Anthony and D. W. Young. Homewood, IL: Richard Irwin.

Marketing for Nonprofit Organizations (1984) by P. Kotler. Englewood Cliffs, NJ: Prentice Hall.

National Directory of Corporate Charity. Available from Regional Young Adult Project, 330 Ellis St, #518, San Francisco, CA.

Program Planning and Proposal Writing. Available from the Grantsmanship Center, 1031 South Grand Avenue, Los Angeles, CA 90015.

Taft Corporate Giving Directory. Available from Taft Corporation, 5125 MacArthur Blvd NW, Washington, DC 20016.

Tax Exempt Status For Your Organization. Internal Revenue Service (IRS) publication, IRS #557. *Tax on Unrelated Business Income of Exempt Organizations*, IRS publication #598.

Check telephone listings for your nearest IRS office.

CHAPTER 6

Advocacy skills for parenting organizations

Mary A. Moran

The *American Heritage Dictionary* defines advocacy as "active support, as of a cause." In everyday parlance, advocacy most often refers to actions taken in a situation that demands assertiveness of one's opinions, needs, values, or interests. Advocacy in this context often takes the connotation of active participation in a decision-making process in which it would be easy to be ignored or viewed as an unimportant component. On a personal level, effective advocacy demands at least two characteristics – awareness and assertiveness. On a group level, advocacy demands that group members have a significant level of awareness of their individual needs and that they share come consensus as to the importance of perceived group needs. However, effective advocacy as a group may occur without all members being assertive about their personal needs nor effective advocates for themselves. Effective advocacy in groups needs both leaders and followers, those who can conceptualize on a large scale and those who can see to small details, those who enjoy making strong public statements and those who can take care of the background work, those who can communicate effectively for the whole group and those who can tell best just their own stories.

My experiences working with groups of parents who have infants and toddlers with special needs lead me to believe that there are two different ways that group advocacy may start. First is the situation in which an ongoing support group decides to undertake an advocacy function; second is the situation in which a group comes together first in order to perform an advocacy function.

In both types of groups a level of personal awareness precedes the decision to organize an advocacy effort. Within the first group, advocacy efforts are often stimulated when the group recognizes that the personal needs, interests, issues and values of the members coincide in an important way. Such efforts most easily flourish when the recognition surrounds an unmet need. In other words, group advocacy is most often born of the recognition of shared feelings and experiences. Not every group member needs to be at the same level of introspection, nor to have made a "similar peace" with his/her own issues and feelings; however each must have some recognition of his/her feelings or there is no common ground from which the group can work. Not all group members can be expected to share all feelings nor an intensity of feeling, but as a group they must have reached a level of development where group members can talk somewhat freely before they are likely to be successful in an ongoing advocacy effort. Otherwise a splinter group or subgroup may devote itself to advocacy while the ongoing group maintains its previous support function. This is often difficult since new advocacy efforts demand a great deal of time and energy commitment from at least a core group in order to succeed. The original group must have a strong ongoing need and usefulness in order for a subgroup to form for advocacy and yet have those members remain active and devoted to the original group functions. Advocacy interests that are not important to the entire group may be divisive and a split (often amicable) is likely to occur.

In a group formed specifically for advocacy purposes, the awareness of personal needs of several individuals must coincide in order to provide the basic impetus for the group – a "mission." In this situation the group members may have met through a variety of informal means. It may begin by two parents sharing views and recognizing a need. It could be stimulated by one parent who recognizes a need and actively seeks other parents with a similar perspective. Either way, conversations with other friends and acquaintances may bring together a core group with advocacy interests.

Every group that undertakes to advocate must grapple with the issue of whether these group members' shared experiences or feelings are representative of a larger constituency or community or whether their burning issues are rather unique to a present situation. That is, the individuals who are forming the group must make some original assessment of whether their goal is time-limited and one-time such as the creation of an early childhood program within their local school system, or a long-term effort such as improving the availability of early intervention services that are also of high quality. In reality, most advocacy groups come together to meet an immediate and short-term need, but in the process may commit themselves to long-term advocacy for a variety of issues related to a population. The vision related to long-term advocacy may flower after the success of a short-term effort or with the frustration that arises with the failure of a first endeavor.

At least some group members must have assertiveness skills in order for the group to be successful in advocating. Not all members will be equally skilled in communicating their personal needs, successful in getting their needs met, nor gifted in exhibiting group advocacy skills. In the early stages, there must be at least one member who is skilled at defining the larger needs – recognizing the similarities or trends in personal needs or issues. Someone must create the spark that says to members in an already existing group that there is an identified need (whether for public awareness, the closing of a service gap, a legislative statement, or the closing of an information gap). In many pre-existing groups, a professional leader may attempt to create that spark. This is a difficult line to walk. Unless the group and the individual members are able to recognize and verbalize the need at some coherent level, it is unlikely that they can organize a successful effort. The role of the professional leader may be to reflect the similarities in views and experiences of group members and to aid them in coming to some sort of decision regarding how to act once the desire to take action is recognized.

In forming a new group, this need for someone to spark interest in the endeavor is more obvious. In groups formed for advocacy purposes the mission is often stated first by that individual who entices others who sense a shared need, interest, and purpose. The decision toward advocacy in an organized manner is frequently based on that mission statement. For example, a parent who feels that there is a strong need for a day care center in the company where he/she works might post a notice on a company bulletin board asking to speak with any parents interested in day care opportunities for young children or frustrated by the lack of options for day care that exist. That simple beginning is likely to bring together interested individuals – if a need exists.

Once the decision toward organizing for advocacy has been made, issues of organization begin to take precedence for a time. Three major issues immediately come to the forefront: group size, leadership, and strategies.

Group size

The issue of group size is a tricky one. There is strength in numbers, but there must be a small and committed core at least in the beginning. The core must share a relatively similar life view at least regarding the initial issue in order for the group to take an advocacy stance effectively. The larger organization, if one is in place, must be inspired by the vision of the leader or the smaller core of members. Especially if interested in impacting a larger system – the general public, the legislature – a larger group can be more effective. The larger group may contain members who are devoted only to a single issue or those who do not share a common core of experience but may have another reason for interest in the problem. For example, a group of allies in the creation of a special needs preschool program within the community might be the faculty of a local college that has a training program for students in that specialty. These people share a common vision and perhaps a set of values, but the reason for their interest, their needs, and their experiences differ. They are more apt to provide peripheral manpower within this advocacy endeavor than to be an essential part of the core of advocates. They might provide vital technical assistance rather than define the initial issue; their commitment is unlikely to be such that they provide the leadership within the group. Effective leadership by more than one person demands a high level of concordance in defining needs, similar experiences, shared values, and short- or long-term interests. It is for this reason that establishing advocacy groups is most successful when a real gap in what is available at present can be identified. If we use the example of the early childhood special needs program, it can be seen that this gap is most easy to identify and the lack most likely to be felt by many people when private programs are not readily available within the general area. If private preschool programs in the area will admit children with mild and moderate special needs and there are adequate therapy opportunities in the area for children who demonstrate those needs, it would be more difficult (but certainly not impossible) to engender the necessary interest and enthusiasm on the part of many parents. Once two parents had found difficulty in meeting needs for themselves or their children in a similar manner, an advocacy group would be easier to establish.

Disseminating information and establishing a target

An individual or small core group must then formulate a strategy for disseminating information about the group's mission. For example, a core of parents within an early intervention program who wish to advocate for the establishment of an early childhood special needs program within the community might first plan a strategy for contacting other parents enroled in the early intervention program. Such strategies might include flyers distributed by program staff, a parent-to-parent telephone chain, a newsletter article written by a parent, or an open letter tacked up in the group space. In order to reach the larger community, they might contact the local newspaper and request stories, send a public service announcement to local newspapers and radio stations, hold an open house at the early intervention program that is run by parents, send letters to parents of program "graduates," or write to the newsletters of local church groups or other parent organizations.

Some people are interested in group membership only to impact a particular issue. They will join a fledgling advocacy group so that they may bring their issue to the forefront. If the first issue that the group chooses is not of their interest, they will not remain active group members. Some will join the group only after the group has chosen and publicized its first issue of interest. A smaller number of individuals are likely to be interested in a broad spectrum of issues and will commit themselves to an advocacy effort that does not address their most clearcut needs.

The charge of choosing their first issue may become, therefore, the nemesis of a group of parents who seek to advocate for themselves, their children, or a larger group of families. Their first task as a group is to turn their personal and group awareness into a knowledge base from which to organize their efforts. They must decide whether their recognized issues are, in fact, representative of those of a larger group of parents or whether they result from their specific ecological circumstances. One of the major tasks of a first meeting is to air the opinions and feelings of those present and then to decide on strategies for gathering more information about those issues and their general significance. Both these activities will help the group to finalize an initial mission and target a first effort.

At the first meeting, one of the organizers should act as a moderator and give a brief opening statement about why the meeting was called. She/he should then open the meeting for comments from those present. This will allow the organizers the opportunity to hear from a range of people with many viewpoints and experiences. Each person at the meeting should be asked to identify most outstanding needs and a list should be made of those. The group should then set out to prioritize these needs in some manner. Each participant might be asked to make their own hierarchy and the group would then pool these lists. An open vote could be used. The group size and the time available will affect how the organizers proceed with this task. If the group is small and the time and interest is available, individuals making their own priority list and then discussing them is useful. In a larger group, an open vote may be attempted. This works best when there is not a sense of strong dissension. The risk is that the group may be fairly evenly divided on the priorities and the need to spend time discussing them at length would then still remain. The group could decide to hold off making a firm decision until more information is gathered.

One way to begin is to seek out the knowledge of other organizations devoted to similar causes – those on a national, state, or local level. Public libraries are good places to start. Professionals within disciplinary areas that relate to the parents' issues are another source of such information. Surveying parents of older children may yield useful information. Contacting national organizations with interests in related topics may be fruitful; they may have knowledge of obscure groups or important trends in the field. Another good source of information is other advocacy groups that focus on different matters. Any access one can get to parents in similar circumstances at present is advantageous. Distributing questionnaires can be a good tactic. These need not be designed in any particular manner, but the questions asked should reflect the group's concerns and should identify concerns that the group may not have recognized. A large general question that addresses how people view the current system or state of affairs should be the lead. More specific questions about those areas that the group identified can then be asked. A place for additional comments should always be left since this is apt to yield the most descriptive information in an original questionnaire that is searching for just a larger knowledge base. Any number of sources for distributing such a questionnaire may be sought. A small newspaper advertisement can be placed. Help may be sought from organizations that may have access to parents with similar concerns – churches, schools, hospitals, counseling centers.

Another particularly good source of information may be the legislative assistants in the offices of any federal or state legislators who are known to have strong interests in the issues related to a particular population. Contacting them is most likely to be helpful if they also serve your district. If this is not the case, making a contact within the legislator's home district is very useful. Telephone calls and personal letters are most likely to initiate a response and yield helpful information. Once the sources of information have been tapped, the group must begin to make some decisions regarding the specific issue that they will target first. Personal commitments of group members are likely to have a strong impact in the decision-making process. The knowledge base that has been built is another source that should be considered. A further knowledge base related to the specific issue targeted may then need to be sought. This will be discussed later in relation to formulating strategies.

A third factor in the decision-making process that must be given some credence if the first advocacy endeavor is to have some chance at recognizable success, is that of feasibility. Four factors must be assessed when the group considers feasibility – time, energy, money, and manpower. For example, if we return to the issue of the early intervention program parents who wish to advocate for an early childhood special needs program within their local school system, the importance of these four factors becomes apparent. The overall long-term goal of this group may be to assure that quality education is available locally for their children throughout their school careers. Their most immediate goal is focussed on the early childhood period. It is on this first, more immediate goal that they should begin to concentrate. This is true regardless of whether they recognize that an adequate program does not exist within the district for high school students as well.

If, at the outset, this group is composed of five parents (three mothers and two fathers), we may see how they might determine the project's feasibility along each of these dimensions. In relation to time, they must consider that one mother and one father hold full-time jobs outside the home during the day for set hours. The other father and one of the mothers work outside their homes at part-time jobs with flexible hours. They each have part-time child care during their work hours. The third mother is a full-time homemaker. Since the two parents who hold full-time jobs outside their homes do not have flexible hours, any meetings that require all participants must happen during the evening hours when they are more available or on week-ends. Because each of the five is intensely interested in the issue, he or she is willing to devote at least five hours a week to the task at hand. They recognize that in time and energy they would like to add to the group of determined parents and interested individuals, but they are willing to begin small. Three of the five involved would describe themselves as energetic individuals who enjoy being in leadership roles. Two of these have strong commitments to other community groups at present. Two of the five would describe themselves as more typically followers who would work hard behind the scenes for issues to which they are committed.

All of the five realize that they have no monetary backing at this point. Each is willing to pledge a small amount of her/his personal finances to cover postage and telephone calls that he/she makes. In additional manpower, one parent is able to donate some secretarial time that is available in a business that she co-owns. Another knows that his older children are willing to run errands, put up signs, etc. A third thinks that his boy scout troop may be willing to do some research on the issue as a public service project.

Once the group has assessed the feasibility of tackling this issue in as realistic a manner as possible, the group must come to some kind of consensus related to their plan. It is particularly useful at this point if one person can act as the organizer or leader. It is often a good strategy to have each person write down what he or she thinks should be the major objective or planned outcome of the effort. Then each should think of all the pros and cons related to achieving the outcome that is sought. The pros and cons should include any risks and benefits related to the outcome as well as an evaluation of the four feasibility factors: time, energy, money and manpower. After the group has fully discussed each member's evaluation of the value and risk involved in undertaking the venture and of the feasibility, they are ready to form a real consensus. Although no process can assure that all members will remain devoted to the endeavor through its completion, a thought-provoking discussion around the issues just noted can ascertain that each begins with some common interest, understanding, and commitment to their group function.

Once a consensus on function has been reached, the group must move to consideration of formulating strategies.

Formulating strategies

Formulating strategies must take into account several factors: further information needed, the issue itself, the target group to be influenced, the advocacy group involved, and the feasibility.

In relation to the specific issue of the absence of an early childhood special needs program within the community, an important source of further information would be the decision-makers. For example, one parent might approach the special education director to ask whether such a program had ever been considered and, if so, the reason it had been rejected. The same questions could be asked of the school committee members (both present members and those in office when the issue was first considered). The superintendent might be questioned. In short, any persons who possess information regarding previous decisions or lack thereof could be an important source of information.

In considering the topic of the issue, three major focii might be examined. The first is whether the topic can be handled through public appeal to general values and principles. For example, advocating for the creation of a neighborhood park for children in an urban setting might be targeted this way. Appealing to a general societal value that children need places to play other than the street may be effective. In other situations, stimulating public awareness of the plight of individuals is helpful. This type of strategy may be especially effective in our main example of a group advocating for the establishment of an early childhood special needs program within the district — most clearly if the present program is a good distance from town. In such a case, telling the story of a three-year-old who must make a long bus ride twice a day may have real appeal to the general public. The third most common strategy is the facts and figures approach. That is, a careful comparison of the costs and benefits of the current situation against those projected for your desired outcome can be advantageous. This might be an effective first step in advocating for a community day care system for after school care. An analysis in this case could include a survey of parents in major community industries, industry executives, school teachers, etc. The survey could answer questions about both what parents do currently regarding after school care for their children and those about potential benefits from having an organized community program. Such a survey should be short and to the point. Many questions can be phrased in a manner that allows "yes" and "no" answers. A space should be left at the end to allow for additional comments so that those who wish can easily add new ideas. The information obtained in the survey should always be made available to those who participated. This assures that their continued participation as information sources is likely. Those who can see that your group will actually use their input are likely to be happy about providing other kinds of help if they can. If the information collected can be disseminated publicly, that is even better. Local newspapers are often happy to provide such coverage.

All of these initial strategies can be used effectively in a variety of situations to spark interest in the issue at hand. It is hoped that the initial effort to spark interest will bring with it a larger manpower base of interested individuals from whom to draw. The type of initial strategy that a group forms is likely to reflect the personalities involved, their problem-solving techniques, and the group process. It should also have been devised with the target group in mind.

If the group is large enough, individuals can formulate initial strategies that are comfortable to them as people while contributing to the overall effort. For example, the group seeking to establish an early childhood special needs program within their school district might agree that they need to target more than one population initially (both the general public and professionals involved in the schools or with young children) in order to accomplish their objectives. As previously noted, different strategies may be most effective for particular target populations. For example, the group may feel that the facts and figures approach may be best used first with the professional audience, and the approach of telling an individual child's story best as a first strategy for the general public. Group members who enjoy collecting data and those who enjoy writing analytical arguments might decide to work on the facts and figures strategy while those who enjoy interviewing people and public relations contact might decide to work on identifying a story for the local newspaper.

Some generalizations may be made about target populations, but the individuals involved may still be most swayed by different methods. Since the group should already have assessed the feasibility of targeting more than one population group, the members should then be able to decide whether more than one type of strategy would be most beneficial. Depending upon the individuals in the group, it may be decided that one strategy can be effective for the entire effort and that the individuals are most comfortable with one type. At this point the decision must also be made about whether subcommittees need to be formed in order to attack different strategies or whether the tasks involved in one major strategy need to be divided among groups. Regardless, responsibility or a leadership role must be assigned for individual tasks or strategies.

If we take the example of the facts and figures approach and use it with the early childhood special needs program problem, several next steps might be taken by the core group of five people. One person might take the responsibility for drafting a questionnaire that she will get to the others for comment. Another might take the responsibility of contacting statewide advocacy groups to ascertain whether other local parent groups have undertaken such efforts successfully. If so, he may also contact them for help and suggestions. A third might compile a list of local officials and professionals who may be important sources of information. A fourth might take charge of asking the early intervention program to help in distributing a questionnaire to both former and current program parents. The fifth could assume responsibility for distributing flyers regarding the advocacy effort to grocery store bulletin boards, churches, etc. These divisions of labor take into account a variety of personalities and styles as well as differences in time and availability among the participants. The person devising the questionnaire may be both articulate in writing and thoughtful in the broad scope. The parent who takes charge of contacting state advocacy groups would probably enjoy personal contact and be verbally articulate. The person who volunteers to compile a list of local officials and professionals may be more detail-oriented and less outgoing or could enjoy networking. The person who takes responsibility for the contact with the early intervention program staff could be one who feels more at ease when dealing with people he knows. While the fifth person may be the one who enjoys being out and on the go, she may also be the one who has more flexible time. Good leadership involves creating an atmosphere where people feel comfortable volunteering for those tasks that they feel that they can do well. Good strategy planning involves not only clear delineation of the tasks involved and an assessment of their feasibility – but a conception of the consensus that can be formed within the group. If no one volunteers for particular tasks, those tasks should be reassessed. If they are too time-consuming, they may be split. Two people may jointly agree to assume responsibility that they would not undertake alone. Tasks must be realistic in scope as well as related to the desired outcome.

Disseminating results of initial efforts

If the group had decided that their first target audience was other parents, the dissemination of the results might be organized very differently from their approach if they had decided that local school officials were their first target. In the first instance, when they had some results, they might ask the early intervention program to give them space and perhaps to help publicize a parent awareness night. At this session they might choose a person to talk about the results of their survey and then leave time open for questions. Or they might ask a parent whose child had moved on into the preschool program to talk about the child's and his or her own experiences within this new setting. That could be used as a lead-in to talk about the survey results.

In a situation where the first target was school officials, the first dissemination strategy would be formulated with consideration given to the expected reception of the survey results. If the officials were expected to be somewhat receptive to the information, the results might first be sent to them in written form and a request for a follow-up meeting made. If it were expected that they would not be receptive to the information, it might also be disseminated to the local newspaper in a "human interest story" manner. It is usually best in the beginning to avoid an antagonistic stance. Such an effort should be reserved for those times when a more cooperative approach to change has obviously failed to gain attention or action. This is especially wise in relation to local endeavors that involve interacting with professionals with whom one may have repeated interactions over several years, e.g., local school officials.

Consensus-building and continuing advocacy

As in any group situation, building a consensus cannot rely on the fantasy of a strong leader's convincing all other group members to be in total agreement with strategy and task assignment. What they must all agree on is some kind of common goal, shared value, or basic philosophy. In the more nitty-gritty aspects of strategies and tasks, consensus demands flexibility in the group so that members are able to support an endeavor that is somewhat different in design from each member's own, and that the individuals within the group make compromises. A group can agree on any rules that it would like to follow as long as the members then do just that. If the group agrees that final decisions will always be put to a vote and that a certain number of members must be present in order for a major vote to take place, the members must follow their own rules if the group is to work. If the group agrees that no more than a certain amount of time will be allowed for any one discussion, a gatekeeper should be appointed who will take responsibility for helping the group to stick to its rules. The group may agree that once tasks are assigned, the responsible people can carry out the task in whatever manner they see fit. They must then agree not to spend a good deal of time analyzing the methods others use. If the group forms its own rules and agrees to evaluate them at a set time, the group is apt to run more smoothly than it will without early and clear discussion of such matters as procedures.

Once an agreement has been struck regarding initial strategies, individuals must commit themselves to the effort. Again, as in the beginning phases, the leadership must be able to spot trends, allow for individual nuances, and redirect when necessary. Groups must maintain some flexibility if they are to succeed, but they must also have some structure.

Group evaluation

At some point, whether a clearcut identifiable success has been demonstrated or not, the group must look at evaluating the success of their efforts. In most cases this reconsideration will not come when an obvious objective has been met. In fact, it often comes when a sense of frustration and exasperation is being felt by some members because there has been no clear and fast resolution. If group members, especially those who belong to the core, are questioning their ongoing commitment, it is time for the group to stop and re-evaluate their mission and target.

Regardless of the success of the first advocacy mission, at its completion the group must evaluate the effort and assess their commitment to any further endeavors. It is often the case that group members differ in how they evaluate their efforts. For some people, anything other than a clear and complete success cannot be acknowledged as a real victory. Others are more willing to accept that their voices may have been heard even if the outcome was not all that they desired. It is these people who are more likely to make a lasting commitment to group advocacy. The group must consider the criteria by which they are judging success at the start of their group evaluation if they are to come to some satisfactory resolution about the outcome. This again requires the individuals involved to think through their measures and to be open to others' interpretations. A successful core group must allow each individual to assess his or her personal commitments whether privately or openly within the group process if an ongoing commitment is sought. Next, the group must reassess the community's continuing needs during their assessment process about whether the group should move on to other advocacy focii.

In the area of evaluation of personal commitments, the group must make an active decision about whether to discuss openly members' thoughts about their personal situations. If the effort they have made together has been difficult or sustained, the group is likely to have enough cohesiveness to desire to do this. Peripheral members may choose not to participate in this process. Whether the group actively encourages self-examination, the individuals are likely to engage in it privately. This is especially true for those people for whom the experience was unusual or especially meaningful. Individuals may come to feel empowered as a result of their participation regardless of whether the advocacy effort was completely successful. If their sense of empowerment is stimulated by group participation, they may be more willing to give their time and energy to a long-term group that will address many needs – some, their burning issues; some, less relevant to their particular situations. Once a commitment to a larger goal has been made on the parts of several individuals, the group is likely to expand to include parents with related but non-identical problems or issues. For example, local associations for retarded citizens have been spurred in recent years primarily by parents of older developmentally disabled individuals. Many feel that this is a result of the availability of better services for younger children – a success of earlier efforts by that same organization. Some parents are still committed to general advocacy for better services throughout the lifespan. Others are active only in efforts that have direct relevance to their individual situations. Parents of young children may be able to commit themselves to issues that they may face in the distant future. Other parents may devote time to efforts to better situations that they faced in the past. Many can only approach issues that are in the present for them. The core of an ongoing advocacy group must be able to commit themselves to the general good or to endeavors that are not always their burning issues. But they do have to represent all families. The associations for retarded citizens have survived regardless of their stronger thrust for the needs of the older citizens at the local level at this point. However, any organization that seeks to be ongoing must keep an eye to attracting new members constantly if they are to remain viable in the long run.

Once a core group has determined that they would like to remain active in ongoing advocacy, members must confront the issue of new membership and the changing group process. A group that plans for long-term advocacy must be able to read and adapt to the changing social climate. They must be willing to confront a variety of changing perspectives in both society at large and also in younger people who cannot understand all the feelings and positions of the earlier group members. New members are what keep the organization vital. The organization must remain empowering to its members and original members must remember that they cannot always offer the benefits of their experiences in a helpful way. Some developing advocacy skills must be re-developed by each new member.

The period when new members develop a crucial role in the organization's continuation is a particularly difficult one for fledgling groups. A group that previously existed primarily as a support group may be able to return to that function successfully. A group formed for advocacy may be able to change its focus and begin to function primarily as a support group. Participants in most advocacy groups do glean support through their shared efforts. Leadership within the group structure is especially important at this juncture. Until the group has been long-established it is likely to face this issue about continuation in a crucial way at the completion of each advocacy project. However, even for long-established groups, new membership and the changing group process are issues of real import at different stages.

The leadership provided within advocacy groups must emanate from an individual or core of individuals who can envision a better reality and who believe that an impact can be made. Groups that decide to forge an ongoing effort should establish a network of information sources. Those local, state and national organizations that they contacted in their initial search for information should be re-contacted at regular intervals in order to maintain a relationship and an awareness on those organizations' parts that the group still exists. The group should seek to be on the mailing lists of a large number of related organizations. This will help assure that the group has important current information. Someone in the group should seek actively to maintain personal contact on a regular basis with any helpful legislative assistants they had found so that they will be advised about proposed and pending legislation of interest.

A fruitful advocacy group demands effort on the parts of several individuals. A committed core of people is vital to a continuing endeavor. Maintaining interest and vigor is a constant challenge. Creating opportunities for involvement at a variety of levels that meet the demands of the interpersonal and problem-solving styles of many individuals also requires much consistent effort. Personal and group awareness must be maintained or constantly sought. The knowledge base must continue to grow. One technique that a group might use in order to enhance their knowledge base and their group sustenance would be a documentation of the strategies that they use in each of their endeavors and of their group growth process. With a good deal of work, confidence and empowerment will enhance the group as well as the individuals involved. Successful advocacy can provide better experiences in the lives of children and families in the present and can influence and enhance the lives and experiences of future generations of children and families.

Further resources

Anyone interested in advocacy related to young children will benefit greatly from an introduction to a national organization known as the Children's Defense Fund, 122 C Street, NW, Washington, D.C. 20001.

Many professional organizations have a growing awareness of public policy interests and have subgroups devoted to these interests, e.g., the Society for Research in Child Development, Committee on Child Development and Social Policy, Washington Liason Office, 100 North Carolina Avenue, SE, Suite 1, Washington, DC 20003; American Academy of Pediatrics, P.O. Box 1034, Evanston, IL 60204; American Psychological Association, 1200 Seventeenth Street, NW, Washington, DC 20036; and the National Association for the Education of Young Children, 1834 Connecticut Avenue, NW, Washington, DC 20009.

Few books have been written specifically for parents trying to organize an advocacy group. However, there are resources directed at self-help groups, assertiveness training for parents, professional advocacy groups, and individual professionals advocating for children's services. The following may be useful to developing advocacy groups for parents:

Gartner, A. and Riessman, F. (1979). *Self-Help in the Human Services*, San Francisco, Jossey Bass.

Markel, G. and Greenbaum, J. L. (1979). *Parents Are To Be Seen And Heard*, San Luis Obispo, CA, Impact Publishers. (Developing assertiveness skills for parents.)

Ornstein, N. and Elder, S. (1978). *Interest Groups, Lobbying, and Policy Making*, Washington, DC, Congressional Quarterly Press. (Professional advocacy.)

Westman, J. (1979). *Child Advocacy*, New York, Free Press. (Professionals advocating for children's services.)

CHAPTER 7

Peer counseling training

C. F. Zachariah Boukydis and Lenette S. Moses

Introduction

This chapter on peer counseling includes: (1) an outline of the main concerns in developing training programs for parenting organizations; (2) an overview of the training program currently in use in one parenting organization; (3) detail on the skills involved; (4) a discussion of some problems involved in training and ongoing concerns in running a peer counseling network, and (5) highlights of further resources for those who want more information on particular aspects of training.

I Main concerns

There are three main areas which form the basis for developing a training program: knowledge of referral resources, counseling process and group process training, and ongoing back-up and supervision for peer counselors.

A knowledge of referral resources

Those planning training should develop a comprehensive list of referral resources for new parents in their area. Important referral resources typically include:

- A list of suggested pediatricians, nurse practitioners, and others in the area who care for children. Parents should be offered more than one recommendation whenever possible.
- Organizations which offer support to parents in typical parenting situations (with no extenuating circumstances). These may include childbirth education groups, nursing mothers' organizations, mother-of-twins clubs, postpartum support, parent and baby exercise programs, support for pregnant teenagers, parents support groups.
- Organizations related to specific medical problems. This list should include both local chapters (e.g., March of Dimes) and national organizations (e.g., American Speech, Language and Hearing Association). Infant Stimulation Programs may be included as well.

A list of many of these organizations is included in Chapter 10 of this book.

- Beareavement support, including days, times and places, of local meetings.
- Family counseling; both free services (e.g. agency provided) and private counselors can be included.
- Support and assistance which can include: Board of Assistance, Children's Aid, Meals on Wheels or similar services, Homemakers, Visiting Nurses, and WIC (Women, Infant and Children's Program).
- Emergency support; search in the local office of a social service agency or telephone blue pages for providers of food, shelter, clothing, money, etc.
- Local hospitals. Names of contact people are particularly important in large institutions.
- Locations for electric breastpump rentals for mothers expressing milk for sick infants. (The companies which make these machines will provide names of stores renting breastpumps.)

The list should include names of agencies, addresses, telephone numbers (including emergency numbers whenever possible), important contact people within the agency, services provided, who is served (what medical problems and conditions), literature available, hours of operation, requirements for making contact, limitations such as financial requirements, meeting times, and so on.

Training should involve people becoming familiar with the referral resources listed, and all the information about contacting them, so that they can give this to parents who request this information. Also, someone in the parenting organization should be responsible for up-dating this listing, keeping track of changes (i.e. in location, referral requirements, contact people), and ideally, a record of problems in contacting and using different referral resources. Having access to a word processor would greatly simplify this process.

Important in these training sessions are discussions about when referrals to different kinds of services are to be made, and how to go about this. Two different issues are involved. First, when a parent asks for information about particular resources, the responsibility of the peer counselor is to give the parent clear, usable information. There are times when a parent may be seeking a particular kind of help indirectly, and the peer counselor can help him to articulate what he needs, and then offer available resources. The second issue, which will be addressed from different angles in this chapter, has to do with identifying problem situations where the peer counselor may need back-up. He needs to recognize that there will be situations in which he will feel unable to be solely responsible for helping, and to be aware of the extra support at his disposal.

As we will see later, collaboration with professional care providers is helpful, and necessary in some areas. Professionals can be used in actual training, as on-call back-up for peer counselors, as referral resources, as co-leaders of discussion groups, and as co-participants in individual involvement efforts such as home visits with parents. Many parenting organizations have professional advisory boards, consisting of professionals from different disciplines who provide help in the areas outlined above. Representatives from parenting organizations also provide "inservice" training and workshops to inform professionals more fully of parents' needs in their area. When necessary, this collaboration can also develop into a team of parents and professionals organized to develop ways to advocate for better services for parents. The earlier chapter on advocacy has information on how to do this effectively.

B Counseling process/group process training

Training in peer counseling should comprise an initial, and potentially ongoing, training program which involves active practive in basic counseling process. The crux or "baseline" of counseling training involves reflective listening and experiential focusing (McGuire, 1981; Boukydis (McGuire), 1984; Gendlin, 1981; Rogers, 1975). More detail and training resources will be outlined below in the section on skills for peer counseling training. When peer counselors enrich the ability in themselves to hear more deeply what parents are saying about their situation, and learn how to help parents "connect up with" and articulate their feelings about what is going on, then peer counselors will have the most essential ability in the counseling process. The feeling of being heard empathically, and learning to hear more fully what one is feeling about one's situation, forms the healthy basis for opening up to difficult decisions which must be discussed and decided upon. The later section, "Overview of peer counseling process", indicates how listening and focusing, and the further articulation of feelings is a necessary prerequisite, and complementary to, more conscious problem solving.

Having experience with group process is also an important part of peer counselor preparation, whether the particular parenting organization runs educational meetings, informal discussions, or more clearly intended "feeling sharing" meetings (see the chapter by Linda Gilkerson and Stephanie Porter for suggestions on running meetings). The basic skills involve practice with organization and running of meetings, leadership styles, attention to group process, and dealing with problems which arise in group meetings (see McGuire, 1981, for useful suggestions in organizing planning meetings, and learning about group process).

C Back-up for peer counselors

There are two kinds of back-up which should be considered: (1) direct back-up for peer counselors so that they can discuss difficult situations that they might encounter, and importantly, back-up for their own lives and concerns; and (2) more coherent referral back-up for situations that peer counselors find themselves unable to handle. One of the most important areas for discussion and role play is the situation of crisis intervention. Although this tends to occur infrequently, it is of the utmost importance that peer counselors have a framework from which to cope with it. An emphasis of the peer counselor's strengths and weaknesses in the counseling experience will help him define when this extra intervention is necessary. A resource list, as described earlier, will offer him instant support and resources when the situation arises. Many parenting organizations also have a back-up counselor who can be called on for advice in difficult situations.

II Overview of a training program

Intensive Caring Unlimited (ICU) is a Philadelphia-area support group which aids parents of premature and hospitalized infants, families going through high-risk pregnancies and those whose babies have died. It has served well over 2,000 families during the past seven years. As the group grew in scope and geographic size, it was obvious that a formal training method was important. Several members of the group wrote a training manual (see Moses, Reilly, Schnaubelt and Gould, 1983), which is used for two training courses each year. With over eighty volunteer parent counselors to date, the manual has been instrumental in maintaining the group's focus and continuity. The manual includes sections on: (1) counseling skills including developing a relationship, listening techniques, crisis intervention, handling telephone calls); and (2) background information such as hospitalization, medical problems, homecoming, bonding, breastfeeding a special care baby, grieving, developmental delays, handicaps, infant stimulation, and high-risk pregnancy. Additional inserts offer information about the group history, its services and resources, and how it works. It is written in outline form for easy referral during the course and when counseling. Open-ended questions and counseling situations are included in each section so that trainees may prepare for discussions during the course. Below are detailed the types of sessions which might be included in a typical course syllabus.

Session 1   Group information, discussion of trainee experiences of having a baby in intensive care.
Session 2   Counseling skills, listening techniques, role playing.
Session 3   Feelings, bonding, counseling.

Session 4 Hospital tour, communicating with hospital staff, medical problems.
Session 5 Grieving, handicaps.
Session 6 Developmental delays, infant stimulation.
Session 7 High-risk pregnancy.*
Session 8 Breastfeeding.*
* These sessions are required only of those who will be actively counseling in these areas.

ICU's course is taught by veteran parent counselors and members of the professional advisory board. The course, which is approximately twenty-four hours long, is held over an eight week period. (Three hours a night for eight Monday nights, for example.) During a typical course, a neonatologist, an infant stimulation therapist, a social worker, a pediatrician, and a representative from a grieving group may offer their expertise and lead discussions and role playing. The tour of a hospital neonatal intensive care unit is also included.

A major emphasis of the course is in discovering and handling parents' feelings. Each evening and each topic includes an overview of how a parent may handle that experience, and how the parent counselor may work with him on his emotions and responses. A natural complement to that thrust is a discussion of parent/hospital staff interaction. Counselors are trained to guide parents in clear communication with the medical team which is caring for their baby. The aims are to: (a) decrease the parents' fears and ignorance about the hospital equipment, routine and staff; (b) make the parents feel an integral part of that care team; (c) increase the parents' awareness of, and interaction with their infant; and (d) enhance the bonding and attachment within the family. This also decreases the parents' dependence on the parent counselor and increases the parent's own feelings of self-worth and assurance.

Those who attend the ICU training course are required to attend each of the meetings, or to listen to a tape recording of a session missed and to discuss it with a veteran counselor. Outside reading is required, and in addition to the manual, trainees are expected to become familiar with the group library, and read books in their area of interest. Articles from medical journals and other periodicals on counseling techniques and other information are reprinted for each trainee to keep.

Eight weeks' time is quite a commitment to make. However, those who are truly concerned about supporting other parents are able to make this time. They are also the ones who will be willing to counsel for a year or more, which is important in the group's continuance. Twenty-four hours' time as a group also allows leaders to detect those parents who have not worked through their own experiences. These parents, who are often aware of their own shortcomings as potential counselors for others, frequently work within the group without coming into peer counseling contact with other parents. As their own situations improve, they may then be offered the position of counselor.

III Skills for peer counseling training

1 Organization of training sessions

Training sessions should happen on a periodic basis to train new peer counselors and provide ongoing updating sessions for everyone. The organization of time will depend on an estimation of when and how frequently people can meet. Some groups arrange a special weekend training, some have training on a weekly basis, for example, every Monday evening for a month, and so on. In addition, for ongoing training, some groups meet once a month for discussion of problems, further training, and support for peer counselors. Some groups arrange for an ongoing monthly series of sessions on topics of concern for peer counselors.

Training sessions should be organized to provide as much active involvement and direct feedback to each participant as possible. This chapter will list relevant training materials which can be used prior to, during, and after training sessions. In addition to training sessions, many organizations use some form of "apprenticeship model" for people learning to be peer counselors. The person who is learning may perhaps team up with someone who has had more experience and help run a meeting, go on an "outreach" or "home visit" to a new parent, or participate in a telephone consult.

It helps to list the important learning points as part of a syllabus. This list may provide the topical focus for each training session, or may provide a guide for people in training to keep track of how they are progressing. The training program listed above gives one example of a syllabus which illustrates how one group arranged their training for peer counselors.

2 Counseling process

A Organization of counseling process training

One model for peer counseling training includes sessions with three to five trainees and one or more trainers (McGuire, 1981; Boukydis (McGuire), 1984). For each session, everyone, including trainers, gets an opportunity to listen, and to be listened to. The group rotates around the circle, with each person listening to the person beside him, and then reversing the responsibility for listening. Before the session begins, there are a few quiet minutes of focusing. As part of this time, each person is asked to concentrate on a concern in his life which deserves attention and which he can choose to talk about for ten to fifteen minutes during the training session.

Overview of phases of training
Phase 1   Reflection of feelings
The first phase of training involves having peer counselors learn to hear accurately and reflect what a parent is really saying. This means responding to the feelings (or main aspects of feelings) rather than the intellectual content of what is being said.

Phase 2   Open-ended pre-focusing questions
In the second phase of training, peer counselors learn to incorporate open-ended questions i.e., "can you say more about . . . ?"; "how does it feel when you . . . ?" along with reflection.

Phase 3   Focusing questions
The third phase of training involves more direct use of "focusing" questions integrated with the listening process. Focusing questions arise out of an understanding of focusing as a process whereby people are able to articulate complex inner meanings (see section on focusing, p. 141). Thus focusing questions on the part of the peer counselor helps the parent to attend to his feeling in a situation, and explore all aspects of his reaction (i.e. "How did it feel when you first walked into the room?"; or "What do you find most difficult about being a parent when this happens?").

Phase 4   Problems with feelings, personal sharing, working on problems
The fourth phase of training involves experience in attending to difficult feelings, helping to discriminate when and how to share personal experience, and when and how to move to problem solving; all areas in which the counselor must gain expertise. In addition to aiding a parent in getting organized, the counselor may also have to assess the parent's readiness for any particular aspect of the situation. For example, a mother who has just delivered a baby may not be able to talk about the baby until she has worked through her feelings about the labor and delivery. After being the center of attention for nine months, a woman will commonly find it difficult to suddenly be "Number 2." She may require an opportunity to relive her part in the miracle of birth before accepting her role as a new mother. The peer counselor must be sensitive to the parent's focus at any particular time.

During the beginning training sessions, the "listener's" responsibility is periodically to reflect the main feeling aspects of what the "listenee" is talking about. After each ten to fifteen minute listening turn, the trainer asks the listenee, and then the listener, for their impressions of the experience. Each person is asked to address what he liked and to identify where, during the session, there may have been a problem. When talking about problems in the listening process, it is important to point to what was actually said, *and* what each person was feeling during this time. The attention is on the "process" and not so much on the "content" of the turn. After hearing from the listenee and listener, the trainer adds her/his comments on the turn, balancing what went well with what was problematic, and pointing to what was being said as a baseline for clarifying problems in how the listener was functioning. After two or three sessions, the listener can begin to look for places during a listening turn where he might ask a simple, open pre-focusing question. Next, he can move to more integral use of focusing questions in the counseling process. Finally, the training can move to how to work with focusing and listening in problem situations, such as when someone appears to be confused, distraught, or discouraged. The training sessions should be used both as an opportunity to learn *and* for the trainers and each trainee to decide mutually when the trainee is ready to become a peer counselor for parents.

B Empathic listening

Those who are involved with the counseling process, are listening to hear another person's perspective about his/her life and how it feels for them to be in a particular situation. Sometimes the listener may decide too quickly that he knows what is going on from what he initially hears the listenee say. In order to listen empathically to what is being said, the listener must continually ask himself: "How is this situation unique for him/her – how does s/he feel in this situation?" This involves recognizing and then setting aside quick judgments about what the listener thinks, or has thought about similar situations, and hearing, freshly, what the listenee is feeling about his own unique life.

When one listens empathically, one is continually trying to detect feelings, even when a person is talking about the concrete details of events that occurred. The practice of empathic listening involves the listener in periodically restating the main "feeling aspects" of what the listenee just said. Figure 7.1 is an example which illustrates this restating of feeling aspects. By this restating, the listener is: (1) trying quietly to demonstrate his care and concern to listen to the listenee's feelings; and (2) by restating, to actively create an exchange whereby the person being listened to can actually hear himself more fully by hearing what he said reflected through the words and caring presence of another.

Even in the process of listening, counselors sometimes mix in their preconceptions of what is being said. In a sense, this "mixing-in" of preconceptions is to be expected because a person cannot put into words all that he is implicitly feeling at one time, in relation to a given situation. We tend to guess at what has not yet been said, and what line of thinking is being used. The job of the peer counselor is to: (1) recognize his own

Type of response	Dialogue
	Listenee: I have trouble being out in public with Ginnie (my baby). Sometimes I feel good watching her talk and smile with different people, but I also feel they're watching me, and waiting. . . .
Reflection	Listener: So, it's mixed, you feel good watching her connect with people, but there's something troublesome for you about feeling people are watching you with her. . . .
Asking for more	Can you tell me more how it feels when people seem to be watching and waiting? Listenee: Yeah, I get edgy, like they're not just watching, but they're waiting for me to foul up, to make a mistake, and there's no room to breathe, and there's no room for error, and I just want to run away.
Reflection	Listener: So their watching has an edge to it like they're waiting for you to make a mistake. . . . Listenee: Yeah, I'll say!
Reflection	Listener: And you get to feel more and more constricted, and you just want to get out of there. . . . Listenee: Yes, yes, surrounded by watching eyes waiting for me to foul up as a mom. Phew! . . . (silence) I never noticed how absolutely boxed in I feel.
Focusing invitation	Listener: Sometimes it helps to talk about a specific time recently when you were feeling this way. . . . Listenee: That's easy, this morning I took her to the cleaner's and sat her on the counter, while they went to get my clothes. She sat and played with a roll of tape, and talked at the other woman behind the counter, and one of the customers. I was o.k. Then, . . . boom, I feel they're watching me, not her, to see if she'll tip over, or grab the box of pins, or. . . . It just came crashing in . . ., and I felt so tight, I'm sure she picked up on it, which makes me tighter. But, the worst is, I'm sure they're gonna yell at me if I make one mistake with her.
Reflection	Listener: So, it was fine for a while, and then all of a sudden, the tightness about being watched hits; and there's something important about: "You can't even make one little mistake" with her as a parent. Listenee: That's it, not one, no sir, not even one, . . . (pause) how severe . . . and I'm afraid I won't be able to function, so I just want to run away . . . (tears).
Reflection	Listener: (After some silence) It happens fast, you're afraid they may be judging, and judging severely: "Not one mistake", and it's all so powerful, you're afraid you won't be able to function, and you just want to get away from the situation. . . . Listenee: Yes, . . . I never noticed how strong this all feels, until right now. [On to explore what this "not being able to make mistakes" reminded her of in her life.]

Figure 7.1 Restating feelings

preconceptions; and (2) help the person articulate more fully what he is feeling. In this attitude of expectancy by the peer counselor, his own acknowledged preconceptions can often be surprisingly violated by what the person says next. In the listening process, when a counselor speaks from his preconceptions, there is often confusion or a subtle rejection on the part of the person being listened to. The job of the peer counselor is not initially to engage the parent in what he (the peer counselor) thinks about the parent's situation, but to help the parent come to his own understanding. One of the main functions of the training phase for peer counselors is to help people identify their preconceptions, and learn to set these to one side in order to empathize with the other person's unique situation (Rogers, 1975; Buber, 1966; Friedman, 1972).

The process of listening has often received a bad name – perceived merely as "parroting," or flatly repeating what a person has said. However, in the peer counseling process just described, the attention of the peer counselor is not just to the words, but to the rich, implicit felt meaning, to the unspoken. Thus, the counselor both emphathizes and enables the person to say or feel more.

A worthwhile training manual, *Building supportive community: Listening and focusing through peer counseling* (Boukydis (McGuire), 1981) has been written to describe concretely the steps of learning to listen and incorporate "experiential focusing" (see p. 141) into the peer counseling process. This publication is being used in numerous training programs for peer counselors as the central training manual for articulating the counseling process. The manual details the four phases of training outlined above.

Thus, the main points required for empathic listening may be summarized as follows:

(a) Look for uniqueness of feeling and situation within what is being spoken.
(b) Listen for feelings, not just intellectual content or external description.
(c) Help the speaker to recognize the feeling aspect of what is being said by restating the main aspects.
(d) Peer counselors must learn to recognize their own preconceptions and set them aside when listening.
(e) Using the above technique, a peer counselor will enable a parent to say more about what he is feeling and further the process of self understanding.

There are a number of other methods of offering trainees experience in listening techniques, some of these include:

• Listening for and trying to match various speech patterns in order to develop rapport. This might include a parent's rate of speech, tone, or intonation.

- Listening for and trying to match the "sense" with which the parent is experiencing his situation. For example:
  Visual: "To you, it looks like. . . ."
  Auditory: "For you, its like all the voices are saying. . . ."
  Visceral: "It's like you feel pinched in. . . ."

- Repeating the parent's last main feeling sense as a statement to communicate understanding and encourage him to attend to the feeling and say more about it.

- Paraphrasing the parent's speech. This may be prefaced with "My understanding of what you are saying is . . ." to clarify that this is one's own understanding of what was said.

- Listening for contradictions, or conflicts. This is a technique akin to just listening for felt meaning, but in this case, the listener is attempting to sift through both sets of messages the parent is presenting and simply reflect, or compare the two.

- Asking appropriate questions. These may allow a parent a chance to "go further with" what has already been said, with the counselor providing a simple structure encouraging the parent to stay with the main feeling(s), or return from some external description back to the central feeling.

In each case from above, the trainee is being asked to concentrate on the words of the speaker and glean a potential deeper meaning than may be apparent on the surface. Gaining insights as to the different aspects of the person's speech encourages the listener to listen more attentively in order to gain more understanding of what is being said (and of what the listenee is unable to say).

Here is one further suggestion for arranging peer counseling training when parent contacts are to be made over the telephone. Trainees are asked to sit back-to-back when doing listening skill practice so that they have the experience of having to listen without the advantage of watching for body language, as will happen during telephone contacts. Some trainers actually use toy telephones, or have trainees in different rooms, to emphasize the conditions under which they will be counseling.

C Experiential focusing in the counseling process

Attentive listening is the "*a priori*," the essential prerequisite in all counseling process. A person cannot move ahead to make difficult decisions, or reflect on situations in his parenting behavior until he has had the opportunity to be protected somewhat from external pressures, and to explore his feelings. Listening to someone carries with it the attitude of enabling him to listen to *himself* more fully. When people are feeling stressed, or confused about a situation, they cannot commit their life energies to difficult decisions, or new patterns of behavior, by making a decision which is *only* intellectual, devoid of emotional, or feeling content.

The process of listening to oneself has been called "experiential focusing" or "focusing" (Gendlin, 1969, 1977, 1981; Boukydis (McGuire), 1984; Boukydis (McGuire), 1981). Focusing involves setting aside the "busyness" in our head, being able to feel more quiet inside, and attending to one's broad felt sense of oneself in a situation. This broad felt sense is not conducive to any particular conventional label (sad, mad, fearful, etc.); it is the "feel of it all" that we have, an intuitive response felt in our body.

You, the reader, can understand what is meant by "felt sense" by remembering how it felt to be around your mother the last time that you saw her. There may be a lot of detail or many activities, or visual images. But beyond that, ask yourself, "How did it feel just to be around her?" Just be quiet and try to suspend active description, as if you had been charged with seriously describing this to someone else, but now you find it is not necessary. Just attend to the feeling rising "in" your body. Your response is not simply a memory or a physical reaction, but a broad intuitive feeling of her presence.

Focusing involves attending more quietly to this broad felt sense, and then letting words or images arise from it. These words and images are not just floating labels; they "resonate with," "interact with," or are "charged with the meaning" of the felt sense. Often in attending to the felt sense and having important words or images arise from this process, there is a perceptible change, sometimes subtle, sometimes massive, a *shift* in the "feel of it all."

Focusing involves further steps in learning to interact with, to question, this felt sense of ourselves in a particular situation. For example, a parent may say something like: "Oh, yes, that's what's going on for me, it's not just that I'm simply irritated by my baby's crying, it's that I get panicky that it will go on forever, and I'll be helpless to stop it." The situation may be the same, but the feeling, the felt sense, has changed. The person may feel subtly better – more able to take the next step in exploration which, in this case, might involve asking: "What's this panicky feeling about?"

Here is a formal outline of the steps of focusing. These steps are not meant to be followed mechanically, but they help to outline the process of focusing, a process which we all do at times, quite naturally.

Step 1 Clearing a space
The first step and the most important involves clearing a space inside oneself. This can mean just noticing, during the busy flow of one's life, that one is feeling "out of sorts," "a bit odd," "spacey;" and asking a simple question like: "What's going on for me?", or "How

am I feeling right now?" A more expansive understanding of clearing a space involves ways that people have learned (or have yet to learn) about becoming less tense and arriving at a quiet, attentive, inner-questioning state. The references include suggestions for helping oneself and others do this.

Step 2 Getting the broad felt sense of oneself in the situation
This step involves suspending the active description of the situation, and what was happening, and asking "How did it feel for me (in my body) to be there – with that going on?" Then one waits for this broad felt sense to arise.

Step 3 Having the key words, crux feelings, felt images, arise
After attending to the broad felt sense for a few moments, there are often some important words, or a key image which emerge. One repeats these key words about how it felt, or sits quietly with the central image.

Step 4 Resonating
In repeating these key words quietly several times, one feels how they match up with (resonate with) the broad felt sense. There can be a change in the "feel of it all," or *other* important feeling aspects emerging or a feeling that the key words are "not quite right." In this case, new words or images may arise.

Step 5 Asking "how come?"
Once one has spent some time with the feel of it all and finding the words or images which resonate, then it is possible, from this feeling base, to ask questions about the situation: "What is it about this situation that makes me feel so . . .?" or "What's going on when this . . . happens?" Again, the attitude is to learn to strengthen exploration, and temporarily put aside the analysis, the closed questions (see below), or the description of the situation.

Step 6 Receptivity to concerns
This step involves a slightly less involved opening to feeling what is central, or conflicting, in the situation. Often the pressure to solve, work through or attack problematic situations pushes people past feeling how it is to be in the situation. Or else, people become caught with tense feelings and cannot help themselves "get a bit outside" to question what is happening. Attention to this intuitive feeling often either: (1) enables new information about the situation to emerge; or (2) enables a change (felt shift) in the bodily felt sense of the situation.

Step 7 Further options for open questioning and attending to the felt sense

There are several options for further questioning and using focusing in a formal counseling or self-help training situation (see McGuire, 1981; Gendlin, 1981).

The learning involved with focusing has to do with asking "open" versus "closed" questions of one's felt sense. *Closed questions* imply a pre-judgment, point toward a specific answer, involve a kind of physical tightening, and often, imply a negative evaluation of behavior: "Why do I always do it this way?"; "What's the matter with me?", and so on. *Open questions* invite something new, something previously felt, but unarticulated to arise. Open questions act as a stimulus for new information to arise, and even acknowledge the serious need for change, but they do not imply the implicit pre-judgment, or self recrimination of closed questions: "What's going on for me when I find myself doing this?"

There is a need for understanding the distinction between open versus closed questions in terms of counseling process. People in stressful situations often have an internal cycle where they are also *stressing themselves* (Achtenberg, Simonton, and Simonton, 1976). The "private voices" that people have in stressful situations are often like closed questions ("I deserve this, this is punishment for me being a bad person," "What do I expect? These things always happen to me, and I can't change them"). Thus, there is not much way out from the internal closed cycle — "I've always done this, I can't change, this always happens to me, no one cares if I try, I don't care any more if I try" — toward dealing with potentially complex external situations. The simple action of listening to someone with this perspective is one way of trying to break their closed internal cycle. The most important aspect is offering caring, attentive human contact. This is what people often mean by "getting outside" of oneself. Helping a person to articulate and see these closed questions may interrupt the cycle as well, as may supporting an outpouring of the experience of tightness and pain they often involve. The latter may kindle a release or discharge of emotion which may be experienced as tears, anger, shaking with fear, etc. Eventually, the listener can introduce open questions which may provide a vehicle for fresh information to be introduced into discussion and decision-making. This is what the existentialists call "the search for meaning" (Frankl, 1959), or the "personal creation of meaning" (Gendlin, 1962).

Another aspect of this understanding of the focusing, listening, and counseling process is what is called "creating an outside." This happens in simple, important ways when one is befriended. This may help someone get a little outside of his internal swirl of feeling, possibly his fears, or stresses, so that he can remember that there is life outside of his troubles, and he can feel partnership in looking at his troubles.

In a basic sense, the peer counselor is helping people to feel their feelings without being immobilized or overpowered by them. The subtle discipline of 'being on the edge" and just experiencing feelings (attending to one's felt sense) is sometimes difficult, especially when a person is living in a stressful situation. However, this is where the attention of a peer counselor must lie. There are times, when we ask "What is the worst, hardest part of this situation for you to deal with?" in order to help someone put something into words that they had only felt implicitly before. There are other times, especially when someone is becoming overly panicked, blocked with fear, talking "all over the place" with anxiety, and so on, where he needs help to calm down and view his situation more objectively.

One way to "get on the outside" is to ask what it would be like if everything was all right. It could sound something like this: "Yes, it's not o.k. right now, there's this problem, this worry, and so on. But would you take a few moments to stay with (let yourself have) your feeling, your view of what it would be like if this situation was all right." It is important once in a while to get out of one's concern a bit, to remember, to feel, a vision of all-rightness, of health. This helps one look at concerns without being paralyzed by the feelings connected with them.

D Defining what is in the way/problem solving
Quite often, after helping people get a little outside, and helping them strengthen their view of what it *would* be like to be all right, it is then possible to help them feel and define what is "in the way," and begin working on the next steps to deal with the problem. This is sometimes called problem solving. However, notice that the approach starts from: (1) hearing the feelings; (2) gaining new understandings from "focusing," from making new distinctions in the feelings; (3) strengthening the vision of "all rightness," of where one is heading; and *then* (4) feeling and defining what one is up against. The phase of defining what is "in the way" again implies a kind of distance. This involves being able, with the help of the peer counselor, to make a list of what is implicitly felt as being in the way. It means, "If only this, and this, and this, were dealt with, then the situation would be all right."

It helps to actually make a list, then explore each item and ask: "what's this about?" Recognize that this is not problem solving yet, but instead exploring as much as possible the feelings and information implicit in each individual item. Next, a "personal hierarchy" can be developed, determining priorities among the areas which must be dealt with. Finally, alternatives can be discussed as to: (1) what can be done, using both people's creativity and experience; or (2) what information, resources, etc., can be approached in order to get help with what needs to be done. When developing their own "personal hierarchies," people sometimes create an order which does not make logical sense when viewed from the outside. However, often when "small" issues, which may personally be felt to be very troublesome, are dealt with in lieu of what appear to be the more pressing, "large" issues, people may gain momentum and the perspective to tackle these larger issues. On the other hand, some people cannot face anything else until their prime concern has been handled.

E Sharing of experience/emotional confirmation

As a "peer counselor", one automatically has a dual responsibility: to let a parent know that one has been through a similar situation, and that one can understand the difficult feelings that he may be having. Further, the counselor will probably want to inform the parent at some point about the counselor's situation and what he did in certain instances with his own child. On the other hand, the counselor will want to attend to what the parent is presently feeling. Peer counselor training involves getting experience with working out this *balance*: knowing when to set aside one's own sharing of their experience and listening, and knowing when to confirm difficult feelings by relating one's own experience.

Training involves practice with these situations, including attention to a questioning process for one's self. For example, one may ask: "What makes me tense when someone starts talking about feeling hopeless (or angry, or tearful)?" The next section gives an overview of the peer counseling process and helps to clarify when to listen, and when to share one's own experience. There are no absolute rights or wrongs in the peer counseling process, but the attention should be on the parent's ongoing experience. If he seems to be getting "overloaded" (seems more confused, tense) by what is being said, the counselor should return to the "baseline" of listening to what the parent is feeling.

F Overview of the peer counseling process

In this outline of the progression which occurs in the peer counseling process, the timing of these events is very much related to what is happening in a parent's life and can influence how the relationship between parent and peer counselor will develop. An overview of this progression can help a peer counselor understand better when to integrate so-called "separate skills" like listening and focusing, sharing from personal experience, emotional confirmation, and so on. The following list illustrates the progression in the peer counseling process.

Phase 1   Befriending
  developing trust;
  help with immediate resources.

Phase 2 Listening for felt aspects
reflecting.

Phase 3 Helping and questioning to:
(a) discover the felt sense; (b) interact with the felt sense; and (c) discover "crux" feelings.

Phase 4 Defining what is "in the way" of things being all right
deciding what is needed, what the next steps are.

Phase 5 Sharing insight, information, peer counselor's own experience
possible further exploration of feelings about what's "in the way."

Phase 6 Further listening
how this is being taken, what difference it makes, etc.

Phase 7 Defining "next steps"
reviewing what happened;
free attention, remembering hopeful events.

Phase 1 The most basic underlying attitude of peer counseling is befriending someone, providing a human contact where he is less likely to feel frightened or judged about difficult feelings, and having someone else who knows and confirms the touching, exciting, joyous feelings associated with parenthood. Befriending someone else draws on all one's natural internal resources, and in this way, cannot be "trained for." Training involves expanding one's ability to respond to confusing or difficult feelings and situations, and training cannot replace, only enhance, the central importance of one's "peerness." In this befriending attitude one cannot take away someone else's confusion or pain, but one can empathize with him, help him to hear himself better, and help him to find and develop more resources. In this way, he may find his path through difficult situations more quickly and efficiently than if he had been alone.

Part of the befriending phase for the peer counselor is continual discovery of qualities in the person which one can care about and ally with. Every one has people to whom one finds it easy to respond and others where there are difficulties in feeling rapport. The back-up system for peer counselors should provide opportunities for peer counselors to look at their initial and ongoing reactions to the people they are befriending. This exploration has two major aspects: (1) checking for reactions; and (2) searching for qualities to care about. *Checking for reactions* can involve asking what happened – how it felt to be with that person, what one's perceptions were of his behavior, and what was going on inside him. Further, given that the counselor perceived him in a particular way, how did that make the counselor feel? Finally, to search out other plausible interpretations for what happened, what the counselor perceived the parent as feeling, communicating, and so on.

Two structured exercises which may be useful in peer counselor training on the befriending phase are: (1) identity checks; and (2) the responsible communication exercise (Rosenberg, 1983). The identity check exercise asks the peer counselor to ask of whom the parent may have reminded him (either specific people in his life, or a "type" of person). The counselor can then list or elaborate on how the person was *similar to* those specific people or type of person, and finally, can elaborate on how that parent was *different from* that particular person or type of person. This exercise helps to clarify to some extent how one may be reacting to a particular parent in similar ways to the ways one responded to particular significant people in one's own past.

The responsible communication exercise helps a peer counselor to distinguish how he perceived a parent, what actions, exchanges affected this perception, and given that he had this perception, how he felt about the parent. Again, this exercise amounts to elaborating on: (1) one's perceptions; (2) what actions, etc. were relevant to perceiving the parent this particular way; and (3) how it felt to be around the parent, given that one was perceiving him this way. Further detail on the responsible communication exercise can be found in Rosenberg (1983).

The "checking of reactions" can take place: (1) in a peer counseling back-up session; (2) by oneself, after a contact with a parent; or (3) during an ongoing discussion with a parent.

Clarifying qualities that one cares about in a parent helps one stay open to empathizing with him, in spite of possible aspects of his behavior to which one feels reactive. This has been characterized as learning to ally with the growing aspects of someone's personality, and balancing those aspects which are stuck, confused, or fearfully "locked in." Finally, it is important for a peer counselor to be able to recognize where, because of his reactions, he is not being helpful to a parent, and to know what to do when this occurs. The most basic aspect of this involves a simple non-condemning statement: "I seem to be having strong reactions to what you are saying;" "I'm finding it hard to listen to you because of my reactions;" "Things seem to be getting muddled." Another aspect is listening to oneself: (1) in potentially tense or confusing interactions; or (2) after being simple or direct. The counselor can indicate that he cannot go on at this time and, either plan a next time to talk, or find another resource(s) for the parent which he can choose to follow up.

Phase 2 When a parent feels befriended, he may choose to talk about more serious and intimate feelings, or he may not. He may want assistance in getting other kinds of help, deciding how to deal with his child, and so on. Although these situations involve personal feelings, people do not automatically attend to such feelings. Help of the kind indicated above may further build the ground for "deeper" explorations later on.

If a person feels accepted in the befriending atmosphere, he may choose to talk about his feelings. In a way, Phases 2–7 are part of the same worthwhile process. When he is listening, a peer counselor is attending to the implicit, felt aspects of what the parent is talking about, and trying to understand as best as possible.

Phase 3 A few gentle "focusing" questions may help a person "connect up with" or articulate for himself what is being felt implicitly. Often this movement is like a spiraling inward toward the most central aspect (the crux), or other aspects of what is being felt in a certain situation. Sometimes, there is a single focus, at other times there is the feeling of two or more aspects in tension or conflict. The crux in the latter case may be the feeling of the conflict or incredulity at the presence of *both* aspects.

Phase 4 After this kind of exploration, there can follow an exploration of what is "in the way," what one is "up against" in a situation. The questioning exercise in the above section on experiential focusing highlights ways of defining, feeling, or touching, what one is facing without being overwhelmed by all the feelings being experienced.

Making a list and devoting time to a parent's outside vision of how it would feel if everything were "all right" in the situation are structured but simple ways to enable him to clarify what he has to handle (what he feels he is up against). This process may occur naturally without questioning on the part of the peer counselor.

Phase 5 This phase involves either exploration of feelings about the problem areas, taking one item at a time, or sharing of some insights or suggestions on the part of the peer counselor.

Phase 6 No matter what happens in the earlier phase, it is important to ask something like: "How would it feel to do it this way?", with the peer counselor listening and potentially investigating what is preventing the parent from trying another alternative.

The counselor should be aware that he is neither trying to make decisions for the parent, nor influence the parent's thought processes. Instead, the counselor is presenting an opportunity for the parent to view the situation from another perspective, a way that someone else might approach it or in which the parent might have looked at it, at another time in his life. He should be direct, not directive. If things become uncertain, the peer counselor goes back to what the parent is feeling, and his definition of the situation they are trying to deal with.

Phase 7 The final phase involves defining the next steps, even though the whole situation may not be resolved or the parents may still be feeling troubled. Having next steps offers someone a constructive line of thought to ponder the situation, which may help him cope successfully with troubled times when he is on his own. Next steps can involve agreement about actions to be taken by parent and/or peer counselor, the next time of talking to explore feelings, and so on. It helps to have a brief time of consolidating to review what was discussed, before parting. Finally, when people have been talking about something confusing or troubling, they sometimes need help to "come out of it" a bit. Structured ways to do this involve: (1) getting one's attention outward (i.e., describing the view outside the window to the peer counselor, naming everything made of wood in the room, etc.); (3) describing something that one likes about oneself (can be problematic, if the person has been feeling generally negative about him or herself); (4) relating some event to which one is looking forward. A suggestion to take a brief walk, or having a few quiet moments can also aid in this process. Further, instead of merely suggesting the exercise to the person, it helps to preface a description of the exercise with "sometimes people can use help coming out a bit of what they've been feeling – here's one way to do this, if you want to."

3 Group process

The main attention in facilitating group process should be devoted to: (1) insuring that each person's remarks about his own situation are given proper attention; (2) decreasing the number of interruptions that can occur while people are speaking, especially when things get tense; (3) deflecting evaluative judgments so that a parent who may be struggling to share his feelings about his situation does not become over-loaded with input (comments from one or more people) which he is not able to consider at the time; (4) assuring that someone who does not choose to share in a group setting does not feel compelled to do so. There are some simple ways of structuring a meeting than can help foster a worth-while process (see McGuire, 1981).

IV Problem areas

Who should be involved in training?

The question often arises in different peer counseling situations as to who should be involved in training, and what different people's motivations are for becoming peer counselors. Because parenting networks tend to be volunteer organizations, there are no clear prerequisites for becoming a peer counselor other than the necessary one of having had a child in a similar situation. Well written guidelines can be useful for giving a fuller description of the responsibilities of a peer counselor in a specific group. There cannot be totally restrictive criteria for who can become a peer counselor and who cannot. The period of training or orientation can be used as the time for experienced trainers and volunteers to come to a *mutual* decision about when a volunteer is ready to become actively involved as a peer counselor. The model in this chapter demonstrates one method of how people can attend to their previous parenting experience and learn to work with difficult feelings in themselves and in others as a part of training. This training experience can allow a volunteer to estimate when, and if, he is ready. This should be a mutual decision because situations have arisen when people have had difficulties which have prevented them from empathizing with the feelings of others (though they have not been cognizant of it themselves). From the beginning, the implications of this mutual decision should be made explicit. It is suggested that rather than rejecting someone who is "not ready," there be clear options such as: (1) further participation in training; (2) working as a team with a veteran peer counselor; or (3) taking on other responsibilities in the operation of the parenting organization (and potentially continuing in training, or participating in a training series at a later date).

There are situations in parenting networks where intensive "pre-training" is not possible. For example, there are networks which operate in remote, large regions to match parents with others who have previously had a child in a similar situation. In these instances the implicit contract should be as clear as possible: (a) for the new parents, "here are some people in your area who have had a child like yours previously, and you may talk to them and share experiences if you'd like to;" and (b) for the "match-up" parents – suggestions for what they can do to be helpful, a listing of referral resources, and a central "back-up" for problem situations. Written materials that may be sent to new parents may also help to decrease the feeling of aloneness. Periodic centralized training sessions in this kind of geographically spread parenting network are helpful.

Guidelines for match-up parents

One of the most important aspects of peer support is having a parent talk with another parent who has already experienced a similar situation, someone who has developed coping mechanisms and "reached the light at the end of the tunnel." The closer the two parents' experiences, the greater chance for developing rapport. Obviously, the larger the support group, the better chance there is for matching situations closely. Likewise, the smaller the scope of the group (i.e., nursing mothers, mothers with babies under three months, parents of premature babies), the greater opportunity there will be for those parents to speak with other parents in like circumstances.

There are other factors to be considered, however, when matching parents. A parent whose child had slightly different experiences but who lives geographically closer to a new parent may be better able to visit;

the new parent may need that type of support more than telephone conversations with a mother with closer circumstances. Matching parents by geography can also be a cost-effective method, preventing extensive telephone bills.

A parent's response to her experiences may also indicate with whom she should be matched. For example, a mother who did not enjoy breastfeeding would probably not be the best support for a nursing mother, even though both have babies who are the same age. A parent who had a bad experience at a particular hospital might not be effective in working with a parent of a baby in the same hospital, even though their infants have identical heart defects.

The personal experiences that support counselors have had may predispose them to handle certain situations better than other parents. A mother who has had many children may be well qualified to help a mother of a colicky baby, for example, even though she did not have such an infant herself. A middle-aged single mother may be able to aid a teenage mother by virtue of the isolation she has experienced. A parent whose own parent has died may be able to understand the feelings of a parent whose baby has died. Since parents with unusual and unexpected situations are often referred to support groups, it is very helpful for the person doing the matching to have a detailed description of the personal experiences of each peer counselor, including some aspects that might not ordinarily be included (e.g., marital status, breastfeeding experience, special problems, previous occupations). Of course, this information should only be provided where a counselor feels comfortable in talking about those experiences.

Some groups also find it beneficial to have more than one parent working with a new parent at a time. One may talk about breastfeeding experiences and another about issues related to teenage parenting, for example; or one about a baby's visual problems and another about heart defects. This type of "team counseling" can offer extended, specific support in a number of situations. It may also be appropriate where a parent is referred to another group for help. The original peer counselor can continue to lend support in a more general way. This dual approach is particularly effective when a baby dies. Though the first peer counselor may not have had this experience, she can offer the resource of another bereavement group while continuing to extend her own support to the grieving parent. Being abandoned at this time can be especially devastating.

In some instances, the referral person may have to be particularly sensitive to a parent's religious beliefs or personality when matching her with a peer counselor. A devout Catholic may have unreconcilable differences with a parent with atheistic beliefs, for example. In some instances, these would not come to the fore, but in others, such as when an ethical decision needs to be made concerning a hospitalized baby, they might make a big difference. Certain basic personalities may clash, as well. Although they may be hard to ascertain at the onset of a relationship, such differences may become more obvious over time. A parent who chooses always to see the bright side of things may have trouble communicating with another more pragmatic parent over a period of time. Other nuances may arise, ones which may be difficult to pinpoint, which may block effective communication between two parents. In this instance, it may be wise for the peer counselor to request that another counselor talk with the parent instead. It is important that all peer support counselors be aware of this option so that they may choose this alternative rather than continuing an unproductive counseling relationship or end the communication before problems have been resolved.

Each group must decide for itself how it will prioritize matching parents. A sensitive, intelligent referral person who knows each group member can be an important asset for initiating effective counseling relationships.

Dealing with death and dying

Relating to parents who have an infant or child who may be dying or who has died draws on the deepest inner resources of compassion from a peer counselor. In some areas, there are support groups or networks for parents concerned with the death of a child. Some of these groups have written extensively about how to help parents. Here are several key resources which will be helpful in starting such a group, or in relating to parents whose child has a serious illness or who has died (Marshall and Cape, 1982; Sawyer, 1982; Wheeler and Von Felts, 1982; Young, 1984).

Parenting stress/anger

A parent who is angry may shout and be accusatory. The counselor can help him to define the source and aim of his anger – they may be two different things. Without focusing on blame, the counselor can quietly guide the parent to be more specific about what is troubling them. It may come to light that there is more than one source of anger. It is important for the peer counselor to learn to be able not to take personally the feelings which may be directed at him. He may be acting as a lightening rod for otherwise undirected anger. It is more constructive to discuss the feelings involved and a way out than to find a scapegoat for a certain situation.

Taking on too much

Training for peer counselors must enable them to develop an understanding of situations that they feel they cannot handle, and must provide referral options which peer counselors can suggest to a parent. Many parenting networks operating with peer counselors provide a central back-up coordinator who is on call to help the peer counselors sort out difficult situations. Further, ongoing periodic training and support provide the opportunity to develop new understanding and enable peer counselors to learn from each other. It is recommended that peer counseling groups keep an ongoing log or resource manual of difficult situations and how they were handled.

One useful model for peer counselors in relating to parents with many difficulties is that of forming a *team*. In this situation, the peer counselor and parent(s) form a list of people in the parent's lives who care about them and who may be willing to help out in some way. People are invited to a team meeting and the peer counselor helps to coordinate what help and resources people are willing to offer. It takes a subtle kind of discipline to help people in the parent's network define what they are most sanely capable of offering (i.e., three hours of baby sitting on Tuesday from 2–5 p.m. for one month) and to help coordinate what resources are available. This model of forming teams derives from the work in crisis intervention, and network support for families (Speck and Attneave, 1973; Howells, 1975), and in many respects is the contemporary equivalent of a "barn raising" or prayer circle for families in need.

References

Achtenberg, J., Simonton, O. C., and Simonton, S. (1976). *Stress, psychological factors, and cancer.* Fort Worth, TX: New Medicine Press.

Boukydis, K. (McGuire) (1981). *Building supportive community: Listening and focusing through peer counseling.* Available from Center for Supportive Community, 186 Hampshire St, Cambridge, MA 02139.

Boukydis, K. (McGuire) (1984). "Changes: Peer counseling supportive communities as a model for community mental health" in D. Larson (ed.), *Teaching psychological skills: Models for giving psychology away.* Monetery, CA: Brooks/Cole.

Buber, M. (1966). *The knowledge of man. The philosophy of the interhuman.* New York: Harper Torchbooks.

Frankl, V. (1959). *Man's search for meaning.* New York: Simon & Schuster.

Friedman, M. (1972). "Dialogue and the unique in humanistic psychology." *Journal of Humanistic Psychology,* 12(2), 7–12.

Gendlin, E. (1962). *Experiencing and the creation of meaning.* Glencoe, IL: Free Press.

Gendlin, E. (1969). "Focusing." *Psychotherapy: Theory, Research and Practice,* 6, 4–15.

Gendlin, E. (1977). "Experiential focusing and the problem of getting movement in psychotherapy" in D. D. Nevill (ed.), *Humanistic psychology: New frontiers.* New York: Gardner Press.

Gendlin, E. (1981). *Focusing.* New York: Bantam.

Howells, M. (1975). *Helping ourselves: Families and the human network.* Boston: Beacon Press.

Marshall, R. and Cape, L. (1982). "Coping with neonatal death" in R.

Marshall, C. Kasman and L. Cape (eds), *Coping with caring for sick newborns.* Philadelphia: W. B. Saunders.

Moses, L., Reilly, M., Schnaubelt, M. and Gould, P. (1983). *Intensive Caring Unlimited: Parent support counselor training manual.* Available from Intensive Caring Unlimited, 910 Bent Lane, Erdenheim, PA 19118.

Rogers, C. (1975). "Empathic: An unappreciated way of being." *Counseling Psychologist*, 5(2), 3–11.

Rosenberg, M. (1983). *A manual for nonviolent communication.* Philadelphia: New Society Publishers.

Sawyer, M. (1982). "Aiding a mother experiencing neonatal death" in R. Marshall, C. Kasman and L. Cape (eds), *Coping with caring for sick newborns.* Philadelphia: W. B. Saunders.

Speck, R. and Attneave, C. (1973). *Family networks.* New York: Pantheon.

Wheeler, J. and Von Felts, L. (1982). "Training a peer counseling and support group" in R. Marshall, C. Kasman and L. Cape (eds), *Coping with caring for sick newborns.* Philadelphia: W. B. Saunders.

Young, V. (1984). *Working with the dying and grieving.* Davis, CA: International Dialogue Press.

PART 4

Overview of models

CHAPTER 8

Innovative models of parenting networks at the national level

Lenette S. Moses

There are a growing number of organizations at the national level which serve to network smaller, regional groups. Some have even become international. It may be advantageous to learn how these networks got started and how they grew. The spark of purpose and enthusiasm which exists in the successful smaller groups is the backbone of these organizations. The unity and cooperative effort which joins the local groups into a network strengthens each organization and helps it to provide better services to each family.

The three organizations detailed in this chapter are the Family Resource Coalition (FRC), Parent Care, Inc. and the International Childbirth Education Association (ICEA). Though their target groups and methods vary, each was formed to support specific problems experienced by many families. In each section, each of the three organizations will be discussed.

Getting started

The Family Resource Coalition was organized as a result of a gathering of professionals at the "Family Resource Forum," sponsored by the Administration for Children, Youth and Families, in May, 1981. It was developed by Family Focus, Inc., of Evanston, Illinois. The coalition is led by a Board of Directors of thirty members from academic positions, national child development organizations, foundations and model family resource programs. Almost 2,000 FRC members represent all fifty states and Canada. A small paid staff, based in Chicago, and a burgeoning decentralized network of member volunteers enable the FRC to act as both a resource and catalyst for the parent education and family support movement.

Parent Care began in 1982 under the name of Parents of Premature and High-Risk Infants, International, Inc., as a joint effort of parents of perinatal professionals concerned with supporting parents of premature and high-risk infants. A core group of fifteen mothers and fathers whose babies had been born prematurely or were hospitalized for other reasons had already formed support groups in their communities. They each felt a strong need for a larger network to join these forces together in an organized fashion. It was apparent that many parents were unable to locate support, and that beginning groups could benefit from the mistakes made by the established groups in their developmental stages. Their major aim was to help to keep these groups working so that families across the country could be supported and educated. This, in turn, would act as a stimulus to encourage the parents to become more actively involved in their infants' care, strengthening bonds and the family itself. The somewhat lugubrious name was changed to Parent Care in 1985.

One hundred and seventy grassroots groups are members of Parent Care, as well as such national organizations as the National Pediatricians Association, National Association of Pediatric Social Workers, and Association of Children's Hospitals. There are no paid staff members.

ICEA was founded in 1960 by a dozen parents and professionals concerned with couples having a positive childbirth experience. It unites groups and people who believe in family-centered maternity care and in freedom of choice based on knowledge of alternatives. These are the only requirements for membership in ICEA. The group is run primarily by volunteers via a network of state and provincial coordinators. As with PPHRIII and FRC, ICEA acts as an umbrella organization for local member groups. These groups are independent, being able to organize their services with just a few guidelines from ICEA. ICEA has remained financially autonomous since its formation, avoiding any ties to specific health care delivery systems. All three of these groups are fully supported by professional advisory boards.

Group philosophy and purpose

All of these organizations were formed to supply support and resources to particular groups of parents. Family Resource Coalition has several major principles that serve as the foundation of their effort. They recognize that parenting can be a very demanding and complex role which can be eased and supplemented by outside support. The individual member groups offer this support, in an effort to determine and build on the families strengths. This type of aid is seen as a preventative measure, to ensure that the family unit remains cohesive and secure and that inner tension does not result in turmoil.

Much support is provided through parent education. The programs' services are further backed through community ties. They are aware that a family isolated from its peers is at risk for developing internal crises. Personal and social networks are offered to bring individuals with similar backgrounds and experiences together for problem solving and peer support. This is provided without regard to sex, race, economic status, religion or ethnic origins.

Parent Care was founded to serve parents of premature and high-risk infants. Its purpose is to provide information, referrals and support to parent groups, families and professionals concerned with infants who require special care at birth. The local groups vary in size and focus. They are the foundation of the network. Parent Care was formed to work together with each group in its own setting, to support these efforts.

The parents of a hospitalized baby have a special set of emotions and crises. Such simple parenting events as breastfeeding, carrying a baby home from the hospital and diapering are often denied these mothers and fathers. The foundation of a new parent's confidence in his ability to care for his child may be greatly shaken. The array of professionals who care for his child may appear more knowledgeable than he is about his own offspring. A critical role for those supporting these parents is having a sensitivity to these individual and very poignant needs. Those representing groups in the Parent Care network know how to promote meaningful bonds between a sick baby and his parents. This, in turn, can prevent critical family disharmony in the future.

For the above reason among others, one of the groups' main focuses is communication. Parent Care acts as a liaison among the various groups, between parents and professionals, and between this movement of parent care and the public, to increase awareness and knowledge.

The International Childbirth Education Association unites people who support family-centered maternity care and believe in freedom of choice based on knowledge of alternatives. The group teachings place an emphasis on education and preparation for childbearing and breastfeeding. They are also concerned with alerting the public to up-to-date research in the childbirth field. Couples are encouraged to understand the childbirth process and to seek individualized care with minimal medical intervention. Research has shown that when parents have understood the physiological process of childbirth and had some methods for handling the labor and delivery, they experienced less fear and less medication was needed. ICEA also promotes the development of safe, low-cost alternatives in childbirth. The Association advocates the awareness of the rights and responsibilities of all involved. A parent who is well-informed will be able to make intelligent decisions and choices before the event, and be better able to accept last-minute alternatives as needed.

Services provided

Parent Care achieves its goals through a number of services. It acts as a link between parents across the country and the local groups via a central telephone number. The smaller groups then offer support by peer counselors via one-on-one telephone contact and in some cases, at-home or at-hospital visits. The names of the member groups and other pertinent information is available in the Parent Care National Resource Directory (see p. 172).

Other written information includes a quarterly newsletter, which provides articles written by perinatal professionals and parents on such topics as prematurity, hospitalization, bonding and developmental delays. The circulation reaches the group members and neonatal intensive care units nationwide.

The organization sponsors an annual conference which brings together he diverse group members, who would ordinarily not have the opportunity to share experiences and ideas. Proceedings from this event are published in an effort further to disseminate the information gained. During the conference, workshops are held which offer the participants practical, working knowledge on areas relating directly to their activity. Typical topics covered include beginning a new group, developing communication between medical staff and parents, and the specifics of breastfeeding a special care baby.

The member groups also offer such services as:

- public education meetings;
- rap sessions/discussion groups;
- group newsletters;
- local resource directories;
- referrals to other area groups for specific problems and situations;
- premie clothing exchanges and sales;
- breastfeeding counseling;
- breast pump rentals and information;
- parent experience books with photographs;
- home visits;
- hospital visits;
- lending libraries/list of recommended books;
- reprint information;
- counselor training;
- referral to area professionals;
- bereavement support;
- support of mothers of twins;
- guidance for other groups in getting started;
- social activities;
- education of hospital staff.

The major aim of Family Resource Coalition is much the same as Parent Care to act as a catalyst for the productivity of smaller, regional groups. It produces conferences to bring together directors of the various programs, to improve the quality and increase the number of these groups. It places an emphasis on public awareness of the importance of family support and acts as an advocate for families at the federal, state and local levels. The Family Resource Coalition conducted an extensive research project to identify and survey family resource programs across the country. These statistics have been compiled in a computerized clearinghouse of information on program services, participants, types of families, staff patterns, funding sources and program evaluation methods. This information is available to FRC members.

The Coalition also acts as a clearinghouse for publications and other information relating to family concerns. It has a national referral service and provides technical assistance to both emerging and existing programs. National conferences are held by the coalition, and regional ones are co-sponsored by the FRC and the individual groups on topics of interest, such as helping parents deal with the economics of raising a family, creating caring communities through family support. Research and evaluation of family resources is encouraged.

Family Resource publishes a newsletter, "The FRC Report." This periodical includes current research, individual programs, advocacy efforts, media access ideas, evaluation techniques and a full range of family support issues. The Coalition also publishes three books, *Programs to strengthen families: A resource guide*, *Sharing resources*, and *Working with teen parents,* all of which are detailed at the end of this chapter.

As with Parent Care, the individual groups provide a wide range of services relating directly to their distinctive populations. Group focuses include parents in low-income, ethnic, and adolescent categories. Fathers, parents in rural areas and working mothers are among some of the others aided by local organizations. Each of these groups has tailored its services to its community needs. Some provide telephone "warmlines", others drop-in centers. In some cases, presentations are offered in schools and community locations or local newsletters are published.

Whatever the emphasis and vehicle for service for the local groups of both Parent Care and FRC, each group shares a commitment to the basic principles described in the first section. Their overall aim is to recognize and support the family's weaknesses and enhance its family strengths in order to make the family itself a smooth working unit.

International Childbirth Education Association provides up-to-date material to groups and individuals about childbirth practices. A large measure of this is done through a number of publications. "ICEA News" is the official newsletter of the organization; "ICEA Sharing" provides additional information for childbirth educators. Group and administrative information is included in the "ICEA Forum." "ICEA Review" has a comprehensive review of literature and research on childbearing issues and "ICEA Bookmarks" reviews current literature and teaching materials on childbirth and early parenting. Additional material is written to present ICEA's position on specific childbirth topics. Printed material on a wide variety of these topics is sold through the ICEA Bookcenter, a mail order bookstore.

ICEA sponsors conventions each year. On even-numbered years, an international conference is held and on odd-numbered years multiple regional conferences are provided. State and provincial meetings are held regularly. Topics include those relating directly to childbirth (i.e., drugs in pregnancy and labor, delivery positions, neonatal ethics), as well as others on parenting in general (i.e., mothering a large family, sibling rivalry, breastfeeding, and grieving).

Individual member groups offer classes relating to birth and early parenting. These vary from group to group, having the prime ICEA guidelines in common. In addition to childbirth preparation, including physiological and emotional aspects, groups often include instruction in cesarean birth, subsequent births including sibling factors, early pregnancy and new parenting. Each of these is designed to educate and prepare families for life passages in order that the new events will not affect the unity of the family in a negative manner.

Meeting problems

Despite the good intentions of those forming such a parent support group, the problems involved are profuse and diverse. Only a group with tenacity and cohesion will be able to override these challenges and continue to provide its defined set of services.

Developing goals

The situations faced by parents are diverse, numerous and often complex. A typical family support group must choose one or more specific area in which they will place their effort. Depending upon the population served, and the availability of funds and volunteers, this focus may be very small or more far-reaching. One comment echoed by directors of these groups is the significance of clearly defining one's goals. Though there is often a strong desire to help anyone who comes for aid, it is more advantageous to develop a local resource guide including names of other organizations and individuals whose services parallel those of the support group. The simpler the structure of the group, the easier it is to achieve the goals.

In developing this specific aim, a wise board of directors will consider the skills of the active members. This means if there is no one who knows how to write, a newsletter should not be a priority at the start. Likewise, if there are a number of members who enjoy public speaking, developing a series of public education meetings may be a smart way to gain initial public awareness and involvement.

All three of the organizations viewed here work in coordination with other groups with similar aims. Professional organizations such as the National Association of Pediatric Social Workers or the National Association for the Education of Young Children have a vested interest in the activities of grassroots parent support organizations. They can provide much-needed research information and knowledge, while gaining first-hand understanding of the needs and feelings of parents from these smaller groups whose members are more in touch with the day-to-day happenings. Legislators, as well, can benefit from hearing the circumstances of their constituency documented with personal experience. This give and take may require some strong resolve and persistence by the members of the local groups, which illustrates the strong need for a clearly defined set of goals from the outset.

Staff *vs* volunteers

ICEA has parents and trained childbirth educators functioning in a group situation. Since the educators are often paid for their professional services and the parents are volunteers, there are sometimes struggles for control of these groups. Regional and state conferences have been held to prepare administrators to face these confrontations on the local level. Unfortunately, these are not always well-attended and have diminished in number.

"ICEA Forum" is the group publication which tries to address this type of problem, as well. Within the structure of ICEA there are Group Services Chairpersons whose responsibility it is to respond to group concerns.

Member groups in Parent Care sometimes have the same type of professional/volunteer conflict. Group administration structure varies, including all professionals, all volunteers or a mix between the two. In some instances, medical professionals feel threatened with the idea of laymen entering their "territory." Many are fearful that the volunteers will give inaccurate information or will interfere with their work. Groups avert this problem by emphasizing to the parent volunteers and professionals alike the aspect of peer support and that no medical information is given out by these parents. A group newsletter can further solve the problem by offering the involved professionals a forum for explaining medical problems and technology on their own terms.

Another reason why hospital staff sometimes do not refer or guide to these groups is that they do not recognize the value of such peer support.

It has been seen that when the nursing and social work staff in particular were exposed to parents' feelings they were apt to be more open to referring other parents to the group. This was done by sharing copies of applicable articles from medical journals and other sources, by having group members speak to staff meetings, and by inviting professionals to attend discussion sessions in which the parents expressed their own experiences and emotions.

In any of these situations, it is crucial to illustrate the fact that peer support groups can supplement and enhance the role of the medical professionals, rather than replace them. Discussing the strengths and differences of each member of the health care team, including volunteer parents, may help to alleviate potential or existing relationship and communication problems.

Burn-out

Another problem faced by most volunteer organizations is that of burn-out. With two-income families on the rise, the number of hours free for volunteer positions has rapidly decreased. For this reason, a few people in each group may take on more and more responsibilities from lack of anyone else to do them. Too, enthusiastic volunteers may want to take on more than they are able to handle and soon become overwhelmed by the entire job.

ICEA has become very candid about the description of each responsibility and the time it may take. Those who take on significant positions are then aware of what they are being asked to do before they agree to do it. A much more aggressive program of volunteer recognition has also helped to keep people involved in group activities.

The groups networked by Parent Care commonly have the burn-out problem as well. One of the biggest thrusts for prevention and treatment of this concern is an active, ongoing search for new volunteers. When a parent support counselor makes a personal recommendation that one of her counselees become a counselor, it tends to give that counselee more confidence and frequently leads to a new counselor. The more willing participants there are to share the group responsibilities, the less pressure each one feels and the less tendency there is for burn-out.

Attrition

Attrition is another challenge facing volunteer groups today. Obviously, as ICEA and FRC find, people keep having babies and facing the experiences that come with them, which provides a new pool of people with interest in their areas. Parent Care has the same situation, and with it the common, automatic desire to help others in a similar situation. But in each instance, as families move on to new and different sets of occurences, they tend to move away from the basic interests of the groups. Except in those special instances when a group can provide services for parents of growing children, each year there are a certain number of parents who will "grow out of" and leave their parent support group. The only answer that groups seem to find is a constant search for new faces. Even when things are running smoothly, a chief aim must be to have the foresight to attract those who will continue the group in the future.

One way that some organizations face attrition is in developing and implementing training programs. These programs enable administrators to discover volunteers' strengths and weaknesses, in order to offer them the responsibilities that they will best be able to handle. Taking the time and effort to attend a training program also instills in a parent a certain group spirit and the confidence that he is well-prepared to take a place in the workings of the organization. Training may also weed out those parents who are not qualified to carry out certain responsibilities, so that someone else who can, will.

None of the groups detailed in this chapter holds a training session at the national level. Workshops at national conferences often fill this need, however. Many Parent Care groups have individual training sessions relating directly to their hospital or community setting. At least one training manual is available (see p. 172). Both Parent Care and ICEA have a "volunteer information questionnaire" which provides information about the volunteers' experiences and interests. In this way, individuals may be matched up with jobs in which they have an interest. Since much communication takes place long-distance, the administration normally starts these volunteers with small projects or gets them involved with others at first to determine how they work best (see Chapters 2 and 3).

Funding

Whether a non-profit group is starting, branching out or just continuing with day-to-day work, funding is a critical source of concern. Without supportive money, the best organized group cannot continue to provide services.

Parent Care is funded by contributions, group memberships, and grants from foundations and major companies whose products and services are directly related to families' health and well-being. Memberships range from $15 for individuals to $500+ for patrons. Those who contribute more than $100 are offered their choice of three books on relating topics, written by Parent Care members. Included in this membership are a subscription to "Parent Care . . . News Briefs", the newsletter, "Zero to Three," the NCCIP newsletter, and a vote at the annual meeting, and a copy of the Resource Directory.

ICEA does not have outside funding. The group relies solely on revenue from the mail order book store, dues, conventions, and subscriptions to the newsletters. Membership benefits include an "ICEA News" subscription, discounts at the Bookcenter and ICEA events, a vote in elections, an opportunity to go through the teacher certification program and an opportunity to subscribe to the other ICEA publications.

FRC is supported by membership dues, conference fees, foundation and federal grants, and by purchase of the group publications. Membership benefits include a subscription to the "FRC Report" and discounts on FRC conference fees and publications as well as access to a computerized clearinghouse on family support programs. Organizational members receive three copies of each "FRC Reports" issue, and additional technical assistance services.

Serving minority populations

One problem that each of these groups has is in reaching all the parents who have hospitalized babies, and could potentially benefit from group services. A special effort is being made in many areas to try to aid teenage, low-income and ethnic families. The problem with a family which speaks a foreign language is obvious yet challenging. Bi-lingual resource people are oftentimes hard to locate and a group's major sources of support, such as telephone counseling, rap sessions, newsletters, classes or resource lists are useless. Mothers and fathers in this situation are apt to be feeling isolated as a result of their inability to communicate in general. When they have a crisis or even a typical parenting question, this feeling of aloneness may be intensified.

A low-income family may not have a telephone, so that direct contact may be difficult to achieve. Teenage parents have special interests and problems and may not be able to relate to other, older parents, even if their babies are in similar situations. The perfect solution would be to have volunteer counselors with the same types of circumstances, but these parents do not normally have the ability either to understand the language of a training course, or a telephone to do telephone counseling. Most importantly, these mothers and fathers do not have the time to devote to helping others when their own needs are so great.

Meeting the needs of a parent with one of these special needs may take more time and effort than helping dozens of parents with more common sets of problems. But it is critical that these mothers and fathers gain access to the same types of information and support as their peers. A local resource list, including representatives of the various cultures and ethnic backgrounds found in the group's population area becomes a prominent way of reaching these parents. If a group at least can find an interpreter, it will be able to share information from which the new parents can benefit.

Facing these problems can be a major time-consuming effort for a group, but developing a clear, concise way to deal with each one will enable an organization to continue on a smooth course.

Future goals

When a parent support group is formed, it has a certain number of goals to achieve. As it develops, the vehicle for meeting these aims may vary as the administration discovers what works best for their particular population. A creative core group will evolve a number of avenues of communication and education and keep a close watch on which ones are effective. In time, the original goals of the group may be modified as the needs of the parents in the community change. This may mean either a decrease in number of services, in an attempt to highlight individual ones, or an increase as more needs are perceived. A group which does not reevaluate its productiveness and merit is in danger of becoming stale and outmoded. Even if the goals remain the same from year to year, methods and resources can vary. This also speaks for the advantages of searching out new people, with new ideas and enthusiasm, at regular intervals.

Parent Care sites the following as some plans for the future: to develop regions and co-sponsor one-day regional workshops; to develop replicable model programs for minorities, teens and siblings; to develop a hotline to connect parents with local resources and to continue to offer annual conferences to bring together parents and professionals involved in the care of special babies.

As information about the research on the development of babies who were born prematurely comes to light, Parent Care will continue to share that with anxious parents, whose access to such vital information is limited. The organization will also act as a liaison to share information about financing a hospitalization, including current reforms and changes.

The Family Resource Coalition has received funding from the Administration for Children, Youth and Families to conduct a large-scale "knowledge transfer project, designed to encourage replication and improvement of family resource programs. The Coalition will synthesize existing materials related to the establishment of local programs into a single, condensed package, combining printed and audio-visual materials. A videotape with an accompanying manual will provide interested parties with an overview of family support programming, theory and practice. These materials will be supplemented with five guidebooks on developing specific program models, parent networks, drop-in centers, home-based programs, warmlines, and parent support and education groups.) A network of regional technical assistance providers will also supply training and consultation for groups interested in developing family resource programs.

The FRC will continue to collect and disseminate information on innovative practices and programs in the primary prevention field, and provide an array of networking and technical assistance services for state and local child welfare officials, under a contract with the National Resource Center on Family-Based Services at the University of Iowa School of Social Work.

ICEA has developed several major goals for the next five years. The organization will continue to provide quality services and information, in order to be recognized internationally as a leader in childbirth education resources, childbirth educator certification and the implementation of the philosophy of family-centered maternity care. This will continue to be achieved through the volunteer organization framework. Priority will be given by the group to the goal of educating the public and the medical field as to the benefits of childbirth education as an effective factor in the reduction of perinatal morbidity and mortality. Further, ICEA will act to counter the threat to freedom of choice posed by the malpractice situation.

Conclusion

The Family Resource Coalition, Parent Care and the Childbirth Education Association are superior examples of how effective national networking organizations can be. Though their constituencies and methods vary, each has found a niche in the international movement of parent support.

The quality of these networks is derived from the effectiveness of the groups they unite. The groups' strength is intrinsic to the families they support. They reach a parent in his environment, in his language and with a full understanding of his problems and needs. Their educational materials and services are up-to-date and practical, full of merit and worth for the parents they inform.

Just as the groups act to support and strengthen the family, the coalitions serve to sustain the grassroots groups. Ongoing research and surveys shared among the groups offer a wider vista of information and creative ideas than would normally be possible in a small, local organization. Most important, however, by offering them supportive autonomy, the networks allow the groups to grow and change with the needs of their communities, yet feel secure and confident with the continuing guidance of their "parent organization." In this way, the integrity of the coalitions depends substantially upon the divestment of their goals.

Group resources

The following publications are available from the groups described in the chapter.

Family Resource Coalition

Membership $20 (U.S.) individuals, $35 organizations (Includes subscription to FRC Report)

(1) "FRC Report"   This twenty-page periodical includes articles on current research, individual programs' highlights, advocacy efforts, media access and a full range of family support issues.

(2) *Programs to strengthen families*   Model family support programs across the nation are described in this book, including prenatal and infant health care, child abuse, early childhood education, parent education and support, school and family linkages, special needs, informal self-help and more.

(3) *Sharing resources*   For those who want to establish new family resource programs or extend existing ones, this is a guide for locating practical "how-to" information. This annotated bibliography describes forty-five resource materials designed to aid in planning for parent groups, drop-in centers, home-based programs, and parent education curricula. Many are aimed at specific populations.

(4) *Working with teen parents*   This is a guide to designing services for teen parents. It includes a survey of promising approaches and discussions of programming issues such as: insuring teen participation, recruiting and training volunteers, building community support and coordinating comprehensive service approaches.

All of these publications may be ordered from: FRC, 230 N. Michigan, #1625, Chicago, IL 60601.

International Childbirth Education Association

Membership $15 (U.S.) individuals, $35 professionals (Includes ICEA News)

(1) "ICEA News"   Newsletter for members. It contains information about family centered maternity care.

(2) "ICEA Sharing"   Newsletter for childbirth educators. Its function is to facilitate exchange of ideas, techniques and materials.

(3) "ICEA Forum"   Newsletter for groups which provides administrative information.

(4) "ICEA Review"   A comprehensive review and commentary on research and literature pertaining to childbearing issues.

(5) *ICEA Membership Directory*
(6) "How to Grow a Parents Group"

Free services:

- ICEA Bookcenter catalog;
- Information on teacher certification, conferences, events, local ICEA groups, breastfeeding, cesarean section resources;
- Help regarding achieving FCMC, group concerns, use of ICEA display or slide/tape presentation, teaching concerns.

All of the above may be obtained from: ICEA, P.O. Box 20048, Minneapolis, MN 55420-0048.

Parent Care, Inc.

Membership $15 (U.S.) individual, $35 professional, $50 local parent group (Includes subscription to newsletter and the Resource Directory)

(1) "Parent Care . . . News Briefs Support Lines" includes articles by professionals and parents about topics relating to prematurity, hospitalization, developmental delays, etc. Includes parent stories and book reviews.
(2) "Parent Care" Conference Proceedings from the Parent Care conferences are available. First Conference "Parental Care," will be available when published.
(3) *Resource Directory* This directory includes listings of local support groups for parents of hospitalized babies, bereaved parents, single parents, parents of twins, national self-help organizations, breastfeeding and nursing supplies and groups, and suggested readings on related topics.

Contact: Parent Care, Inc., 50 North Medical Drive, Room 2A210, Salt Lake City, UT 84132. Telephone: (801) 581–5323.

PART 5

Resource directory

CHAPTER 9

Tools for planning a parenting network

Lauri Lowen

Introduction

The material in this section was written by Lauri Lowen, who has been president of Parents of Prematures, Bellevue, Washington, USA since 1978. Parents of Prematures is a parenting network for parents who have had, or anticipate having, a premature or high risk baby which provides emotional and educational support through peer counseling, parent education, and parenting publications.

The section is divided into two parts. The first part comprises a list of advantages and risks for participation in a parenting network for parents, children, "helping parents," and professionals. While the issues presented are directed toward the operation of a parenting network for parents of premature or high risk babies, they are of general concern for people developing a parenting network for similar populations of parents. This section may be used as the basis for discussion by a "core group" of parents and professionals involved in planning a parenting network.

The second part presents a detailed listing of choices to be considered in: (1) assessing the need for a parenting network; and (2) determining the priorities and direction a core group can follow in planning a parenting network. Again, some of the options presented are specifically for parents of premature or high risk babies, but the questions are suitable for those planning for similar populations of parents. This section can serve as a model for those people who are planning a "needs assessment" for determining the demand for a parenting network in a given location, *and* for helping with decisions about priorities for which functions are of highest priority in developing a parenting network.

Part 1 will describe the advantages and risks for participation in a parent support group for families of prematures. Part 2 will cover the choices in organizing a parent support group for families of premature and ill infants. It is a tool to assess the need for and determine the direction of a parent support group.

Part 1   Advantages and risks of participation in a parent support group for families of prematures

Parents receiving the services of the parent support group

Advantages
- Parents may experience a boost in their self-image, confidence and pride.
- Parents who are better prepared for the remainder of their premature experience may have more appropriate expectations.
- Parents are encouraged to play an active role in the care of their child.
- Educational and emotional support may reduce feelings of frustration, anxiety, guilt and loss. Reduction in stress may eliminate some obstacles to attachment.
- Contact with the parent support group provides continuity of care from pre-discharge, through post-discharge and well beyond.
- The parent support group can give recognition not found elsewhere to parents of premature or ill infants.
- Because parents may identify with others who have had the same experience, they may reveal feelings that they may not have shared with a professional.
- Parents have access to expert speakers at meetings, educational materials to borrow and handouts to reinforce what they have learned.
- Breastfeeding counseling specifically tailored to their situation is available. Breastfeeding parents are helped not only by the knowledge of the lactation counselor, but also by the vicarious experiences of hundreds of other mothers who have breastfed their premature infants.
- Parents are not obligated to participate to an extent more than they feel appropriate. They may choose from a broad range of services and can be part of the parent support group without effort.
- Meetings may provide an opportunity for close and informal contact with other similar parents and with professionals.
- Information parents obtain from the parent support group may save the parents time and effort.
- Services usually are provided at no cost to the families served.
- Practical items and services such as breast pumps, tiny clothes and premie diapers may be available through the parent support group.

Risks
- Parental needs may be partially unmet or parents may be dissatisfied as a result of:
    1 inadequate recognition of parental needs;

  2 inefficient administration of the program;
  3 incomplete followup when lack of feedback allows inadequate amounts of contacts to go undetected;
  4 helping parents acting inappropriately.

- Parents may be contacted without obtaining parental permission.
- Some parents (teenagers, minorities, single parents, very low-income families) may not identify with those in the parent support group, which is typically made up of middle-class and married parents.
- Certain emotions, such as disappointment, regret or envy, cannot be alleviated by contact with the parent support group.

Expectant parents

Advantages
- Expectant parents, if provided with resource information in advance, may be more prepared if the birth of their offspring does occur prematurely.

Risks
- Information about premature birth may frighten some expectant parents.

Premature children

Advantages
- Parents may behave more appropriately with and increase attachment to their child if they are informed, confident and aware of developmental milestones as a result of receiving educational and emotional support from the parent support group.

Risks
- The premature child may be considered different from, rather than similar to, other children.

Parents providing the services in the parent support group

Advantages
- Helping parents may satisfy their own needs to help others.
- Parents may benefit from a sense of community gained through their self-help participation.
- Experience in the parent support group may spark interest in pursuing a career in counseling, medical social work, nursing, etc.

Risks
- Priorities may be disordered.
- Responsibilities may be too heavy.
- Helping parents may "burn out" and leave, or may remain with the group but not reveal that they are providing only minimal service.
- Workers may experience a difficult transition as the parent support group moves from a professionally run group to a parent run group.
- Parent support group representatives may display an inappropriate degree of parent advocacy.
- Helping parents may not have been well selected or trained adequately.
- Lack of cooperation and acceptance from community professionals may be discouraging.

Medical and other helping professionals

Advantages
- Meetings and panels provide a non-threatening opportunity to hear feedback directly from parents.
- The professional can rely on the parent support group to provide continuity of care after the parent is no longer at the professional's agency.
- Professionals can be assured that the parent support group will refer parents to the appropriate agency if there are problems requiring professional help.
- The parent support group provides a model for and assistance with developing other parent support groups or in-hospital support systems.
- Many parent support groups offer free inservice training, often with academic credit.
- Professionals may receive regular parent support group member benefits, such as a newsletter, invitations to meetings, resource information and library materials.
- Professionals may have an opportunity to participate in the parent support group's planning, projects and meetings, or to serve on their Professional Advisory Board.

Risks
- The professional may see the parent support group as competition or as implying that they have left parental needs unmet.
- Some professionals may not feel comfortable supporting the parent support group, especially if another agency initiated the group.
- The professional may not trust the parent support group or may

feel burdened by their requirements (such as obtaining parental permission before referral or following screening guidelines).
- Some may question how the power of the group influences new parents.

Community

Advantages
- The parent support group provides an additional resource for a specialized portion of the community.

Risks
- Some may see the parent support group as competing with family and spiritual support.
- The high risk parents needing the services of the parent support group may not become aware of the group's existence.

Part 2 Choices in organizing a parent support group for families of premature and ill infants: A tool to assess the need for and determine the direction of a parent support group

This tool presents alternatives for those initiating or continuing a parent support group for families of premature or ill infants. By selecting choices listed under each category question, the design of the parent support group can be tailored to meet the needs of both the community and the group.

A Who will you be serving? Will you limit your services to only one group, or offer them to more than one group?

1 Parents of babies during hospitalization;
2 parents of babies already discharged;
3 parents of growing children who were premature or sick and have significant residual problems;
4 parents of growing children who were premature or sick and have no significant residual problems;
5 the hospitalized babies;
6 the hospital;
7 the general community of all ages;
8 potential parents of childbearing age;
9 pregnant women, during uncomplicated pregnancies;
10 pregnant women, during pregnancies with complications;
11 families who have lost a baby due to prematurity or neonatal illness.

B Do you have a sponsor, a source of funding or an affiliation which will determine the group that you will serve?

1 Individual hospital;
2 university affiliated School of Medicine, Nursing, Social Work, etc.;
3 Public Health Department;
4 childbirth education organization;
5 parent education organization;
6 health related public foundations;
7 government funding;
8 private funding.

C What services do you want to provide?

Emotional:
1 visits;
2 telephone calls;
3 letters.

Educational:
1 visits;
2 telephone calls;
3 distribution of material produced outside the parent support group;
4 distribution of material produced within the parent support group;
5 audio-visual material produced outside the parent support group;
6 audio-visual material produced within the parent support group;
7 lending library based in hospital;
8 lending library based outside hospital;
9 newsletter for parents;
10 newsletter for professionals;
11 presentations to parents of hospitalized children by members of parent support group;
12 presentations to parents of discharged children by members of parent support group;
13 presentations to professionals by members of parent support group;
14 presentations to the general public by members of parent support group;
15 presentations to parents of hospitalized children by professionals, on behalf of the parent support group;
16 presentations to parents of discharged children by professionals, on behalf of the parent support group;
17 presentations to professionals by professionals, on behalf of the parent support group;

18 presentations to the general public by professionals, on behalf of the parent support group;
19 assistance in starting similar parent support groups.

Social:
1 gatherings of families of hospitalized infants;
2 gatherings to acquaint families of hospitalized infants with staff;
3 gatherings of families of discharged children;
4 gatherings of families of both hospitalized and discharged children.

Fundraising:
1 to benefit the parent support group;
2 to benefit the hospital;
3 to benefit the sponsoring organization.

Practical:
1 providing breast pumps (__free, __loaned for rental fee, __sold);
2 providing premie diapers (__free, __sold);
3 providing premie clothes (__free, __loaned, __sold);
4 providing infant equipment (__free, __loaned, __sold);
5 providing premie clothing patterns (__free, __sold);
6 providing transportation to families of hospitalized infants (__free, __for fee);
7 providing temporary housing for families of hospitalized infants (__free, __for fee);
8 providing financial subsidies for needy parents of hospitalized or discharged infants;
9 blood donations to benefit hospitalized infants;
10 babysitting services for siblings or discharged infants (__free, __for fee, __coop).

D What subjects will your educational services cover? Will these subjects be discussed during a visit, by telephone, in printed educational materials, at meetings, in a newsletter or in a presentation?

1 Practical aspects of dealing with the hospital experience;
2 emotional aspects of dealing with the hospital experience;
3 care of a hospitalized premie;
4 care of a discharged premie;
5 general baby care;
6 breastfeeding the premature baby;
7 community resources;
8 child development (physical, intellectual, emotional);
9 nutrition;
10 parenting (including fathering);

11 high risk pregnancies;
12 financial concerns;
13 emergency first aid and CPR;
14 dealing with a handicapped child;
15 ethics of neonatal intensive care;
16 twins;
17 attachment;
18 premature followup and outcome;
19 genetic counseling;
20 allergies;
21 child abuse;
22 sudden infant death syndrome;
23 the value of play;
24 when a child does not survive;
25 parent support group news;
26 research.

E Who will provide services?

1 Parents within the parent support group (__paid, __volunteer);
2 professional within the parent support group (__paid, __volunteer);
3 parents outside of parent support group (__paid, __volunteer);
4 professionals outside of parent support group (__paid, __volunteer).

F When will parents be contacted by the parent support group? What will be the duration of the contact?

1 During childbearing years;
2 during an uncomplicated pregnancy;
3 during a pregnancy with complications;
4 while mother is hospitalized prenatally;
5 while mother is hospitalized postnatally;
6 while baby is hospitalized: contacted when visiting hospital;
7 while baby is hospitalized: contacted when at home;
8 at or soon after baby's discharge;
9 unlimited amount of time after baby's discharge;
10 designated limited amount of time after baby's discharge.

G Who will make referrals of new parents to the parent support group?

1 Staff physicians;
2 staff nurses;
3 staff social workers;
4 staff clerical and other personnel;
5 private physicians;

6   private nurses;
7   private social workers;
8   private clerical or other personnel;
9   public health nurses;
10 childbirth educators;
11 parenting class teachers;
12 lactation counselors;
13 community members;
14 the new parents themselves.

H How will new parents learn about the existence of the parent support group?

1   Staff physicians;
2   staff nurses;
3   staff social workers;
4   staff clerical and other personnel;
5   private physicians;
6   private nurses;
7   private social workers;
8   private clerical or other personnel;
9   public health nurses;
10 childbirth educators;
11 parenting class teachers;
12 lactation counselors;
13 community members;
14 other new parents;
15 posters;
16 flyers;
17 brochures;
18 newsletter;
19 television;
20 radio;
21 exhibits;
22 resource lists;
23 newspapers and periodicals.

I How will tasks be divided within the parent support group?

Professionals:
1   Coordinator;
2   Consultant;
3   Professional Advisory Board.

Parents:
1   President;
2   Vice-President;
3   Corresponding secretary;
4   Recording secretary;
5   Treasurer;
6   professional liaison;
7   community education coordinator;
8   inservice coordinator;
9   outreach (parent-to-parent counseling) coordinator;
10 breastfeeding help coordinator;
11 parent education coordinator;
12 parent meeting coordinator;
13 fundraising coordinator;
14 public relations and publicity coordinator;
15 newsletter editor;
16 newsletter circulation coordinator;
17 membership coordinator;
18 librarian;
19 branch coordinator;
20 project coordinators (__visitation, __letters to parents,
    __emotional support, __breast pumps, __diapers, __clothes,
    __equipment, __patterns, __transportation, __housing,
    __donations made by parent support group, __welcoming,
    __sunshine, __babysitting, __blood donations, __audio-visual
    material production, __written material production, __other
    projects).

J How will outreach parents (parent-to-parent counselors) be selected?

1   All volunteers accepted;
2   selected from new parents only;
3   selected from experienced parents only;
4   personal recommendation required from within group;
5   personal recommendation required from professional;
6   parent support group committee approval required;
7   professional approval required;
8   certification exam required.

K How will outreach parents (parent-to-parent counselors) be trained?

Method:
1   Parents in parent support group;
2   parents outside of parent support group;

3 professionals within parent support group;
4 professionals outside of parent support group;
5 educational material prepared within parent support group;
6 educational material prepared outside of parent support group;
7 workshops within parent support group;
8 workshops outside of parent support group;
9 unsupervised apprenticeship;
10 supervised apprenticeship.

Duration of training:
1 single orientation;
2 completion of course;
3 ongoing training.

Subjects:
1 Parent support group and counseling procedures;
2 grieving;
3 adolescent parents;
4 facts and statistics about prematurity and neonatal illness;
5 child development and premie outcome;
6 breastfeeding the premature or ill infant;
7 counseling skills;
8 community resources;
9 ethics of neonatal intensive care;
10 psychological aspects of parenting the premature;
11 premie care;
12 general baby care.

L Where will the parent support group obtain funding?

1 Grants (__hospital, __university, __government, __health oriented public foundations, __organizations);
2 private funding;
3 sales;
4 dues.

M What expenses might the parent support group have?

1 Employee wages;
2 newsletter;
3 publicity;
4 educational materials produced within the parent support group;
5 educational materials produced outside of the parent support group;
6 postage;

7   office supplies;
8   library books and supplies;
9   art supplies;
10   project supplies;
11   fees;
12   long distance calls;
13   social event supplies.

N Other issues to consider

Policies:
1   Defined in bylaws or other document;
2   defined but not recorded;
3   undefined;
4   made by parent support groups;
5   made by professionals;
6   made by sponsoring agency;
7   enforceable;
8   unenforceable.

Privacy:
1   Sharing of information concerning families referred expected of parent support group;
2   sharing of information concerning families referred restricted in parent support group;
3   sharing of information concerning families referred expected of staff;
4   sharing of information concerning families referred restricted for staff;
5   parental permission required to accept referral;
6   parental permission not required to accept referral;
7   parental permission required to refer to another agency;
8   parental permission not required to refer to another agency;
9   parental notification required when referred to another agency;
10   parental notification not required when referred to another agency.

Power:
1   Goal is to build new parents' power; demands of staff by parent support group considered inappropriate;
2   goal is to build parent support group's power; demands of staff by parent support group considered appropriate;

Status:

1 Non-profit corporation;
2 tax-exempt status determined by IRS;
3 affiliate of other organization;
4 independent.

Limits:

1 Restrictions on medical advice given;
2 restrictions on other advice given;
3 no restrictions on advice given;
4 families referred to other agencies when their needs are beyond the scope of the parent support group;
5 families not referred to other agencies when their needs are beyond the scope of the parent support group;
6 outreach parents (parent-to-parent counselors) work independently;
7 outreach parents (parent-to-parent counselors) report to a coordinator;
8 outreach parents (parent-to-parent counselors) supervised by professional;
9 outreach parents (parent-to-parent counselors) report back to referring individual.

Suggested reading

Boukydis, C. F. Z. (1982). "Support groups for parents with premature infants in NICU's" in Marshall, R. E., Kasman, C. and Cape, L. S. (eds), *Coping With Caring For Sick Newborns*, Philadelphia, W. B. Saunders.
Erdman, D. (1977). "Parent to parent support: The best for those with sick newborns," *Maternity-Child Nursing Journal*, September/October, pp. 291–2.
Garrand, S., Sherman, N., Rentchler, D. and Jung, A. (1978). "A parent to parent program," *Family and Community Health*, vol. 1, no. 3, November, pp. 103–13.
Lowen, L. (1980). "Breastfeeding the premature baby: Considerations in parent education" in Freier, S. and Eidelman, A. (eds), *Human Milk. Its Biological and Social Value*, Amsterdam, Excerpta Medica, pp. 260–3.
Mangurten, H., Slade, C. and Fitzsimons, D. (1979). "Parent-parent support in the care of high-risk newborns," *Journal of Obstetrical and Gynecological Nursing*, September/October, pp. 275–7.
Mason, D., Jenson, G. and Ryzewicz, C. (1979). *How To Grow A Parents Group*, Milwaukee, WI, International Childbirth Education Association.
Minde, K., Shosenberg, N., Marton, P., Thompson, J., Ripley, J. and

Burns, S. (1980). "Self-help groups in a premature nursery – A controlled evaluation," *Journal of Pediatrics*, vol. 96, no. 5, pp. 933–40.

CHAPTER 10

Parenting organizations and resources

C. F. Zachariah Boukydis

Appendix 1 Self-help groups for parents in the US

American Academy of Husband Coached Childbirth
PO Box 5224,
Sherman Oaks, CA 91413

American College of Home Obstetrics
664 North Michigan Ave, Suite 600
Chicago, IL 60611

American Society for Psychoprophylaxis in Obstetrics (ASPO)
1411 K Street, NW,
Washington, DC 20005

Association of Children with Learning Disabilities (ACLD)
4156 Library Road,
Pittsburgh, PA 15234
412-341-1515
ACLD is a "nonprofit organization whose purpose is to advance the education and general welfare of children of normal or potentially normal intelligence who have learning disabilities of a perceptual, conceptual or coordinative nature."

Black Parents for Quality Education
Detroit, MI,
313-934-7721
Black Parents for Quality Education is a citywide organization dedicated to improving the quality of Detroit's educational system.

Candlelighters
123 C Street, SE,
Washington, DC 20003
202-544-1696
A national organization of parents of children with cancer, Candlelighters includes other family members as well, and provides for mutual support and legislative action designed to improve research and treatment of childhood cancer.

Cesarean Birth Council International
PO Box 6081, San Jose, CA 95150

C-Sec, Inc.
66 Chistopher Road,
Waltham, MA 02154

Cesarean Birth Council International Association (ICEA)
PO Box 20048, 8060 26th Ave. South,
Minneapolis, MN 55422

Cesarean Connection
PO Box 11,
Westmont, IL 60559

Childbirth Without Pain Education League
3940 11th Street,
Riverside, CA 92501

Compassionate Friends, Inc.
PO Box 1347,
Oak Brook, IL 60521
A self-help and mutual-support group for bereaved parents.

Family Resource Coalition
230 North Michigan Ave, Suite 1625
Chicago, IL 60601
A North American network of family support programs.

Fathers United for Equal Justice (FUEJ)
339 Auburn St,
Auburndale (Newton), MA 02156
617-965-5460
FUEJ is an organization that provides guidance and mutual support to fathers before, during, and after divorce and custody proceedings. FUEJ also works for reform of divorce laws and legislative and court actions that promote joint child custody arrangements. Many similar groups operate under different names in numerous communities in the country.

Hydrocephalus Parent Support Group
225 Dickinson St H-893,
San Diego, CA 92103

International Association of Parents of the Deaf (IAPD)
814 Thayer Avenue,
Silver Springs, MD 20910
301-585-5400
An international organization that helps put parents of deaf children in touch with each other, encourages mutual support among parents, and works for legislative and other changes in public policy that favor the participation of deaf children in educational services, TV captioning, TT-Y telephone communications, and other opportunities.

International Childbirth Education Association
PO Box 20852,
Milwaukee, WI 53220

La Leche League International
9616 Minneapolis Avenue,
Franklin Park, IL 60131
312-455-7730
An international organization of parents who provide information and support to mothers who are breastfeeding their babies.

National Association for Parents and Professionals for Safe Alternatives in Childbirth (NAPSAC)
PO Box 267
Marble Hill, MO 63764

National Organization of Mothers of Twins Clubs
5402 Amberwood Lane,
Rockville, MD 20853
301-460-9108
An organization that provides information and encourages mutual support among mothers of twins.

National Society for Autistic Children (NSAC)
1234 Massachusetts Ave NW, Suite 1017,
Washington, DC 20005
NSAC is "an organization of parents, professionals and other interested citizens working together to bring into being programs of legislation, education and research for the benefit of all children with severe behavior disorders." Organized primarily by parents, NSAC's membership at present is comprised primarily of

parents, and its board of directors is totally made up of parents of autistic children.

Nursing Mothers Counsel
PO Box 50063,
Palo Alto, CA 94303

Parent and Childbirth Education Society (PACES)
PO Box 213,
Western Springs, IL 60558

Parent Care (Parents of Premature and High Risk Infants International)
c/o Parent Care,
50 North Medical Drive,
Room 2A210,
Salt Lake City,
Utah 84132
(801) 581–5323

Parents Anonymous (PA)
22330 Hawthorne Boulevard, Suite 208,
Torrance, CA 90505
213-371-3501
Toll-free: 800-421-0353
California toll-free: 800-352-0386
A self-help group for persons with child-abuse problems, which strongly encourages mutual support and provides a toll-free telephone service for parents seeking information or help.

Parents Campaign for Handicapped Children and Youth
1201 16th NW, Suite 606E,
Washington, DC 20036
The Parents' Campaign for Handicapped Children and Youth is an "organization of parents dedicated to working for the right of handicapped individuals to be full participants in the mainstream of society." The Parents' Campaign distributes information about education for handicapped children under federal and state law and about other rights to equal opportunity.

Parents Concerned for Hospitalized Children
Redbook Magazine, Box HC,
230 Park Avenue,
New York, NY 10017

Parents Without Partners International (PWP)
7910 Woodmont Avenue,
Bethesda, MD 20014
301-654-8850
A self-help group for single parents.

Encourages mutual support and practical assistance among single parents.

Resolve
PO Box 474,
Belmont, MA 02178
Infertility problems.

Sisterhood of Black Single Mothers
1360 Fulton St, Room 423,
Brooklyn, NY 11216
212-638-0413
The Sisterhood is a "self-help organization comprised of Black women who are raising their children alone." Encourages mutual support and practical assistance among black single mothers.

Sudden Infant Death Syndrome Foundation
310 S. Michigan Avenue,
Chicago, IL 60604
312-663-0650
A national organization that provides information and mutual support to parents whose infants have died unexpectedly and apparently without cause, a disease diagnosed as "sudden infant death syndrome."

Twinline
6421 Telegraph Avenue,
Oakland, CA 94609
415-654-0613
Phone advice, information, and referrals. Services available in Spanish and Chinese by appointment. Resource library. The following leaflets are available free with a self-addressed, stamped legal-sized envelope for up to three handouts per envelope: "The Symptoms of a Plural Pregnancy," "Advice for New Parents of Twins and Triplets," "Breastfeeding Your Twins," "What to Read" – a bibliography of popular and research literature on twins," "The Multiple Birth Book" – information on how parents can contribute the story of their multiple birth experience to this project.

Appendix 2 Parenting organizations in other countries

A resource for locating parenting organizations in countries not currently listed in this Appendix is: The International Information Center on Self-Help and Health, c/o The World Health Organization, E. van Evanstraat 2C, B-3000, Leuven, Belgium. Telephone: Leuven, Belgium: 32 (016) 237145, or 236507.

Australia

Allergy Association of Australia
26 Erin Street,
Richmond, Victoria 3121

Australian Multiple Birth Association
71 Valley Road,
Park Orchards, Victoria 3114

Childbirth Education Association Australia (Victoria) Ltd
116 Glenferrie Road,
Malvern, Victoria 3144

Childbirth Education Association of North Brisbane,
PO Box 208,
Chermside, Q4032

Childbirth Education and Parenting Association of Victoria
13 Hull Road,
Croydon, Victoria 3136

Children's Protection Society
14 Gertrude Street,
Fitzroy, Victoria 3065

The Lightweight Club Support Group for Parents of Premature Children
PO Box 255,
North Mulgrave, Victoria 3170

NIPPA
8 Grove Street,
Guildford, New South Wales 6058

Noah's Ark
28 The Avenue,
Windsor, Victoria 3181

Nursing Mothers' Association of Australia
5 Glendale Street,
Nunawading, Victoria 3131

Parents Anonymous
156 Collins Street,
Melbourne, Victoria 3000

Parents of Preterm Infants (POPI)
PO Box 63
Unley, South Australia 5061

PIPA
47 Anderson Road,
Forrestfield, Western Australia 6058

**Preterm Infants' Parents' Association
(PIPA)**
9 Heathfield Street,
Eight Mile Plains, Queensland 4123

Royal Victorian Institute for the Blind
557 St Kilda Road,
Melbourne, Victoria 3000

**Stillbirth and Neonatal Deaths Support
Group (SANDS)**
63 Menin Road,
Forest Hill, Victoria 3131
Also miscarriage.

Sudden Infant Death Research Foundation
283 Wattletree Road,
Malvern, Victoria 3144

Canada

Aide directe a l'enfance malheureuse,
Terre des Hommes,
53 Lakeshore Road
Pointe Claire, Quebec H9S 4H4

**Association for Care of Children in
Hospital, Southwestern Ontario Affiliate,**
C/O Recreation Dept.
Hospital for Sick Children
555 University Avenue
Toronto, Ontario M5G 1X8

Birthright Montreal,
1280 St. Mark Street, Room 204
Montreal, Quebec H3H 2G1

Canadian Association for Young Children,
323 Chapel St
Ottawa, Ontario K1N 7Z2

Canadian Cerebral Palsy Association,
1 Yonge St, Suite 2110
Toronto, Ontario M5E 1E8

**Canadian Cleft Lip and Palate Family
Association,**
4981 Bathurst St., Apt. 215
Willowdale, Ontario M2R 1Y5

Canadian Diabetic Association,
123 Edward St., Suite 601
Toronto, Ontario M5G 1E2

**Canadian Foundation for the Study of
Infant Deaths,**
4 Lawton Blvd.
Toronto, Ontario M4B 1Z4

Canadian Hearing Society,
60 Bedford Road,
Toronto, Ontario M5R 2K2

Canadian Institute of Child Health,
410 Laurier Avenue West, Suite 803,
Ottawa, Ontario K1R 7T3

Canadian Medical Association,
1867 Alta Vista Drive,
Ottawa, Ontario K1G 0G8

Canadian Mental Health Association,
2160 Yonge St,
Toronto, Ontario M4S 2Z3

Canadian Mothercraft Society,
32 Heath Street West,
Toronto, Ontario M4V 1T3

Canadian National Institute for the Blind,
1929 Bayview Avenue,
Toronto, Ontario M4G 3E8

Canadian Paediatric Society,
Centre Hospitalier Universitaire de
Sherbrooke,
Sherbrooke, Quebec J1H 5N4

Canadian Physiotherapy Association,
25 Imperial Avenue,
Toronto, Ontario M5P 1C1

Canadian Red Cross Society,
95 Wellesley Street East,
Toronto, Ontario M4Y 1H6

Canadian Young Family,
37 Hanna Avenue, Box 8, Station C
Toronto, Ontario M6J 3M8

Capital Families Association,
517–620 View St,
Victoria, British Columbia V8W 1J6
(604) 383-4222

Children's Book Center,
86 Bloor Street West, Suite 200,
Toronto, Ontario M5S 1M5

Children's Broadcast Institute,
3 Charles Street West, Suite 202,
Toronto, Ontario M4Y 1R4

College of Family Physicians,
4000 Leslie St,
Willowdale, Ontario M2K 2R9

Consumer Association of Canada,
261 Laurier Avenue West, Room 801,
Ottawa, Ontario K1P 5Z7

Consumer and Corporate Affairs Canada,
Consumer Service Branch,
480 University Avenue, 9th Floor,
Toronto, Ontario M5G 1V2

Early Additions,
c/o Jewish General Hospital, Room 6618,
3755 Cote Ste. Catherine Road
Montreal, Quebec H3T 1E2

Family Leukemic Association,
22 Davisville Avenue,
Toronto, Ontario M4S 1E9

Family Planning Federation of Canada,
1226 A rue Wellington St.
Ottawa, Ontario K1Y 3A1

Family Planning Resource Center, Family Planning Division, Health and Welfare, Canada,
Brooke Claxton Bldg., Suite 658
Ottawa, Ontario K1A 1B5

L'Association Canadian pour les jeunes Enfants,
323 Chapel St,
Ottawa, Ontario K1N 7Z2

L'Institute de Radio-Telediffusion Pour Enfants,
724 Charles Lussier,
Boucherville, Quebec

La Leche League Canada,
PO Box 11, Station Z,
Toronto, Ontario M5N 2Z3

Ligue La Leche du Canada,
C.P. 118, Succursale Laval Ouest,
Laval, Quebec H7R 5B7

Mental Hygiene Institute, Department of Family Education Services,
3690 Peel St,
Montreal, Quebec

Mississauga Parents of Twins,
2380 Broms Grove, Apt. 15,
Mississauga, Ontario L5J 4E6

National Institute and Canadian Association for the Mentally Retarded,
4700 Keele St, Kinsman Bldg,
Downsview, Ontario M3J 1P3

One Parent Family Association of Canada,
2279 Yonge St, Suite 17,
Toronto, Ontario M4P 2C7

Parent Relief Services for Multihandicapped Children,
Children's Services Committee,
18 Kempford Blvd,
Willowdale, Ontario M2N 2B9

Parents Anonymous,
Box 843, Attn Susan Parker
Burlington, Ontario

Parents Without Partners, Inc,
Canadian Office,
205 Yonge Street, Suite 13
Toronto, Ontario M5B 1N2

Parents of Twins Club,
Metro Toronto and North York,
57 Wortham Drive,
Scarborough, Ontario M1G 1W6

Pilot Parents,
c/o National Institute and Canadian Association for the Mentally Retarded,
4700 Keele St, Kinsman Bldg,
Downsview, Ontario M3J 1P3

Provincial Medical Associations' Child Welfare Committees;
Provincial Ministries of Community and Social Services;
Provincial Ministries of Health Publications;
contact local offices.

Service Social Ville-Marie,
874 Est rue Sherbrooke
Montreal, Quebec H2L 1L1

Sex Information and Education Council of Canada,
c/o Dr M. Barrett,
423 Castlefield Avenue,
Toronto, Ontario M5N 1L4

Denmark

Parents and Birth/Foroeldre og Foedsel,
Secretariat: Anne Olsen
GL: Soestvej 142
6200 Aadenraa
Denmark
Telephone: 99045 4 620525
This organization has listings of local support groups for parents and infants.

England

The Association for Post-Natal Illness,
Institute of Obstetrics and Gynaecology,
Queen Charlotte's Maternity Hospital,
Goldhawk Road
London, W6 0XG

The Association of Post-Natal Illness,
7 Gowan Avenue,
Fulham, London SW6

Ceasarian Support Group of Cambridge,
7 Green Street,
Willingham, Cambridge

Cry-Sis
63 Putney Road,
Freezy Water,
Enfield, Middlesex

The Family Forum,
Cambridge House,
131 Camberwell Road,
London, SE5 0HF

Homestart,
61B Mansfield Road,
Nottingham, NG1 3FN
This organization was started in Leicester
and is at present in many towns
throughout the Midlands area of Great
Britain.

Meet-A-Mum Association,
26A Cumnor Hill,
Oxford, OX2 9HA

The National Childbirth Trust,
9 Queensborough Terrace
London, W2 3TB
This is a nationwide organization running
neighborhood groups to support women
through pregnancy and childbirth, now
running postnatal support groups which
help young mothers through the early
stages of child rearing.

**National Information for Parents of
Prematures Education, Resources and
Support (NIPPERS),**
c/o Perinatal Research Unit, St Mary's
Hospital,
Praed St,
London, W2 1PG

**Organisations for Parents Under Stress
(OPUS),**
26 Manor Drive,
Pickering,
Yorkshire, YO18 8DD

Twins Clubs Association,
c/o Gillian Lee, M.D.

Contact the National Health Service health
visitor in a particular area. Health visitors
are aware of parenting organizations for
parents and infants.

France

**Association Nationale d'Entraide des
Parents de Naissances Multiples,**
5 rue de la Poste
77114 Gouaix
Telephone: (6) 400 74 18

La Leche League, France,
B.P. 18
78620 L'Etang-la-Ville

L'Ecole des Parents et des Educateurs,
4 rue Brunel
75017 Paris
Telephone: (1)380 29 00 and (1)766 51 52

**Les Lieux de Parentalité, Association
MIRE,**
12 rue Clairaut
75017 Paris
Telephone: (1)229 45 51

**Union Nationale des Associations de
Parents d'Enfants Inadaptes (UNAPEI),**
15 rue Coysevox
75018 Paris
Telephone: (1)263 84 33

Israel

**Association of Community Centers in
Israel,**
Early Childhood Division
Givat Ram
Jerusalem
Parenting groups are often established
informally or through women's
organizations. This organization is kept
aware of special interest groups related to
parents and infants.

Ireland

Department of Paediatrics
Rotunda Hospital,
Dublin

Netherlands

**Association of Parents of Incubator
Babies,**
c/o Dr Richard de Leeuw, Department of
Neonatology,
University of Amsterdam, Wilhelmina
Gasthuis, Amsterdam

New Zealand

Auckland Neonatal Parent Support Unit,
63 Cliff Road,
St Heliers,
Auckland

Catholic Social Services,
PO Box 4038,
Hamilton,
Waikato

Norway

Mental Barnehjelp,
General Secretary: Elsa Boasson
Arbiensgt 1
0253 Oslo 2
Telephone: (02) 44 14 51
This organization is working to develop
parenting networks and collaboration
between parents and professionals.
Contact this organization for a listing of
local groups.

Scotland

Cry-Sis
21 Falkland Gardens,
Edinburgh EH12 6UW

Scottish Premature Baby Support Group,
c/o National Information for Parents of
Prematures: Education Resources &
Support (NIPPERS)
Perinatal Research Unit, St Mary's
Hospital,
Praed St,
London, W2 1PG, U.K.

Sweden

**"Amningshjälpen" (Breast Feeding
Association)**
c/o Carina Sjögren,
Fågelvägen 4,
S–141 40 Huddinge

Appendix 3 Resources for parenting organizations

Action for Child Transportation Safety
400 Central Park West, 15P,
New York, NY 10025

Allergy Foundation of America
801 Second Ave,
New York, NY 10017

American Academy of Pediatrics
1801 Hinman Avenue,
Evanston, IL 60204
(312) 869-4255
Offers literature on child care and the
health needs of children.

**American Association for the Education of
the Severely/Profoundly Handicapped**
Exper. Ed. Unit, CDMRC, WJ-10
University of Washington,
Seattle, WA 98195

**American Association for Maternal and
Child Health**
PO Box 965,
Los Altos, CA 94022

American Cancer Society
777 Third Avenue,
New York, NY 10017

American College of Nurse-Midwives
1000 Vermont Avenue NW, Suite 1210,
Washington, DC 20005

**American College of Obstetricians and
Gynecologists**
Resource Center,
1 E. Wacker Drive,
Chicago, IL 60601

American Foundation for the Blind
15 West 16th Street,
New York, NY 10011

American Institute of Family Relations
5287 Sunset Blvd,
Los Angeles, CA 90027

American Medical Association
535 N. Dearborn St,
Chicago, IL 60610

American Optometric Association
7000 Chippewa St,
St Louis, MO 63119

American Speech and Hearing Association
10801 Rockville Pike,
Rockville, MD 20852

**Association for the Care of Children in
Hospitals, Inc.**
Box H,
Union, WV 24983

Association for the Care of Children's Health (ACCH)
3615 Wisconsin Avenue, NW
Washington, DC 20016
(202) 244-1801
ACCH is an international group of parents and health care professionals dedicated to humanizing health care for children and their families.

Association for Childhood Education, International
3615 Wisconsin Avenue, NW,
Washington, DC 20016

"Because We Care So Much"
Tressler-Lutheran Associates
25 West Springettsbury Avenue,
York, PA 17403
Free monthly newsletter for adoptive and/ or foster parents who have 5 or more children. Families share budget ideas, recipes, holiday traditions, problems, solutions, and most of all the joys and frustrations of large families.

Center for Parenting Studies
Wheelock College,
200 The Riverway,
Boston, MA 02215
(617) 734-5200, X-214
Call to be placed on mailing list for courses, workshops, and seminars on family issues, special needs children, and parenting.

Center for Study of Multiple Birth
333 E. Superior St, Suite 463-5,
Chicago, IL 60611
(312) 266-9093
Publications on twins. Call or write for current list.

Center for Supportive Community
186 Hampshire St,
Cambridge, MA 02139,
(617) 492-5559
Manual on peer counseling, decision making. Consultation with self-help groups, parenting organizations.

Child Study Association of America
853 Broadway,
New York, NY 10003

Child in Hospitals, Inc. (CIH)
31 Wilshire Park,
Needham, MA 02192
An organization that seeks to educate the public about the needs of children and

parents for "continued and ample contact" when either is hospitalized, and encourages hospitals to adopt flexible visiting policies and provide live-in accommodation whenever possible.

Coalition for Children and Youth
1910 K Street NW, Suite 800,
Washington, DC 20006

Coalition of Healthy Mothers and Healthy Babies
c/o National Center for Clinical Infant Programs,
733 15th St. NW, Suite 912,
Washington, DC 2005

Consumer Information Center
Pueblo, CO 81009
Send for the Consumer Information Catalogue, a listing of booklets on many topics including children, education, health, money management, and housing.

Council for Exceptional Children
1920 Association Drive,
Reston, VA 22091

DES Action National
East Coast Office:
Long Island Jewish-Hillside Medical Center,
New Hyde Park, NY 11040
West Coast Office:
1638-B Haight St,
San Francisco, CA 94117

Early Childhood Nutrition Programs
Division Nutritional Sciences,
Cornell University,
Ithaca, NY 14853

Fathering Support Services
3248 N. Racine Ave,
Chicago, IL 60657
(312) 327-3752

Federation for Children with Special Needs
120 Boylston St, Suite 347,
Boston, MA 02116
(617) 482-2915

Footsteps
Government Printing Office,
Pueblo, CO 81101
Free, extensive resource book – Viewer Guide to Footsteps Weekly Parenting Series.

Good Housekeeping Children's Center
959 Eighth Avenue,
New York, NY 10019

Guardians of Hydrocephalus Research Foundation
2618 Avenue Z,
Brooklyn, NY 11235

Handicapped Children's Early Education Program
400 Maryland Ave, SW
Washington, DC 20202

Home Oriented Maternity Experience
511 New York Avenue,
Takoma Park,
Washington, DC 20012

Know Problems of Hydrocephalus Association
South River Road, Route 1
Joliet, IL 60436

Maternity Center Association
48 East 92nd Street,
New York, NY 10028

Mothers Against Drunk Drivers (MADD)
PO Box HC,
Fair Oaks, CA 95628
(916) 966-7433
MADD is directed primarily by parents whose children have been killed or injured in alcohol-related car crashes; however, it is also a citizen's organization whose membership comprises both other relatives of victims and a variety of individuals concerned about drunk driving. MADD works for stronger anti-drunk-driving laws at the federal, state, and local levels, and educates the public against driving under the influence of alcohol. Many local groups help bereaved parents with practical support and referrals to mutual-help organizations and counseling services.

Mothers' Center Development Project
129 Jackson St,
Hempstead, NY 11550
(516) 486-6614 in New York State
(800) 645-3828 elsewhere
This project disseminates information nationally about the Mothers' Center and helps parents form "a community program where women/mothers, in conjunction with members of the professional community, provide services, research and advocacy on mothering, pregnancy, childbirth and health care."

National Alliance Concerned with School-age Parents
7315 Wisconsin Avenue NW,
Suite 211-W,
Washington, DC 20014

National Association for Mental Health
1800 N. Kent St,
Rosslyn, VA 22209

National Center for Prevention and Treatment of Child Abuse and Neglect
University of Colorado Medical Center,
Denver, CO 80210

National Association for Retarded Citizens
2709 Avenue E East,
Arlington, TX 76011
(817) 261-4691

National Clearinghouse for Smoking and Health
Rockville, MD 20852

National Association for the Visually Handicapped
305 East 24th Street,
New York, NY 10010

National Association of Hearing and Speech Agencies
1800 H Street, NW,
Washington, DC 20006

National Coalition of ESEA Title 1 Parents
The Parent Center, Suite 520,
1341 G Street, NW,
Washington, DC 20005
(202) 538-5466
The National Coalition provides a voice at federal, state, and local levels for parents of children eligible for federally funded educational services for economically disadvantaged children. The Coalition also brings parents together for workshops and training conferences and distributes information which helps parents in local communities design and carry out an advisory role.

National Council on Family Relations
1219 University Avenue SE,
Minneapolis, MN 55414

National Easter Seal Society for Crippled Children and Adults
2023 West Ogden Ave,
Chicago, Il 60612

National Foundation, March of Dimes
PO Box 1275,
White Plains, NY 10605

National Health Information
Clearinghouse
PO Box 1133,
Washington, DC 20013
(800) 336-4797

National Safety Council
444 N. Michigan Avenue,
Chicago, IL 60611

National Society for the Prevention of
Blindness
79 Madison Avenue,
New York, NY 10016

National Sudden Infant Death Syndrome
Foundation,
310 S. Michigan Avenue, Suite 1904,
Chicago, IL 60604

North American Council on Adoptable
Children (NACAC)
1346 Connecticut Avenue NW, Suite 229,
Washington, DC 20036
(202) 466-7570
NACAC is a national federation of local
and state citizens' groups that serves "as
a voice for waiting children and adoptive
families." NACAC works for legislative
and other activities that ensure legal
adoptive placement of every child eligible
for adoption, provides information and
support during the adoption process and
after placement, and speaks for the rights
of children in foster care to permanent
homes.

Orton Dyslexia Society, Inc.
724 York Road
Baltimore, MD 21204

Parents' Campaign for Handicapped
Children and Youth
Box 1492,
Washington, DC 20013
Send for free publications, information
packets, and newsletters from a national
information center for parents of children
with special needs.

The Parents' Network
National Committee for Citizens in
Education (NCCE),
410 Wilde Lake Village Green,
Columbia, MD 21044
(301) 997-9300
Toll-free: 800-NETWORK

The Parents' Network is a project of the
National Committee for Citizens in
Education (NCCE) which links together
and provides information to state and
local parent-citizen groups working to
improve public schools.

Parents' Union for Public Schools
401 N. Broad St, Room 704,
Philadelphia, PA 19108
Parents' Union is a "city-wide independent
organization *of*, *by* and *for* parents"
which focuses on school system-wide
issues such as the budget, desegregation,
discipline, special education, and reading.

Pediatric Projects Incorporated
PO Box 1880
Santa Monica, CA 90406

Planned Parenthood
810 Seventh Avenue,
New York, NY 10019
(212) 541-7800
Direct services, referrals and counseling
concerning birth control and infertility.

Resources in Human Nurturing
International
PO Box 6861
Denver, CO 80206
This organization publishes the "Keeping
Abreast" journal, which is concerned
with breastfeeding and related topics.

Society for the Protection of the Unborn
Through Nutrition
17 N. Wabash Avenue, Suite 603,
Chicago, IL 60602

Spina Bifida Association of America
343 South Dearborn, Suite 319,
Chicago, IL 60604

United Cerebral Palsy Association, Inc.
66 East 34th Street,
New York, NY 10016

United Infertility Organization
PO Box 23,
Scarsdale, NY 10583

US Department of Health, Education and
Welfare
Children's Bureau,
Washington, DC 20201

Volunteer: The National Center for
Citizen Involvement
PO Box 4179,
Boulder, CO 80306

Appendix 4 Periodicals/parenting magazines and newsletters/mail-order services

Periodicals

These periodicals deal with issues related to infant development, relations between parents and babies, and developing parenting organizations.

Birth (formerly Birth and the Family Journal)
110 El Camino Real,
Berkeley, CA 94705
Published quarterly.

Family Resource Coalition Report
c/o Family Resource Coalition,
230 N. Michigan, #1625
Chicago, IL 60601

Infant Mental Health Journal
110 W. Downie,
Alma, MI 48801
Can be included with membership in International Association for Infant Mental Health.

Infant Behavior and Development
Ablex Publishing Corporation,
355 Chestnut St,
Norwood, NJ 07648

Journal of Voluntary Action Research
Rutgers University, Camden College,
311 N. Fifth St,
Camden, NJ 08102

Perinatal Press
The Perinatal Center, Sutter Memorial Hospital,
52nd and F Streets,
Sacramento, CA 95819

Support Lines
c/o Parent Care (Parents of Premature/High Risk Infants International), Inc.
Parent Care Inc.
50 North Medical Drive,
Room 2A210,
Salt Lake City, Utah 84132

Zero To Three
National Center for Clinical Infant Programs,
733 15th St NW, Suite 912,
Washington, DC 20005

Parenting magazines and newsletters

There are numerous books available on how to parent. In addition, there are many newsletters and magazines that deal with issues related to early parenting.

American Baby
575 Lexington Ave,
New York, NY 10022

Baby Care
52 Vanderbilt Ave,
New York, NY 10017

Baby Talk
185 Madison Ave,
New York, NY 10016

Building Blocks
314 Liberty, Box 31,
Dundee, IL 60118

Closer Look
National Information Center for the Handicapped,
Box 1492,
Washington, DC 20013
Information for handicapped children, their parents, and people who work with them.

Crisscross
1301 East 38th Street,
Indianapolis, IN 46205
Newsletter for parents of children with health problems or developmental disabilities.

Doubletalk
Box 412,
Amelia, OH 45102
Newsletter about twins.

Early Years Parent
Allen Raymond, Inc.
11 Hale Lane, Box 1223
Darien, CT 06820

Exceptional Parent (newsletter)
296 Boylston St, Third Floor,
Boston, MA 02116
For parents of children with health problems or developmental disabilities.

Exceptional Parent (magazine)
PO Box 4944,
Manchester, NH 03108

Family Journal
1205 University Ave,
Columbia, MO 65201

Family Resource Coalition Report
230 North Michigan, #1625
Chicago, IL 60601

For Parents
Interpersonal Communication Services,
7052 West Lane,
Eden, NY 14057

Growing Parent; Growing Child
22 North Second St, Box 101,
Lafayette, IN 47902

Health Connection
Childrens Better Health Institute,
1100 Waterway Blvd,
Indianapolis, IN 46202

Mothering
PO Box 2046,
Albuquerque, NM 87103

Mother's Manual
441 Lexington Ave,
New York, NY 10017

New Parent Adviser
505 Market St,
Knoxville, TN 37902

Parent Express
Cooperative Extension, U./Cal. Berkeley
317 University Hall,
Berkeley, CA 94720
A month-by-month description of infant
growth and development in the first year.
Suggested play activities. Emotional
support for parents.

Parent's Magazine and **Better
Homemaking**
52 Vanderbilt Ave,
New York, NY 10017

**Pediatrics for Parents: The Monthly
Newsletter for Caring Parents**
Box 1069,
Bangor, ME 04401

Pediatric Mental Health
PO Box 1880
Santa Monica, CA 90406
Newsletter for parents and professionals
working with ill, disabled, and
hospitalized children.

Practical Parenting
18318 Minnetonka Blvd,
Deephaven, MN 55391

Redbook's Young Mother
230 Park Ave,
New York, NY 10017

Parent Care (Support Lines)
c/o 50 North Medical Drive,
Room 2A210,
Salt Lake City,
Utah 84132
Newsletter for parents of prematures/high
risk infants.

Totline
Warren Publishing,
1004 Harborview Ln.
Everett, WA 98203

Mail-order services

The following specialized bookstores offer
mail-order service for book buyers:

Birth and Life Bookstore,
PO Box 70625,
Seattle, WA 98107

ICEA Bookcenter,
PO Box 20048,
Minneapolis, MN 55420

The Orange Cat,
442 Church St,
Garberville, CA 95440

US Government Printing Office,
Superintendent of Documents,
Washington, DC 20402

Appendix 5 Finding books and articles

American Guidance Service
Publisher's Building,
Circle Pines, MN 55014

Birth and Life Bookstore
PO Box 70625,
Seattle, WA 98107
Mail order service for book buyers

The Center for Medical Consumers
237 Thompson St,
New York, NY 10013
(212) 674-7105
The Center accepts mail requests for
medical information. The staff offers in-
depth searches of the medical literature on
specific topics. Call or write for details.

Children's Book and Music Center
2500 Santa Monica Blvd,
Santa Monica, CA 90404

Consumer Information Center
Pueblo, CO 81009

Family Resource Coalition
230 N. Michigan, Suite 1625,
Chicago, IL 60601
A network and clearinghouse for
information on programs that support
families.

**The International Childbirth Education
Association (ICEA)**
Bookcenter,
PO Box 20048,
Minneapolis, MN 55420
(612) 854-8660
Source for both professional and non-
professional literature on birth, child care,
and family issues. Call or write for their
extensive catalog of publications.

Learn Me Bookstore
642 Grand Ave,
St. Paul, MN 55105

Meadowbrook Press
Practical Parenting Catalog, Dept. DM
18318 Minnetonka Blvd,
Deephaven, MN 55391

National Self-Help Clearinghouse
Graduate School and University Center,
City University of New York,
33 West 42nd St, Room 1227,
New York, NY 10036
A source of information on national and
local self-help groups.

The Orange Cat
442 Church St,
Garberville, CA 95440
Mail-order service for book buyers.

**Parent Care (Parents of Premature/High
Risk Infants International)**
50 North Medical Drive,
Room 2A210,
Salt Lake City,
Utah 84132

Planetree Health and Resource Center
2040 Webster St,
San Francisco, CA 94115
(415) 346-4636
Planetree Health and Resource Center
accepts mail requests for medical
information. The staff offers in-depth
searches of the medical literature on
specific topics. Call or write for details.

Special People Library
641 Park Road,
West Point, PA 19486
Books and articles on children with
disabilities.

US Government Printing Office
Superintendent of Documents,
Washington, DC 20402

**Volunteer: The National Center for
Citizen Involvement**
PO Box 4179,
Boulder, CO 80306
Non-profit organization that offers
information and advice on volunteerism.

Index

advocacy groups, 129–30, 133; assertiveness, 117, 118; awareness, 117, 118, 130; Children's Defence Fund, 130; concensus-building, 127; contacts with other groups, 121; core-group, 128–9; disseminating information, 120, 126; feasibility of, 122–3; formulating strategies, 123–6; group advocacy, 118–19; group evaluation, 127–30; group size, 119–20; individual tasks, 125–6; leadership, 123, 126, 129; need for information, 123–4; publicity, 120; resources for, 130; self-examination, 128; skills, 2, 6, 129; target of, 121
American Academy of Pediatrics, 130, 195
American Association of University Women, 45, 50, 55
American Speech, Language and Hearing Association, 131
Association of Children's Hospitals, 160
Association of Parents of Incubator Babies, 3
Ayer, S., 29, 30

Bank Street College, New York, 96
Baby Sitting Cooperative, 49
Barrera, M., 11
Behavior Associates, 32
Benedek, T., 89–90
Berman, W., 30–1
'Booth Buddies', Philadelphia, PA, 94
Boukydis, C.F.Z., ix, 3, 5, 13, 28, 133, 140, 142
Bowlby, John, 84

California Parenting Institute, 94
Cassidy, Florence G., 46
Center for Fathers in Transition, 93–4
child abuse, 28, 32–3
childbirth classes, 5
Children's Defence Fund, Washington, D.C., 130
Cohn, Ann, 32–3
Compassionate Friends, 106
conferences, x, 162, 163, 164
constitution, 72–81
contextual assessment, 13
Coping with the Overall Pregnancy/ Parenting Experience (COPE), 47–8
Crnic, K., 15–16
Crockenburg, S., 12–13, 16, 28
Cronenwett, L. R., 21–2, 25

Dawson, P., 26–7, 28, 31–2
Demos, John, 82–3

early intervention projects, 30–1
early parenting, 5, 6; social support, 11–19; effect of parenting networks on, 19–26

families, ix, 5, 6, 11
Family Birth Center, San Mateo, CA, 95
Family Focus, Evanston, IL, 45
Family Resource Coalition (FRC), 1, 53, 56, 159, 170; attrition, 166–7; formation of, 159; funding, 168; future goals, 169–70; principles of, 160, 163; "Programs to strengthen families", 26–7, 45–6; publications, 171; services provided, 163